PRAISE FOR THE TWO-INCOME TRAP

"Why are so many millions of parents earning more but enjoying it less in our modern economy? Why are mothers the only group of women worse off financially now than a generation ago? Why can't today's hardworking families afford the happier lifestyle of their parents? How can they escape the "two-income trap" and prevent a financial meltdown? In this excellent book, Warren and Tyagi tell the shocking story of that trap, and offer real hope for a better future."

—Senator Edward M. Kennedy

"A provocative new book. . . the authors suggest ambitious solutions."

—*Newsweek*

"At a time when many middle-class families are just an accident or an illness away from financial disaster, this book provides a well-researched road map of where we are, as well as viable escape routes."

—*Boston Globe*

"An eye-opening, well-documented thesis set out in a succinct and easy-to-read fashion."

—*Washington Post*

"THE TWO-INCOME TRAP goes a long way toward explaining. . . why so many Americans, even quite affluent ones, are convinced they aren't doing as well as their parents did or that they could have their success snatched away much more easily."

—*Los Angeles Times Book Review*

"One of the best books that explains this historic moment and describes what families are going through."

—Senator John Edwards

"Original solutions that go beyond ideology. . . . I highly recommend to my viewers that they get THE TWO-INCOME TRAP."

—Bill Moyers

"[Warren] argues movingly that the misery and shame of bankruptcy is as pungent as ever — it's just more widely experienced . . . The book is brimming with proposed solutions to the nail-biting anxiety that the middle class finds itself in: subsidized day care, school vouchers, new bank regulations, among other measures."

—*Wall Street Journal*

"Astounding."

—Mortimer B. Zuckerman, editor-in-chief, *U.S. News & World Report*

"Warren and Tyagi argue persuasively that mass 'over-consumption' is not the problem . . . Moreover, the book does offer unexpectedly fresh discussions of "deadbeat dads" (it turns out there aren't very many of them) and the credit-card industry (where the current business strategy is to get financially troubled families 'to borrow [still] more money')."

—*National Review*

"In their groundbreaking book, Elizabeth Warren and Amelia Warren Tyagi demonstrate that . . . even when a two-earner family today brings in almost twice the income of a one-earner family in the 1970s (in inflation-adjusted constant dollars), the 1970s family had more discretionary income than today's."

—*Atlantic Monthly*

"Warren and Tyagi masterfully demonstrate how parents' quest for high-quality public schools often lies at the heart of their precarious economic position. . . . [I]nnovative . . . ingenious approach to a difficult and divisive issue."

—Judith A. Winston, Former Undersecretary and General Counsel, U.S. Department of Education

"Presenting carefully researched economic data to support their arguments, the authors contend that, contrary to popular myth, families aren't in trouble because they're squandering their second income on luxuries. On the contrary, both incomes are almost entirely committed to necessities . . . The authors recommend a number of useful societal solutions to get families out of this trap . . . this is a needed examination of an emerging social problem."

—*Publishers Weekly*

"[This] sobering analysis of the widespread and largely unaddressed erosion of middle-class stability presents a carefully crafted, persuasive indictment of a financial industry preying on the hardships and vulnerabilities of middle-class families, and the argument is perhaps most effective in its careful accounting of the families of public education to serve equitably the needs of those families."

—*Ruminator Review*

"[A]ccurately characterizes the plight of the middle class and illuminates the problems that arise when families become dependent upon two incomes without adequately saving."

—*The Hill*

"The book persuasively argues that the rise of dual-income families is increasing the chances of a middle-class financial disaster."

—*St. Petersburg Times*

"My advice for a great way to start on the road back to fiscal solvency, or to avoid falling into this trap altogether, is to invest $26 of your dwindling discretionary income on THE TWO-INCOME TRAP. The solutions and advice it provides might change the financial future for you and your children, today, tomorrow, and forever."

—*Lowell Sun*

"The book should be mandatory reading for any couple before they begin a family."

—*Pensacola News Journal*

"Well-constructed book [with a] very persuasive argument"

—"Sound Money," NPR

"An extremely thoughtful, well-presented, relevant book that challenges some of the basic assumptions in America today . . . this excellent work deserves to be considered by all, and most currently by policy-makers looking for creative solutions."

—*Tampa Tribune*

"[A] comfort to parents who are sick of being told it is their own fault their families are struggling financially. Here, finally is another interpretation of the data, one that says we're going broke not because we over-spend on things we don't need but because we're good parents . . . It is a sound policy document . . . Whether you agree with their suggestions or not, [Warren and Tyagi] offer plenty of food for thought and a welcome break from the guilt that comes with each month's efforts to keep up with the mounting bills."

—*Chicago Parents Magazine*

The Two-Income Trap

ALSO BY ELIZABETH WARREN:

As We Forgive Our Debtors

The Fragile Middle Class

The Two-Income Trap

Why Middle-Class Parents Are Going Broke

ELIZABETH WARREN

AMELIA WARREN TYAGI

A Member of the Perseus Books Group
New York

Published by Basic Books,
A Member of the Perseus Books Group

Hardback first published in 2003 by Basic Books
Paperback first published in 2004 by Basic Books

Designed by Brent Wilcox.

Warren, Elizabeth.
The two-income trap : Elizabeth Warren and Amelia Warren Tyagi.
p. cm.
ISBN-13 978-0-465-09090-7 (alk. paper)
ISBN-10 0-465-09090-7 (pbk)
1. Dual-career families—United States. 2. Family—Economic aspects—United States. 3. Bankruptcy—United States. I. Tyagi, Amelia Warren, 1971– . II. Title.

HQ536.W35 2003
306.3'6'973—dc21

2003010496

08 09 / 10 9 8 7 6 5

This book is dedicated to all parents who wake up with hearts thudding over the possibility that buying school shoes and Girl Scout uniforms will mean that there won't be enough left over to pay the mortgage. These people are our neighbors, our brothers and sisters, our friends and coworkers. They travel anonymously among us, but we know them. They went to college, had kids, bought a home, played by the rules—and lost. It is time to rewrite the rules so that these families are winners again.

CONTENTS

Introduction

The Two-Income Trap shipped to bookstores on September 2, 2003—an easy day to remember, because it happens to be Amelia's birthday. (Amelia's co-author, Elizabeth, also celebrates that day, since she's Amelia's mom.) Within two weeks, *The Two-Income Trap* had been featured in *Newsweek*, *Time*, *The New York Times*, and *Business Week*, and on The Today Show, National Public Radio's "All Things Considered," and so on.

At the end of September, we took a deep breath. Wasn't that exciting! Now, time to get back to life as usual—research projects, teaching classes at Harvard Law School, a demanding toddler.

Then Dr. Phil called. And Lou Dobbs. And Bill Moyers. And Senator John Edwards. And *USA Today, Houston Chronicle, Los Angeles Times, Boston Globe, Wall Street Journal, Marketplace,* CNN. And the calls kept coming.

Their message added up to one thing: *The Two-Income Trap* is a phenomenon.

Most of the time, we talked with reporters who just wanted to quiz us about our book. "How did you find out about the Two-Income Trap?" (We completed the largest study ever on financial failure in America.) "What should families do to protect themselves from the Two-Income Trap?" (Take their own Financial Fire Drill.) And so on.

But sometimes the attention was far more personal. A reporter, a secretary, a neighbor taking out her groceries, or a mom dropping off her son at preschool would lean in close, dropping her voice to a whisper. "*The Two-Income Trap* is *my life.* No one has any idea. Thank you for writing this book."

At book signings we met retired couples who asked us to sign three copies, one for each of their grown children who, they said, were caught in the trap. On radio call-in programs we talked with pastors and rabbis who worried about families in their congregations who were sliding into debt and needed help. We received emails from stay-at-home moms who said this book helped them rethink their choices and from young couples who decided to pause before committing to an oversized mortgage that would chew through both of their incomes.

This book touched a nerve with families around the country. Perhaps we should not have been surprised. Families are facing economic stress as never before:

- This year, more women will file for bankruptcy than will graduate from college.
- Seventy percent of all Americans (roughly 140 million people) say that they are carrying so much debt that it is making their home lives unhappy.
- The number one New Year's resolution in America in 2004 is to get out of debt (overtaking losing weight for the first time).
- This year, more children will live through their parents' bankruptcy than their parents' divorce.

And we heard from another group of Americans: those who shape the policies that mold this country. In a few short months, *The Two-Income Trap* was quoted publicly by Senators John Kerry, John Edwards, and Ted Kennedy, Representative Richard Gephardt, and former Vermont Governor Howard Dean. They told moving stories of the drastic changes that have taken the American family by storm in a few short decades. And they spoke of the need for change—and of policies that can move toward a better America. Credit industry regulation and limits on usury, which are featured prominently in this book, were endorsed by nearly all of the Democratic presidential candidates. Disability insurance has gotten a new look from legislators on both sides of the aisle. Leading thinkers in public education are considering the implications of the *Two-Income Trap* on school reform. The Center for American Progress, The New America Foundation, Drum Major, Demos, and The Century Fund have all turned up the volume in pressing issues related to families' economic stability. In a remarkably short time, there are stirrings of change in the political landscape, changes that may move the economic plight of the middle class to the forefront of the national agenda.

Changes are also occurring at dinner tables across America. Families have shared their stories with us—and their plans to change. Every day we talk with mothers and fathers, grandmas and young singles, who are concerned about their futures and who are determined to make their families more secure. Families are taking to heart the lessons of the Financial Fire Drill, as they evaluate the risks they face in a whole new light.

This book is dedicated to improving the lives of the hard-working, play-by-the-rules families who are learning the hard way that the rules have changed. These pages speak to the hopes and fears of today's middle class. It is our deepest desire that we can help Americans understand how the financial rules have changed, and how they must now play smarter than ever. We hope that we can help more families make changes—the kind that can protect them from disaster and help them build a brighter future.

The past several months have strengthened our faith in America's great middle class. They are under assault, but they are fighters. They want to know the truth about what is going on, and they are willing to work hard to protect themselves. *The Two-Income Trap* tells a harrowing tale, but it also speaks of survival and triumph. America's middle class is ready to fight back.

APRIL 2004

1

Just the Way She Planned

Ruth Ann smiles when she talks about the summer she was pregnant with Ellie.[1] Those were the good days, when life was working out just the way she had planned.

Dexter was five and learning to swim. Ruth Ann would pick him up from day care in the late afternoon, and the two of them would head for the town swimming pool. While Dexter thrashed about in the water, Ruth Ann would dangle her feet in the pool, waiting for her husband, James, to swing by on his way home from work. Dinners were late and haphazard, but no one cared. Ruth Ann's life was exactly as she had wanted it, exactly as she had planned.

And Ruth Ann was a planner. In college, she had majored in accounting. It was respectable and dependable, a little bit the way Ruth Ann saw herself. After graduation, she resisted the lure of Houston or Dallas and moved back to her hometown, Wylie, Texas, where she could live near her parents, get some experience doing payrolls and tax returns, and build up a little savings while waiting to begin what she always thought of as her "real life."

Real life began when she saw James Wilson, a friend from her high school days, who was managing a carpet and flooring store in Wylie. It was his hands, she would later say, his capable hands, the sure hands of a carpenter, that drew her to him. But it was something else as well. During her junior year at Texas Tech, Ruth Ann had broken off an engagement because she couldn't shake the feeling that her intended was not the kind of guy she could count on. With James she felt she was marrying someone who would work as hard as she did to build a life together.

After a brief courtship, they married. A year later, in January 1994, Dexter was born. Ruth Ann was back at work in six weeks.

Three years later, Ruth Ann and James took a deep collective breath and jumped. They bought their first home. It wasn't the house of their dreams, but it was the house they thought they could afford. The roof needed to be replaced and the kitchen hadn't been updated in fifty years, but the house had three nice-sized bedrooms, a big yard, and, most important, at $84,000 it was within the couple's price range. Ruth Ann recalls the day they moved, a happy confusion of uncles and cousins carrying furniture, while Ruth Ann's Aunt Ida set up a big picnic in the front yard of the new home to feed both the movers and the neighbors. That night, Ruth Ann sank down in the big old tub in the upstairs bathroom and let the joy run through her.

Two years later, in September 1999, there was another cause for celebration: Ruth Ann gave birth to a little girl, Ellie. Nine weeks later, Ruth Ann returned to work and life settled down again.

Then it happened. Just after the 1999 Christmas season, when Dexter was six and Ellie was five months old, James's boss announced that he was closing the store. A national megastore had opened a few miles away, and its huge floor-covering department was sucking away business. To save on costs, layoffs were effective immediately. James was out of work in one day.

James was frantic about finding another job. Like Ruth Ann, he didn't want to disturb the life they had put together. But nothing came through that matched his previous salary. "After I lost my job I did odd jobs. Carpet cleaning, crazy stuff. I figured any work is better than no work." Ruth Ann asked for extra hours at work, but her office was already overstaffed.

Cutting back was hard to do because they weren't really spenders in the first place. Most of their money went for the basics—the mortgage, car payments, day care, and food on the table. They hadn't realized just how tight their budget really was until they missed a mortgage payment three months after James lost his job. Both had been raised to pay their bills, and as an accountant, Ruth Ann had seen what happened to people who didn't. But they held on to the belief that their situation was temporary.

Within six months they were two payments behind on the mortgage. To raise cash, they had had two garage sales; then they sold the antique dining set that James had refinished. Ruth Ann quietly asked family and neighbors if she could prepare their tax returns for $50 apiece.

As Ruth Ann and James learned, the dance of financial ruin starts slowly but picks up speed quickly, exhausting the dancers before it ends. Few families have substantial savings, so they usually run out of cash within a month or so. Soon the charges start mounting up for the basics of life—food, gasoline, and whatever else can go on "the card." When there still isn't enough to go around, the game of impossible choices begins. Pay the mortgage or keep the heat on? Cancel the car insurance or the health insurance? Meanwhile, interest and late fees have piled on, making everything more expensive. Ruth Ann and James got a small reprieve from family. James's parents kicked in $4,000 and Ruth Ann's brother lent them $1,500. But these temporary infusions of money were just that—they covered the minimum payments for a few months, but they didn't begin to provide a way out of the hole. Before it was over, Ruth Ann had taken to parking the station wagon behind the elementary school and walking the six blocks home, figuring the bankers wouldn't repossess her car if they couldn't find it.

A neat stack of manila folders on Ruth's bedroom bureau told the story of how quickly their carefully planned lives had unraveled. The first folder held a letter from the county threatening to foreclose on their home for failure to pay taxes, along with past due notices from the mortgage company. Other files held a variety of bills totaling $12,000, and Ruth Ann's carefully documented IOUs to their families.

The end for Ruth Ann and James came with a bang. One evening Ruth Ann walked into the living room to hear Dexter, now seven, on the phone, talking to a bill collector. "My mom doesn't do that, and you shouldn't call here any more. Leave us alone." When he heard her enter the room, he whirled around, his eyes wide. He slammed down the phone and ran out of the room. Ruth Ann wasn't sure whether Dexter was afraid or angry, but she knew this had to stop.

Ruth Ann was more financially sophisticated than most women. As an accountant, she knew that it was time to see a bankruptcy attorney. Filing for bankruptcy would give them some time to repay their bills, and it would prevent the bank from foreclosing on their home, at least for a few more months. It would also ensure that Dexter wouldn't have to answer any more collection calls. That night Ruth Ann told her husband what they needed to do. James never said a word. He just walked out to his pickup truck, sat in the front seat, and cried.

One in Seven

Ruth Ann and James didn't know anyone at their church or at work who couldn't pay their utility bills or make their car payments, let alone someone in so much trouble they would have to file for bankruptcy. Or at least, that's what they thought.

In fact, Ruth Ann and James probably knew plenty of families who were in just as much trouble as they were. The odds were certainly in favor of it. Over the past generation, the number of American families who have found themselves in serious financial trouble has grown shockingly large. In a world in which our neighbors seem to be doing fine and the families on television never worry about money, it is hard to grasp the breadth or depth of financial distress sweeping through ordinary suburbs, small towns, and nice city neighborhoods. People like Ruth Ann and James, typical American families who are doing their best to make a good life for their children—working hard, paying their bills, and playing by the rules—lose it all when disaster strikes.

Because they filed for bankruptcy in 2001 in northern Texas, Ruth Ann and James were among the 2,220 families interviewed as part of a Harvard University–based research project. One of us (Elizabeth) has been studying families in financial trouble since graduating from law school in 1976. I am a professor at Harvard Law School, where I teach the commercial law curriculum, which means that I specialize in the laws about debts and money. The other of us (Amelia) has an MBA from Wharton and a businessperson's view of economics. We are both working mothers, representing two generations of families. And we have something else in common: We are mother and daughter.

The idea behind this book took root in the spring of 1999, when Elizabeth was reviewing some preliminary data from an early phase of the Consumer Bankruptcy Project. I had begun to thumb through a stack of computer printouts to verify the accuracy of the sample. All the points were checking off fine, when my attention was suddenly drawn back to a single line on the page: the number of women in the sample. In 1981, about 69,000 women had filed for bankruptcy.[2] The data on my printout indicated that by 1999 that figure had jumped to nearly *500,000*—an unimaginable leap. I guessed that the data had been entered wrong—maybe someone had added a couple of zeroes somewhere—or, worse still, our research team had somehow pulled way too many women into their sample, inadvertently producing a huge distortion in the numbers. Frustrated, I tossed the printout in the trash, assuming we would be forced to throw out months of work.

The research team went back into the field for more data, initiating the 2001 Consumer Bankruptcy Project, which would evolve into the largest study ever conducted about families that had failed financially. I soon learned that there was something wrong, but it wasn't the data sampling. In just twenty years, the number of women filing petitions for bankruptcy had, in reality, increased by 662 percent.[3] As I soon discovered, divorced and single women weren't the only ones in trouble; several hundred thousand married women filed for bankruptcy along with their husbands.

Our research eventually unearthed one stunning fact. The families in the worst financial trouble are not the usual suspects. They are not the very young, tempted by the freedom of their first credit cards. They are not the elderly, trapped by failing bodies and declining savings accounts. And they are not a random assortment of Americans who lack the self-control to keep their spending in check. Rather, the people who consistently rank in the worst financial trouble are united by one surprising characteristic. They are parents with children at home. *Having a child is now the single best predictor that a woman will end up in financial collapse.*

Consider a few facts. Our study showed that married couples with children are more than twice as likely to file for bankruptcy as their childless counterparts. A divorced woman raising a youngster is nearly three times more likely to file for bankruptcy than her single friend who never had children.[4]

Over the past generation, the signs of middle-class distress have continued to grow, in good times and in bad, in recession and in boom.[5] If those trends persist, more than 5 million families with children will file for bankruptcy by the end of this decade. That would mean that across the country nearly *one of every seven families with children* would have declared itself flat broke, losers in the great American economic game.[6]

Bankruptcy has become deeply entrenched in American life. This year, more people will end up bankrupt than will suffer a heart attack. More adults will file for bankruptcy than will be diagnosed with cancer. More people will file for bankruptcy than will graduate from college. And, in an era when traditionalists decry the demise of the institution of marriage, Americans will file more petitions for bankruptcy than for divorce.[7] Heart attacks. Cancer. College graduations. Divorce. These are markers in the lives of nearly every American family. And yet, we will soon have more friends and coworkers who have gone through bankruptcy than any one of these other life events.

And the lines at the bankruptcy courts are not the only signs of financial distress. A family with children is now 75 percent more likely to be late on credit card payments than a family with no children.[8] The number of car repossessions has doubled in just five years.[9] Home foreclosures have more than tripled in less than 25 years, and families with children are now more likely than anyone else to lose the roof over their heads.[10] Economists estimate that for every family that officially declares bankruptcy, there are seven more whose debt loads suggest that they *should* file for bankruptcy—if only they were more savvy about financial matters.[11]

Unseen Dangers

Who are the families in so much trouble? Most are like Ruth Ann and James—ordinary, middle-class people united by their determination to provide a decent life for their children. Like James, many had been felled by a layoff or a business failure; someone who glanced at this year's tax return might label them as poor. But very few were chronically poor. For most, poverty was only temporary, a setback in an otherwise solidly middle-class life. When membership in the middle class is defined by enduring criteria that don't disappear when a pink slip arrives—criteria such as going to college, owning a home, or having held a good job—more than 90 percent of those in bankruptcy would qualify as middle class.[12] By every measure except their balance sheets, the families in our study are as solidly middle class as any in the country. And they are united by another common thread: Most of these families sent two parents into the workforce.

By the usual logic, sending a second parent into the workforce should make a family *more* financially secure, not less. But this reasoning ignores an important fact of two-income life. When mothers joined the workforce, the family gave up something of considerable (although unrecognized) economic value: an extra skilled and dedicated adult, available to pitch in to help save the family during times of emergency. When Junior got sick, the stay-at-home mother was there to care for him full-time, without the need to hire a nurse. If Dad was laid off, Mom could enter the workforce, bringing in a new income until Dad found another job. And if the couple divorced, the mother who had not been working outside the home could get a job and add *new* income to support her children. The stay-at-home mother gave her family a safety net, an all-purpose insurance policy against disaster.

If two-income families had saved the second paycheck, they would have built a different kind of safety net—the kind that comes from having plenty of money in the bank. But families didn't save that money. Even as millions of mothers marched into the workforce, savings declined, and not, as we will show, because families were frittering away their paychecks on toys for themselves or their children. Instead, families were swept up in a bidding war, competing furiously with one another for their most important possession: a house in a decent school district. As confidence in the school system crumbled, the bidding war for family housing intensified, and parents soon found themselves bidding up the price for other opportunities for their kids, such as a slot in a decent preschool or admission to a good college. Mom's extra income fit in perfectly, coming at just the right time to give each family extra ammunition to compete in the bidding wars—and to drive the prices even higher for the things they all wanted.

The average two-income family earns far more today than did the single-breadwinner family of a generation ago. And yet, once they have paid the mortgage, the car payments, the taxes, the health insurance, and the day-care bills, today's dual-income families have *less* discretionary income—and less money to put away for a rainy day—than the single-income family of a generation ago. And so the Two-Income Trap has been neatly sprung. Mothers now work two jobs, at home and at the office. And yet they have less cash on hand. Mom's paycheck has been pumped directly into the basic costs of keeping the children in the middle class.

At the same time that millions of mothers went to work, the family needed the stay-at-home mom (or a costly replacement) more than ever. The number of frail elderly, most of whom must depend on family for daily care, spiraled upward. Hospitals began discharging patients "quicker and sicker," expecting the family to pick up the task of nursing them back to health. With Mom in the workforce, parents were faced with a painful choice between paying for expensive care and taking time off work. At the same time, the divorce rate continued its upward climb. This situation was compounded by a leaner-and-meaner business climate that closed plants and laid off workers with alarming frequency. In this tougher world, millions of two-income families learned the price of living without a safety net.

Inevitably, the Two-Income Trap affected the one-income family too. When millions of mothers entered the workforce, they ratcheted up the price of a middle-class life for everyone, including families that wanted to keep Mom at home. A generation ago, a single breadwinner who worked diligently and spent carefully could assure his family a comfortable position in the middle class. But the frenzied bidding wars, fueled by families with two incomes, changed the game for single-income families as well, pushing them down the economic ladder. To keep Mom at home, the average single-income family must forfeit decent public schools and preschools, health insurance, and college degrees, leaving themselves and their children with a tenuous hold on their middle-class dreams.

What about single-parent families, the group that has no choice about getting by on one income? Not surprisingly, they are in even worse shape than their married counterparts. But the magnitude of the problem for single-mother families shocked us. If current trends persist, *more than one of every six single mothers will go bankrupt by the end of the decade.*[13] The usual explanations for why these women are in trouble—"deadbeat dads" who don't pay child support, discrimination in the workplace, and so forth—cannot account for the growing distress. Today's middle-class single mothers have better legal protection, higher salaries, more child support, and more opportunities in the workplace than their divorced counterparts of a generation ago, yet they face a much greater likelihood of financial collapse. We estimate that over the past twenty years, the number of single mothers in bankruptcy has increased more than 600 percent.

So why are these women in so much trouble? We will show that changes in the family balance sheet *before* a couple divorces explain much about the vulnerability of today's single mothers. Married parents are in trouble because they have spent every last penny and then some just to buy a middle-class life for their children. As a result, today's newly divorced mother is already teetering over a financial abyss the day she signs her divorce papers. She has nothing in the bank, and the family's fixed costs stretched the limits of *two* incomes, let alone one. She hasn't a prayer of competing with double-income families to provide her children with what have come to be seen as the basic requirements of a middle-class upbringing.

Is the only solution for all the mothers to scurry pell-mell back to the hearth? It may sound like a tidy resolution, but it won't work. Like it or not, women now need those paychecks to pay the mortgage and the health insurance bills. Their incomes are committed, and calling for them to abandon those financial commitments would mean forcing them to give up their families' spot in the middle class. No, the real solution lies elsewhere—in addressing the reasons behind the bidding war and helping *all* families, both dual- and single-income, to get some relief.

The Two-Income Trap is thick with irony. Middle-class mothers went into the workforce in a calculated effort to give their families an economic edge. Instead, millions of them are now in the workplace just so their families can break even. At a time when women are getting college diplomas and entering the workforce in record numbers, their families are in more financial trouble than ever. Partly these women were the victims of bad timing: Despite general economic prosperity, the risks facing their families jumped considerably. Partly they were the victims of optimistic myopia: They saw the rewards a working mother could bring, without seeing the risks associated with that newfound income. And partly they were the victims of one another. As millions of mothers poured into the workplace, it became increasingly difficult to put together a middle-class life on a single income. The combination has taken these women out of the home and away from their children *and* simultaneously made family life less, not more, financially secure. Today's middle-class mother is trapped: She can't afford to work, and she can't afford to quit.

A Mother's Story

Both mothers and fathers are trapped in the same sinking boat, but it is mothers who have been the special targets of change over the past generation. It is mothers who left the home en masse, transforming generations of family economics. It is mothers who must do it all, tending to home and children while managing full-time jobs outside the home. And it is nearly always mothers who preserve the remnants of the family in the aftermath of divorce.

Even for a married couple, financial failure is disproportionately a woman's problem. A husband and wife who have been struck by financial disaster look more or less the same on paper. They share the same assets, they owe the same debts, and they have the same black marks on their credit reports. But behind the curtain of marriage, there are important differences.

In this age of nominal equality between husbands and wives, in the most intimate aspect of their lives—family finance—couples reveal a surprising traditionalism. Research shows that on average, a husband is three times more likely than a wife to take primary responsibility for managing the family's money.[14] But as a couple sinks into financial turmoil, this responsibility tends to shift. As families fall behind on their bills, it is wives who roll up their sleeves and do what must be done. Wives who deal with foreclosure notices, wives who plead with creditors for more time to pay, and wives who insist on seeking credit counseling or legal help. And, like Ruth Ann, it is wives who ultimately decide when it is time to file for bankruptcy. Among couples who seek credit counseling or file for bankruptcy, the split over who was responsible for dealing with the bills was exactly reversed from that of secure families: three-quarters of the wives were exclusively responsible for trying to extract their families from their financial quagmire.[15]

This shift is not merely a mundane realignment of responsibilities within the household, a simple variation on the routine decisions that he will mow the lawn while she folds the laundry. Rather, it is a signal of serious discord within a marriage. In financially troubled families, women who managed the money alone were twice as likely to describe themselves as very dissatisfied with the arrangement than the men who took on that task. Many women, exhausted and frustrated by all that accompanies the descent into financial ruin, find that just when they most need help, their husbands have disappeared.

Men, for their part, often feel that their failure to provide for their families calls into question not just their abilities in the labor force but also their identities as husbands, as fathers, and as men. Perhaps it should come as no surprise to discover that financial problems and marital problems are statistically linked. Study after study shows that money is a source of contention in most marriages, but it is particularly problematic for couples that are financially unstable.[16] For a family living on the edge, every purchase must be scrutinized, creating flash points for conflict in marriages that are already overly stressed. With no one close at hand to blame for layoffs at work or exclusions in the health insurance policy, it is all too easy to turn frustration and anger on one another. Couples slip into an endless round of "should haves," second guessing themselves—and each other—for decisions long past. He should have worked the night shift when he had the chance, she should have kept driving the old car, he should have bargained for a better price on the home, she should have spent less on groceries. For some, words give way to physical blows in an ever-escalating battle to assess blame. A bankruptcy trustee we interviewed explains that by helping families use the bankruptcy courts to get protection from their creditors, "I'm in the abuse-prevention business. Every time I help a family get straightened out financially, I figure I saved someone a beating."

Make no mistake: Financial distress is a problem for both men and women. Accordingly, we will tell the stories of both mothers and fathers in the pages of this book. But we do not want to leave the impression that these phenomena are entirely gender-neutral. They are not. Mothers are 35 percent more likely than childless homeowners to lose their homes, three times more likely than men without children to go bankrupt, and seven times more likely to head up the family after a divorce.[17] And so, in the pages of this book, we will tell a story about families, about children, and, especially, about mothers.

Having Children, Going Broke

This book will tell the story of how having children has become the dividing line between the solvent and the insolvent, and how today's parents are working harder than ever and falling desperately behind even with two incomes. It is also the story of how this state of affairs is not some unavoidable feature of the modern economy, or, for that matter, the inevitable by-product of women's entry into the workforce.

We write this book so that Ruth Ann and all the mothers like Ruth Ann, along with politicians and pundits, child advocates and labor organizers, pro-family conservatives and liberal feminists, will take a serious look at the economic forces that have battered the American family. We want them to see the hard numbers—and to gasp. But most of all, we want them to see that there is a way out. There are changes that can happen—real changes, practical changes, meaningful changes. Changes that can be made in Congress, in state legislatures, in school boards, and in families. Changes that can make it so that the average parent can once again spend her nights fretting about potty training and prom dresses, not about home foreclosures and overdrawn bank accounts. Changes that can make America's great middle class secure once again.

2

The Over-Consumption Myth

During the past generation, a great myth has swept through America. Like all good myths, the Over-Consumption Myth tells a tale to explain a confusing world. Why are so many Americans in financial trouble? Why are credit card debts up and savings down? Why are millions of mothers heading into the labor force and working overtime? The myth is so deeply embedded in our collective understanding that it resists even elementary questioning: Families have spent too much money buying things they don't need. Americans have a new character flaw—"the urge to splurge"[1]—and it is driving them to spend, spend, spend like never before.

The drive for all that spending is almost mystical in origin. John de Graaf and his coauthors explain in *Affluenza: The All-Consuming Epidemic,* "It's as if we Americans, despite our intentions, suffer from some kind of Willpower Deficiency Syndrome, a breakdown in affluenza immunity."[2] Economist Juliet Schor blames "the new consumerism," but the results are the same. She points to "mass 'over-spending' within the middle class [in which] large numbers of Americans spend more than they say they would like to, and more than they have. That they spend more than they realize they are spending, and more than is fiscally prudent."[3]

Many maladies are explained away by the Over-Consumption Myth. Why are Americans in debt? Sociologist Robert Frank claims that America's newfound "Luxury Fever" forces middle-class families "to finance their consumption increases largely by reduced savings and increased debt."[4] Why are schools failing and streets unsafe? Juliet Schor cites "competitive spending" as a major contributor to "the deterioration of public goods" such as "education, social services, public safety, recreation, and culture."[5] Why are Americans unhappy? *Affluenza* sums it up: "The dogged pursuit for more" accounts for Americans' "overload, debt, anxiety, and waste."[6] Everywhere we turn, it seems that over-consumption is tearing at the very fabric of society.

The Over-Consumption Myth rests on the premise that families spend their money on things they don't really need. Over-consumption is not about medical care or basic housing; it is, in the words of Juliet Schor, about "designer clothes, a microwave, restaurant meals, home and automobile air conditioning, and, of course, Michael Jordan's ubiquitous athletic shoes, about which children and adults both display near-obsession."[7] And it isn't about buying a few goodies with extra income; it is about going deep into debt to finance consumer purchases that sensible people could do without.

The beauty of the Over-Consumption Myth is that it squares neatly with our own intuitions. We see the malls packed with shoppers. We receive catalogs filled with outrageously expensive gadgets. We think of that overpriced summer dress that hangs in the back of the closet or those power tools gathering dust in the garage. The conclusion seems indisputable: The "urge to splurge" is driving folks into economic ruin.

But is it true? Intuitions and anecdotes are no substitute for hard data, so we searched deep in the recesses of federal archives, where we found detailed information on Americans' spending patterns since the early 1970s, carefully sorted by spending categories and family size.[8] If families really are blowing their paychecks on designer clothes and restaurant meals, then the expenditure data should show that today's families are spending more on these frivolous items than ever before. (Throughout our discussion, in this chapter and elsewhere, all figures will be adjusted for the effects of inflation.[9]) But we found that the numbers pointed in a very different direction, demonstrating that the over-consumption explanation is just a myth.

Consider clothing. *Newsweek* recently ran a multipage cover story about Americans drowning in debt. The reason for widespread financial distress and high bankruptcy rates? "Frivolous shopping is part of the problem: many debtors blame their woes squarely on Tommy, Ralph, Gucci, and Prada."[10] That certainly sounds reasonable. After all, Banana Republic is so crowded with shoppers we can barely find an empty fitting room, Adidas and Nike clad the feet of every teenager we meet, and designer shops rake in profits selling nothing but underwear or sunglasses. Even little children's clothes now carry hip brand names, and babies sport "GAP" or "YSL" on their T-shirts and sleepers.

And yet, when it is all added up, including the Tommy sweatshirts and Ray-Ban sunglasses, the average family of four today spends 21 percent *less* (inflation adjusted) on clothing than a similar family did in the early 1970s. How can this be? What the finger-waggers have forgotten are the things families *don't* spend money on anymore. I (Elizabeth) recall the days of rushing off to Stride Rite to buy two new pairs of sensible leather shoes for each of my children every three months (one for church and one for everyday) plus a pair of sneakers for play. Today, Amelia's toddler owns nothing but a pair of $5 sandals from Wal-Mart. Suits, ties, and pantyhose have been replaced by cotton trousers and knit tops, as "business casual" has swept the nation. New fabrics, new technology, and cheap labor have lowered prices. And discounters like Target and Marshall's have popped up across the country, providing reasonable, low-cost clothes for today's families. The differences add up. In 1973, Sunday dresses, wool jackets, and the other clothes for a family of four claimed nearly $750 more a year from the family budget than all the name-brand sneakers and hip T-shirts today's families are buying.[11]

OK, so if Americans aren't blowing their paychecks on clothes, then they must be overspending on food. Designer brands have hit the grocery shelves as well, with far more prepared foods, high-end ice creams, and exotic juices. Families even buy bottles of *water,* a purchase that would have shocked their grandparents. Besides, who cooks at home anymore? With Mom and Dad both tied up at work, Americans are eating out (or ordering in) more than ever before. The authors of *Affluenza* grumble, "City streets and even suburban malls sport a United Nations of restaurants. . . . Eating out used to be a special occasion. Now we spend more money on restaurant food than on the food we cook ourselves."[12]

They are right, but only to a point. The average family of four spends more at restaurants than it used to, but it spends less at the grocery store—a lot less. Families are saving big bucks by skipping the T-bone steaks, buying their cereal in bulk at Costco, and opting for generic paper towels and canned vegetables. Those savings more than compensate for all that restaurant eating—so much so that today's family of four is actually spending 22 percent *less* on food (at-home and restaurant eating combined) than its counterpart of a generation ago.[13]

Outfitting the home? *Affluenza* rails against appliances "that were deemed luxuries as recently as 1970, but are now found in well over half of U.S. homes, and thought of by a majority of Americans as necessities: dishwashers, clothes dryers, central heating and air conditioning, color and cable TV."[14] These handy gadgets may have captured a new place in Americans' hearts, but they aren't taking up much space in our wallets. Manufacturing costs are down, and durability is up. When the microwave oven, dishwasher, and clothes dryer are combined with the refrigerator, washing machine, and stove, families are actually spending 44 percent *less* on major appliances today than they were a generation ago.[15]

Vacation homes are another big target. A financial columnist for *Money* magazine explains how life has changed. A generation ago, the dream vacation was a modest affair: "Come summer, the family piled into its Ford country wagon (with imitation wood-panel doors) and tooled off to Lake Watchamasakee for a couple of weeks." Now, laments the columnist, things have changed. "The rented cabin on the lake gave way to a second home high on an ocean dune."[16] But the world he describes does not exist, at least not for the middle-class family. Despite the rhetoric, summer homes remain the fairly exclusive privilege of the well-to-do. In 1973, 3.2 percent of families reported expenses associated with owning a vacation home; by 2000, the proportion had inched up to 4 percent.[17]

That is not to say that middle-class families never fritter away any money. A generation ago no one had cable, big-screen televisions were a novelty reserved for the very rich, and DVD and TiVo were meaningless strings of letters. So how much more do families spend on "home entertainment," premium channels included? They spend 23 percent more—a whopping extra $170 annually. Computers add another $300 to the annual family budget.[18] But even that increase looks a little different in the context of other spending. The extra money spent on cable, electronics, and computers is more than offset by families' savings on major appliances and household furnishings.

The same balancing act holds true in other areas. The average family spends more on airline travel than it did a generation ago, but it spends less on dry cleaning. More on telephone services, but less on tobacco. More on pets, but less on carpets.[19] And, when we add it all up, increases in one category are offset by decreases in another. In other words, there seems to be about as much frivolous spending today as there was a generation ago.

Yet the myth remains rock solid: Middle-class families are rushing headlong into financial ruin because they are squandering too much money on Red Lobster, Gucci, and trips to the Bahamas. Americans cling so tightly to the myth not because it is supported by hard evidence, but because it is a comforting way to explain away some very bad news. If families are in trouble because they squander their money, then those of us who shop at Costco and cook our own pasta have nothing to worry about. Moreover, if families are to blame for their own failures, then the rest of us bear no responsibility for helping those who are in trouble. Their fault, their problem. We can join the chorus of experts advising the financial failures to "simplify"—stay away from Perrier and Rolex. Follow this sensible advice, and credit card balances will vanish, bankruptcy filings will disappear, and mortgage foreclosures will cease to plague America.

Reality is not nearly so neat. Sure, there are some families who buy too much stuff, but there is no evidence of any "epidemic" in overspending—certainly nothing that could explain a 255 percent increase in the foreclosure rate, a 430 percent increase in the bankruptcy rolls, and a 570 percent increase in credit card debt.[20] A growing number of families are in terrible financial trouble, but no matter how many times the accusation is hurled, Prada and HBO are not the reason.

Where Did the Money Go?

If they aren't spending themselves into oblivion on designer water and DVDs, how did middle-class families get into so much financial trouble? The answer starts, quite literally, at home.

We could pile cliché on cliché about the home, but we will settle for this observation: The home is the most important purchase for the average middle-class family. To the overwhelming majority of Americans, home ownership stands out as the single most important component of "the good life."[21] Homes mark the lives of their children, setting out the parameters of their universe. The luck of location will determine whether there are computers in their classrooms, whether there are sidewalks for them to ride bikes on, and whether the front yard is a safe place to play. And a home will consume more of the family's income than any other purchase—more than food, more than cars, more than health insurance, more than child care.

As anyone who has read the newspapers or purchased a home knows, it costs a lot more to buy a house than it used to.[22] (Since the overwhelming majority of middle-class parents are homeowners, we focus this discussion on the costs of owning, rather than renting.[23])

What most of us have forgotten, however, is that today's home prices are *not* the product of some inevitable demographic force that has simply rolled its way across America. Quite the opposite. In the late 1980s, several commentators predicted a spectacular collapse in the housing market. Economists reasoned that the baby boomers were about to become empty nesters, so pressure on the housing market would undergo a sharp reversal. According to these experts, housing prices would reverse their forty-year upward trend and drop during the 1990s and 2000s—anywhere from 10 to 47 percent.[24]

Of course, the over-consumption critics have a ready explanation for why housing prices shot up despite expert predictions: Americans are bankrupting themselves to buy over-gadgeted, oversized "McMansions.". *Money* magazine captures this view: "A generation or so ago . . . a basic, 800-square-foot, $8,000 Levittown box with a carport was heaven. . . . By the 1980s, the dream had gone yupscale. Home had become a 6,000-square-foot contemporary on three acres or a gutted and rehabbed townhouse in a gentrified ghetto."[25]

Where did so many people get this impression? Perhaps from the much ballyhooed fact that the average size of a new home has increased by nearly 40 percent over the past generation (though it is still less than 2,200 square feet).[26] But before the over-consumption camp declares victory, there are a few more details to consider. The overwhelming majority of middle-income families don't live in one of those spacious new homes. Indeed, the proportion of families living in older homes has increased by nearly 50 percent over the past generation, leaving a growing number of homeowners grappling with deteriorating roofs, peeling paint, and old wiring. Today, nearly six out of ten families own a home that is more than twenty-five years old, and nearly a quarter own a house that is more than fifty years old.[27]

Despite all the hoopla over the highly visible status symbols of the well-to-do, the size and amenities of the average middle-class family home have increased only modestly. The median owner-occupied home grew from 5.7 rooms in 1975 to 6.1 rooms in the late 1990s—

an increase of less than half of a room in more than two decades.[28] What was this half a room used for? Was it an "exercise room," a "media room," or any of the other exotic uses of space that critics have so widely mocked? No. The data show that most often that extra room was a second bathroom or a third bedroom.[29] These are meaningful improvements, to be sure, but the average middle-class family in a six-room house has hardly rocketed to McMansion status.

For the Children

The finger-waggers missed another vital fact: The rise in housing costs has become a *family* problem. Home prices have grown across the board (particularly in larger urban areas), but the brunt of the price increases has fallen on families with children. Our analysis shows that the median home value for the average childless couple increased by 26 percent between 1984 and 2001—an impressive rise in less than twenty years.[30] (Again, these and all other figures are adjusted for inflation.) For married couples with children, however, housing prices shot up 78 percent during this period—*three times faster.*[31] To put this in dollar terms, in 1984 the average married couple with young children owned a house worth $72,000. Less than twenty years later, a similar family bought a house worth $128,000—an increase of more than $50,000. The growing costs made a big dent in the family budget, as monthly mortgage costs made a similar jump, despite falling interest rates.[32] No matter how the data are cut, couples with children are spending more than ever on housing.

Why would the average parent spend so much money on a home? The over-consumption theory doesn't offer many insights. We doubt very much that families with children have a particular love affair with "bathroom spas" and "professional kitchens" while the swinging singles are perfectly content to live in Spartan apartments with outdated kitchens and closet-sized bathrooms.

No, the real reason lies elsewhere. For many parents, the answer came down to two words so powerful that families would pursue them to the brink of bankruptcy: *safety* and *education*. Families put Mom to work, used up the family's economic reserves, and took on crushing debt loads in sacrifice to these twin gods, all in the hope of offering their children the best possible start in life.

The best possible start begins with good schools, but parents are scrambling to find those schools. Even politicians who can't agree on much of anything agree that there is a major problem in America's public schools. In the 2000 election campaign, for example, presidential candidates from both political parties were tripping over each other to promote their policies for new educational programs. And they had good reason. According to a recent poll, education now ranks as voters' single highest priority for increased federal spending—higher than health care, research on AIDS, environmental protection, and fighting crime.[33]

Everyone has heard the all-too-familiar news stories about kids who can't read, gang violence in the schools, classrooms without textbooks, and drug dealers at the school doors. For the most part, the problems aren't just about flawed educational policies; they are also depicted as the evils associated with poverty.[34] Even President Bush (who didn't exactly run on a Help-the-Poor platform) focused on helping "failing" schools, which, by and large, translates into help for schools in the poorest neighborhoods.

So what does all this have to do with educating middle-class children, most of whom have been lucky enough to avoid the worst failings of the public school system? The answer is simple—money. Failing schools impose an enormous cost on those children who are forced to attend them, but they also inflict an enormous cost on those who don't.

Talk with an average middle-class parent in any major metropolitan area, and she'll describe the time, money, and effort she devoted to finding a slot for her offspring in a decent school. In some cases, the story will be about mastering the system: "We put Joshua on the wait-list for the Science Magnet School the day he was born." In other cases, it will be one of leaving the public school system altogether, as middle-class parents increasingly opt for private, parochial, or home schooling. "My husband and I both went to public schools, but we just couldn't see sending Erin to the [local] junior high." But private schools and strategic maneuvering go only so far. For most middle-class parents, ensuring that their children get a decent education translates into one thing: snatching up a home in the small subset of school districts that have managed to hold on to a reputation of high quality and parent confidence.

Homes can command a premium for all sorts of amenities, such as a two-car garage, proximity to work or shopping, or a low crime rate. A study conducted in Fresno (a midsized California metropolis with 400,000 residents) found that, for similar homes, school quality was *the single most important determinant of neighborhood prices*—more important than racial composition of the neighborhood, commute distance, crime rate, or proximity to a hazardous waste site.[35] A study in suburban Boston showed the impact of school boundary lines. Two homes located less than half a mile apart and similar in nearly every aspect, will command significantly different prices if they are in different elementary school zones.[36] Schools that scored just 5 percent higher on fourth-grade math and reading tests added a premium of nearly $4,000 to nearby homes, even though these homes were virtually the same in terms of neighborhood character, school spending, racial composition, tax burden, and crime rate.

By way of example, consider University City, the West Philadelphia neighborhood surrounding the University of Pennsylvania. In an effort to improve the area, the university committed funds for a new elementary school. The results? At the time of the announcement, the median home value in the area was less than $60,000. Five years later, "homes within the boundaries go for about $200,000, even if they need to be totally renovated."[37] The neighborhood is otherwise pretty much the same: the same commute to work, the same distance from the freeways, the same old houses. And yet, in five years families are willing to pay more than *triple* the price for a home, just so they can send their kids to a better public elementary school. Real estate agents have long joked that the three things that matter in determining the price of a house are "location, location, location." Today, that mantra could be updated to "schools, schools, schools."

This phenomenon isn't new, but the pressure has intensified considerably. In the early 1970s, not only did most Americans believe that the public schools were functioning reasonably well, a sizable majority of adults thought that public education had actually *improved* since they were kids. Today, only a small minority of Americans share this optimistic view. Instead, the majority now believes that schools have gotten significantly worse.[38] Fully half of all Americans are dissatisfied with America's public education system, a deep concern shared by black and white parents alike.[39]

Even Juliet Schor, a leading critic of over-consumption, acknowledges the growing pressure on parents. For all that she criticizes America's love affair with granite countertops and microwave ovens, she recognizes that parents can find themselves trapped by the needs of their children:

> Within the middle class, and even the upper middle class, many families experience an almost threatening pressure to keep up, both for themselves and their children. They are deeply concerned about the rigors of the global economy, and the need to have their children attend "good" schools. This means living in a community with relatively high housing costs.[40]

In other words, the only way to ensure that a beloved youngster gets a solid education is to spring for a three-bedroom Colonial with an hour-long commute to a job in the city.

Today's parents must also confront another frightening prospect as they consider where their children will attend school: the threat of school violence. The widely publicized rise in shootings, gangs, and dangerous drugs at public schools sent many parents in search of a safe haven for their sons and daughters. Violent incidents can happen anywhere, as the shootings at lovely suburban Columbine High

School in Colorado revealed to a horrified nation. But the statistics show that school violence is not as random as it might seem. According to one study, the incidence of serious violent crime—such as robbery, rape, or attack with a weapon—is more than three times higher in schools characterized by high poverty levels than those with predominantly middle- and upper-income children.[41] Similarly, urban children are more than twice as likely as suburban children to fear being attacked on the way to or from school.[42] The data expose a harsh reality: Parents who can get their kids into a more *economically* segregated neighborhood really improve the odds that their sons and daughters will make it through school safely.

Newer, more isolated suburbs with restrictive zoning also promise a refuge from the random crimes that tarnish urban living.[43] It may seem odd that families would devote so much attention to personal safety—or the lack thereof—when the crime rate in the United States has fallen sharply over the past decade.[44] But national statistics mask differences among communities, and disparities have grown over time. In many cities, the urban centers have grown more dangerous while outlying areas have gotten safer—further intensifying the pressure parents feel to squeeze into a suburban refuge.[45] In Baltimore and Philadelphia, for example, the crime rate fell in the surrounding suburbs just as it increased in the center city. The disparities are greatest for the most frightening violent crimes. Today a person is *ten times* more likely to be murdered in center city Philadelphia than in its surrounding suburbs, and twelve times more likely to be killed in central Baltimore.[46]

Dyed-in-the-wool urbanites would be quick to remind us that although the crime rate may have climbed in many urban areas, the average family faces only minuscule odds of being killed in a random act of violence in downtown Baltimore or any other city. That may be true, but it is beside the point, because it ignores a basic fact of parental psychology—worry. Parents are constantly mindful of the vulnerability of their children, and no amount of statistical reasoning can persuade them to stop worrying.

Emily Cheung tells a story that resonates with millions of parents. A psychotherapist and longtime city dweller, Emily had rented an apartment in a working-class neighborhood. For years, she sang the praises of city living. But as her boys got older, her views began to change. "We were close to The Corner and I was scared for [my sons]. I didn't want them to grow up there." After a series of break-ins on her block, Emily started looking for a new place for her family to live. "I wasn't looking to buy a house, but I wanted to rent something away from [this neighborhood] to get my boys out to better schools and a safer place." It wasn't as easy as she had hoped. Emily couldn't find any apartments in the neighborhood she wanted to live in. When her real estate agent convinced her that she could qualify for a mortgage, she jumped at the chance to move to the suburbs.

> The first night in the house, I just walked around in the dark and was so grateful. . . . At this house, it was so nice and quiet. [My sons] could go outdoors and they didn't need to be afraid. [She starts crying.] I thought that if I could do this for them, get them to a better place, what a wonderful gift to give my boys. I mean, this place was three thousand times better. It is safe with a huge front yard and a back yard and a driveway. It is wonderful. I had wanted this my whole life.

Emily took a huge financial gamble buying a house that claimed nearly half of her monthly income, but she had made up her mind to do whatever she could to keep her boys safe.

Families like Emily's have long acknowledged crime as an unfortunate fact of life, but the effect on parents has changed. A generation ago, there just wasn't much that average parents could do to escape these hazards. A family could buy a guard dog or leave the lights on, but if the suburbs were about as troubled as the cities—or if crime wasn't framed as a *city* problem—then the impetus to move wasn't very compelling. Today, however, cities and suburbs seem to present two very distinct alternatives. When the car is stolen or the news features a frightening murder on a nearby street, families are more inclined to believe that the suburbs will offer them a safer alternative. According to one study, more than one-third of families who had left central Baltimore and over half of families who had considered leaving "were moved to do so by their fear of crime."[47]

Ultimately, however, it did not matter whether there was a meaningful gap between the schools in the center cities and those in the surrounding suburbs, or whether the streets really were safer far away from the big city. It didn't even matter whether there really was a crisis in public education, as the politicians and the local news might insist. What mattered was that parents *believed* that there was an important difference—and that the difference was growing.[48] The only answer for millions of loving parents was to buy their way into a decent school district in a safe neighborhood—whatever the cost.

Bidding War in the Suburbs

And so it was that middle-class families across America have been quietly drawn into an all-out war. Not the war on drugs, the war about creationism, or the war over sex education. Their war has received little coverage in the press and no attention from politicians, but it has profoundly altered the lives of parents everywhere, shaping every economic decision they make. Their war is a bidding war. The opening shots in this war were fired in the most ordinary circumstances. Individual parents sought out homes they thought were good places to bring up kids, just as their parents had done before them. But as families saw urban centers as increasingly unattractive places to live, the range of desirable housing options began to shrink and parents' desire to escape from failing schools began to take on new urgency. Millions of parents joined in the search for a house on a safe street with a good school nearby. Over time, demand heated up for an increasingly narrow slice of the housing stock.

This in itself would have been enough to trigger a bidding war for suburban homes in good school districts. But a growing number of families brought new artillery to the war: a second income. In an era when the overwhelming majority of mothers are bringing home a paycheck and covering a big part of the family's bills, it is easy to forget that just one generation ago most middle-class mothers—including those in the workforce—made only modest contributions to the family's regular expenses. A generation ago, the average working wife contributed just one-quarter of the family's total income.[49] In many families, Mom's earnings were treated as "pin money" to cover treats and extras, not mortgages and car payments. Unenlightened husbands weren't the only ones to foster this attitude. Banks and loan companies routinely ignored women's earnings in calculating whether to approve a mortgage, on the theory that a wife might leave the workforce at any moment to pursue full-time homemaking.[50]

In 1975 Congress passed an important law with far-reaching consequences for families' housing choices. The Equal Credit Opportunity Act stipulated, among other things, that lenders could no longer ignore a wife's income when judging whether a family earned enough to qualify for a mortgage.[51] By the early 1980s, women's participation in the labor force had become a significant factor in whether a married couple could buy a home.[52] Both families and banks had started down the path of counting Mom's income as an essential part of the monthly budget.

This change may not sound revolutionary today, but it represents a seismic shift in family economics. No longer were families constrained by Dad's earning capacity. When Mom wanted a bigger yard or Dad wanted a better school for the kids, families had a new answer: Send Mom to work and use her paycheck to buy that nice house in the suburbs.

The women's movement contributed to this trend, opening up new employment possibilities and calling on mothers to reconsider their lifetime goals. For some women, the decision to head into the workplace meant personal fulfillment and expanded opportunities to engage in interesting, challenging occupations. For many more, the sense of independence that accompanied a job and a paycheck provided a powerful incentive. But for most middle-class women, the decision to get up early, drop the children off at day care, and head to the office or factory was driven, at least in part, by more prosaic reasons. Millions of women went to work in a calculated attempt to give their families an economic edge.[53]

The transformation happened gradually, as hundreds of thousands of mothers marched into the workforce year after year. But over the course of a few decades, the change has been nothing short of revolutionary. As recently as 1976 a married mother was more than twice as likely to stay home with her children as to work full-time. By 2000, those figures had almost reversed: The modern married mother is now nearly twice as likely to have a full-time job as to stay home.[54] The transformation can be felt in other ways. In 1965 only 21 percent of working women were back at their jobs within 6 months of giving birth to their first child. Today, that figure is higher than 70 percent. Similarly, a modern mother with a three-month-old infant is more likely to be working outside the home than was a 1960s woman with a five-year-old child.[55] As a claims adjuster with two children told us, "It never even occurred to me not to work, even after Zachary was born. All the women I know have a job."

Even these statistics understate the magnitude of change among middle-class mothers. Before the 1970s, large numbers of older women, lower-income women, and childless women were in the workforce.[56] But middle-class mothers were far more likely to stay behind, holding on to the more traditional role of full-time homemaker long after many of their sisters had given it up. Over the past generation, middle-class mothers flooded into offices, shops, and factories, undergoing a greater increase in workforce participation than either their poor or their well-to-do sisters.[57] Attitudes changed as well. In 1970, when the women's revolution was well under way, 78 percent of younger married women thought that it was "better for wives to be homemakers and husbands to do the breadwinning."[58] Today, only 38 percent of women believe that it is "ideal" for one parent to be home full-time, and nearly 70 percent of Americans believe it doesn't matter whether it is the husband or the wife who stays home with the children.[59]

It is also the middle-class family whose finances have been most profoundly affected by women's entry into the workforce. Poorer, less educated women have seen small gains in real wages over the past generation. Wealthy women have enjoyed considerable increases, but those gains were complemented by similar increases in their husbands' rapidly rising incomes.[60] For the middle class, however, women's growing paychecks have made all the difference, compensating for the painful fact that their husbands' earnings have stagnated over the past generation.[61]

For millions of middle-class families hoping to hold on to a more traditional mother-at-home lifestyle, the bidding wars crushed those dreams. A group of solidly middle-class Americans—our nation's police officers—illustrate the point. A recent study showed that the average police officer could not afford a median priced home in *two-thirds* of the nation's metropolitan areas on the officer's income alone.[62] The same is true for elementary school teachers. Nor is this phenomenon limited to high-cost cities such as New York and San Francisco. Without a working spouse, the family of a police officer or teacher is forced to rent an apartment or buy in a marginal neighborhood even in more modestly priced cities such as Nashville, Kansas City, and Charlotte. These families have found that in order to hold on to all the benefits of a stay-at-home mom (which we will discuss in chapter 3), they will be shoved to the bottom rungs of the middle class.

What about those families with middle-class aspirations who earned a little less than average or those who lived in a particularly expensive city? Even with both parents in the workforce, they have fallen behind. Rather than drop out of the bidding war and resign themselves to sending their kids to weaker schools, many middle-class couples have seized on another way to fund their dream home: take on a bigger mortgage. In 1980, the mortgage lending industry was effectively deregulated (see chapter 6). As a result, average families could find plenty of banks willing to issue them larger mortgages relative to their incomes. As the bidding war heated up, families took on larger and larger mortgages just to keep up, committing themselves to debt loads that were unimaginable just a generation earlier.

With extra income from Mom's paycheck and extra mortgage money from the bank, the usual supply and demand in the market for homes in desirable areas exploded into an all-out bidding war. As millions of families sent a second earner into the workforce, one might expect that they would spend *less* on housing as a proportion of total income. Instead, just the opposite occurred. A growing number of middle-class families now spend *more* on housing relative to family income.[63] As demand for the limited stock of desirable family housing continued to grow, prices did not reach the natural limit that would have been imposed by the purchasing power of the single-income family confined to a conventional 80 percent mortgage. Instead, monthly mortgage expenses took a leap of 69 *percent* at a time that other family expenditures—food, clothing, home furnishings, and the like—remained steady or fell.[64]

Parents were caught. It may have been their collective demand for housing in family neighborhoods that drove prices up, but each individual family that wanted one of those houses had no choice but to join in the bidding war. If one family refused to pay, some other family would snatch up the property. No single family could overcome the effects of millions of other families wanting what it wanted.

Each year, a growing number of stay-at-home mothers made the move into the workforce, hoping to put their families into solidly middle-class neighborhoods. But the rules quietly changed. Today's mothers are no longer working to get ahead; now they must work just to keep up. Somewhere along the way, they fell into a terrible trap.

Out of the Housing Trap?

Can families extract themselves from the two-income housing trap? We could make all the obvious suggestions here. Families should "downshift," taking on no more mortgage debt than they can afford. If that means renting for another ten years or living in a neighborhood with lousy schools, well, that's just too bad. This advice would certainly be sensible from a financial point of view. The problem is that families don't find it particularly compelling. The experts have been dispensing these words of wisdom for at least a decade with no discernible effect, and we're pretty sure that adding our own voices to the chorus would be useless.

Alternatively, we could take the usual liberal approach, calling for more government regulation of the housing market such as price caps. But we don't think the solution lies with such complex regulations. Indeed, any effort to eliminate the fundamental forces of supply and demand with such artificial constraints might actually worsen the situation by diminishing the incentive to build new houses or improve older ones. Nor would we argue for outright government subsidies. Such programs may be appropriate to help a small number of low-income families get a decent place to live, but America simply cannot afford mass subsidies for its middle class to buy housing. Besides, direct subsidies are likely to add more ammunition to the already ruinous bidding wars, ultimately driving home prices even higher.

In order to free families from the trap, it is necessary to go to the heart of the problem: public education. Bad schools impose indirect—but huge—costs on millions of middle-class families. In their desperate rush to save their children from failing schools, families are literally spending themselves into bankruptcy. The only way to take the pressure off these families is to change the schools.

The concept of public schools is deeply American. It is perhaps the most tangible symbol of opportunity for social and economic mobility for all children, embodying the notion that merit rather than money determines a child's future. But who are we kidding? As parents increasingly believe that the differences among schools will translate into differences in lifetime chances, they are doing everything they can to buy their way into the best public schools. Schools in middle-class neighborhoods may be labeled "public," but parents have paid for tuition by purchasing a $175,000 home within a carefully selected school district.

It is time to sound the alarm that the crisis in education is not only a crisis of reading and arithmetic; it is also a crisis in middle-class family economics. At the core of the problem is the time-honored rule that where you live dictates where you go to school. Any policy that loosens the ironclad relationship between location-location-location and school-school-school would eliminate the need for parents to pay an inflated price for a home just because it happens to lie within the boundaries of a desirable school district.

A well-designed voucher program would fit the bill neatly. A taxpayer-funded voucher that paid the entire cost of educating a child (not just a partial subsidy) would open a range of opportunities to all children. With fully funded vouchers, parents of all income levels could send their children—and the accompanying financial support—to the schools of their choice. Middle-class parents who used state funds to send their kids to school would be able to live in the neighborhood of their choice—or the neighborhood of their pocketbook. Fully funded vouchers would relieve parents from the terrible choice of leaving their kids in lousy schools or bankrupting themselves to escape those schools.

We recognize that the term "voucher" has become a dirty word in many educational circles. The reason is straightforward: The current debate over vouchers is framed as a public-versus-private rift, with vouchers denounced for draining off much-needed funds from public schools. The fear is that partial-subsidy vouchers provide a boost so that better-off parents can opt out of a failing public school system, while the other children are left behind.

But the public-versus-private competition misses the central point. The problem is not vouchers; the problem is parental choice. Under current voucher schemes, children who do not use the vouchers are still assigned to public schools based on their zip codes. This means that in the overwhelming majority of cases, a bureaucrat picks the child's school, not a parent. The only way for parents to exercise any choice is to buy a different home—which is exactly how the bidding wars started.

Short of buying a new home, parents currently have only one way to escape a failing public school: Send the kids to private school. But there is another alternative, one that would keep much-needed tax dollars inside the public school system while still reaping the advantages offered by a voucher program. Local governments could enact meaningful reform by enabling parents to choose from among *all* the public schools in a locale, with no presumptive assignment based on neighborhood. Under a public school voucher program, parents, not bureaucrats, would have the power to pick schools for their children—and to choose which schools would get their children's vouchers. Students would be admitted to a particular public school on the basis of their talents, their interests, or even their lottery numbers; their zip codes would be irrelevant. Tax dollars would follow the children, not the parents' home addresses, and children who live in a $50,000 house would have the same educational opportunities as those who live in a $250,000 house.

Children who required extra resources, such as those with physical or learning disabilities, could be assigned proportionately larger vouchers, which would make it more attractive for schools to take on the more challenging (and expensive) task of educating these children. It might take some re-jiggering to settle on the right amount for a public school voucher, but eventually every child would have a valuable funding ticket to be used in any school in the area. To collect those tickets, schools would have to provide the education parents want. And parents would have a meaningful set of choices, *without* the need to buy a new home or pay private school tuition. Ultimately, an all-voucher system would diminish the distinction between public and private schools, as parents were able to exert more direct control over their children's schools.[65]

Of course, public school vouchers would not entirely eliminate the pressure parents feel to move into better family neighborhoods. Some areas would continue to have higher crime rates or better parks, and many parents might still prefer to live close to their children's schools. But a fundamental revision of school assignment policies would broaden the range of housing choices families would consider. Instead of limiting themselves to homes within one or two miles of a school, parents could choose a home five or even ten miles away—enough distance to give them several neighborhoods to choose from, with a broad range of price alternatives.

School change, like any other change, would entail some costs. More children might need to take a bus to school, pushing up school transportation expenses. On the other hand, many parents might actually shorten their own commutes, since they would no longer be forced to live in far-flung suburbs for the sake of their children. The net costs could be positive or negative.

An all-voucher system would be a shock to the educational system, but the shakeout might be just what the system needs. In the short run, a large number of parents would likely chase a limited number of spots in a few excellent schools. But over time, the whole concept of "the Beverly Hills schools" or "Newton schools" would die out, replaced in the hierarchy by schools that offer a variety of programs that parents want for their children, regardless of the geographic boundaries. By selecting where to send their children (and where to spend their vouchers), parents would take control over schools' tax dollars, making them the de facto owners of those schools. Parents, not administrators, would decide on programs, student-teacher ratios, and whether to spend money on art or sports. Parents' competitive energies could be channeled toward signing up early or improving their children's qualifications for a certain school, not bankrupting themselves to buy homes they cannot afford.

If a meaningful public school voucher system were instituted, the U.S. housing market would change forever. These changes might dampen, and perhaps even depress, housing prices in some of today's most competitive neighborhoods. But these losses would be offset by other gains. Owners of older homes in urban centers might find more willing buyers, and the urge to flee the cities might abate. Urban sprawl might slow down as families recalculate the costs of living so far from work. At any rate, the change would cause a one-time readjustment. The housing market would normalize, with supply and demand more balanced and families freed from ruinous mortgages.

The Price of Education

Even with that perfect house in a swanky school district, parents still are not covered when it comes to educating their kids—not by a long shot. The notion that taxpayers foot the bill for educating middle-class children has become a myth in yet another way. The two ends of the spectrum—everything that happens before a child shows up for his first day of kindergarten and after he is handed his high-school diploma—fall directly on the parents. Preschool and college, which now account for one-third (or more) of the years a typical middle-class kid spends in school, are paid for almost exclusively by the child's family.

Preschool has always been a privately funded affair, at least for most middle-class families. What has changed is its role for middle-class children. Over the past generation, the image of preschool has transformed from an optional stopover for little kids to a "prerequisite" for elementary school. Parents have been barraged with articles telling them that early education is important for everything from "pre-reading" skills to social development. As one expert in early childhood education observes, "In many communities around the country, kindergarten is no longer aimed at the entry level. And the only way Mom and Dad feel they can get their child prepared is through a pre-kindergarten program."[66]

Middle-class parents have stepped into line with the experts' recommendations. Today, nearly two-thirds of America's three- and four-year-olds attend preschool, compared with just 4 percent in the mid-1960s.[67] This isn't just the by-product of more mothers entering the workforce; nearly half of all stay-at-home moms now send their kids to a prekindergarten program.[68] As *Newsweek* put it, "The science says it all: preschool programs are neither a luxury nor a fad, but a real necessity."[69]

As demand has heated up, many families have found it increasingly difficult to *find* a prekindergarten program with an empty slot. Author Vicki Iovine describes the struggle she experienced trying to get her children into preschool in southern California:

> Just trying to get an application to any old preschool can be met with more attitude than the maitre d' at Le Cirque. If you should be naïve enough to ask if there will be openings in the next session, you may be reminded that there are always more applicants than openings, or the person might just laugh at you and hang up.[70]

Ms. Iovine's remarks are tongue-in-cheek, and pundits love to mock the parent who subscribes to the theory that "if little Susie doesn't get into the right preschool she'll never make it into the right medical school." But the shortage of quality preschool programs is very real. Child development experts have rated day-care centers, and the news is not good. The majority are lumped in the "poor to mediocre" range.[71] Not surprisingly, preschools with strong reputations often have long waiting lists.[72]

Once again, today's parents find themselves caught in a trap. A generation ago, when nursery school was regarded as little more than a chance for Mom to take a break, parents could consider the economics in a fairly detached way, committing to pay no more than what they could afford. And when only a modest number of parents were shopping for those preschool slots, the prices had to remain low to attract a full class. Today, when scores of experts routinely proclaim that preschool is decisive in a child's development, but a slot in a preschool—any preschool—can be hard to come by, parents are in a poor position to shop around for lower prices.

The laws of supply and demand take hold in the opposite direction, eliminating the pressure for preschool programs to keep prices low as they discover that they can increase fees without losing pupils. A full-day program in a prekindergarten offered by the Chicago *public* school district costs $6,500 a year—more than the cost of a year's tuition at the University of Illinois.[73] High? Yes, but that hasn't deterred parents: At just one Chicago public school, there are ninety-five kids on a waiting list for twenty slots. That situation is fairly typical. According to one study, the annual cost for a four-year-old to attend a child care center in an urban area is more than *double* the price of college tuition in fifteen states.[74] And so today's middle-class families simply spend and spend, stretching their budgets to give their child the fundamentals of a modern education.

The Promise of Public Education

The solution here is pretty obvious: Extend the scope of public education. If Americans generally believe that educational programs should begin at age three, why should public education wait to kick in at age five or six? The decision about how old children should be when they start school was made more than a century ago, when views about the learning capacity of young children were very different. The absence of publicly funded preschool is an anachronism, one that could easily be remedied. A host of politicians, including 2000 Democratic presidential candidate Al Gore and Congressman Richard Gephardt, have proposed publicly funded, universal preschool.[75] We agree—it is high time.

At this point, the reader might expect us to join the chorus calling for taxpayer-funded day care as well. Unlike preschool, the primary mission of most day-care programs is not to educate children but to provide surrogate child care when parents are at work. For more than two decades, women's groups, labor unions, and liberal politicians have been pressing the government to foot the bill for day care. Blocked by conservatives, advocates of free day care have had little success, but that hasn't stopped the clamor.

It is time for a hard look at this sacred cow. How much help would subsidized day care really offer to middle-class families? It would certainly be a big help for poorer families whose paychecks can barely cover even low-quality child care. But what about the average two-parent middle-class family? Government-sponsored day care would ease the immediate cost pressures on some families, but the long-term financial implications are more complex. Unlike the money that the government spends on public safety or education, which benefit every child, subsidized day care benefits only some kids—those whose parents both work outside the home. Day-care subsidies offer no help for families with a stay-at-home mother. In fact, such subsidies would make financial life more difficult for these families, because they would create yet another comparative disadvantage for single-income families trying to compete in the marketplace. Every dollar spent to subsidize the price of day care frees up a dollar for the two-income family to spend in the bidding wars for housing, tuition, and everything else that families are competing for—widening the gap between single- and dual-income families. Any subsidy that benefits working parents without providing a similar benefit to single-income families pushes the stay-at-home mother and her family further down the economic ladder. In effect, government-subsidized day care would add one more indirect pressure on mothers to join the workforce.

Does that mean that publicly supported day care is a bad idea? Not necessarily. If it were part of a package that also improved public education from kindergarten through high school, the bidding-war implications of a day-care subsidy would be muted. Moreover, day-care subsidies could be accompanied by offsetting support for single-income families, such as tax credits for stay-at-home parents, which would help level the playing field between single- and dual-income families. Besides, publicly supported day care would have very real benefits for society at large, not the least of which would be to raise the standard of care for millions of children who currently receive inadequate attention while their parents are at work.

That All-Important Degree

Finally, we come to the other end of the education spectrum, for which American parents are advised to start stashing away money before their little ones can even fingerpaint, let alone choose a major: college.

Americans are a contentious lot. They express an astonishing variety of opinions about politics and religion, sports teams and movies, vitamin supplements and workplace dress codes. They even disagree on the basic facts of history. According to one recent poll, 6 percent of our fellow citizens believe that the Apollo moon landings were faked.[76] But there is one topic on which Americans overwhelmingly agree: the importance of a college education. According to a recent survey, 97 percent of Americans agree that a college degree is "absolutely necessary" or "helpful," compared with a scant 3 percent claiming that a degree is "not that important."[77] In other words, Americans are *twice* as likely to believe that man never walked on the moon as they are to believe that a college degree doesn't matter! In a diverse culture full of contrarians who relish their differences with one another, faith in the power of higher education is the new secular religion. Americans now see a college degree as the *single most important* determinant of a young person's chances of success—even more significant than getting along well with others or having a good work ethic.[78]

A generation or so ago, Americans were more likely to believe that there were many avenues for a young person to make his way into the middle class, including paths that didn't require a degree. I (Elizabeth) recall my parents encouraging me to attend college, since my grades were high and they hoped I might become a teacher one day. But they were equally pleased when my eldest brother joined the Air Force, my middle brother entered a skilled trade, and my youngest brother became a pilot—even though all three of the boys had given up on college. My parents' views were pretty typical a generation or two ago. Education was valued, but no one in our neighborhood would have claimed it was the "single most important determinant of a young person's success."

Today, 77 percent of adults say that getting a college education is more important than it was just ten years ago, and 87 percent believe that "a college education has become as important as a high school diploma used to be."[79] Middle-class parents—obeying the dictate that college is essential in the new economy—have found themselves combatants in yet another active bidding war. Once again, supply and demand are out of balance. The number of students aiming for a spot in a decent four-year institution is rising every year, while the number of openings at the major public and private universities stays essentially the same. This is true not just at Harvard and Princeton, but also at the big state universities. The "open admission" policies that once ensured pretty much everyone a slot at State U. have virtually disappeared. Indeed, many state universities no longer have room even for average students, let alone struggling ones. The University of Wisconsin, for example, recently announced that the majority of its student body graduated in the top 10 percent of their high school classes.[80] Not every child can be in the top 10 percent, and parents can find themselves in a bind. For the growing number of parents whose kids don't make it into the local public university, there may be little choice but to come up with $25,000 (or more) a year for tuition, room, and board at a private college.[81]

With more applications flooding admissions offices every year, colleges are in the catbird seat, free to increase the price of admission with relative impunity. Parents may complain and students may protest, but since nearly two-thirds of parents view a degree for Junior as "*absolutely essential*," universities can safely assume that families will find a way to pay.[82] And that is precisely what has happened. After adjusting for inflation, in-state tuition and fees at the average state university have nearly doubled in less than twenty-five years.[83] To put that in perspective, the price of college has grown twice as fast as the average professor's salary, three times faster than the cost of food, and eight times faster than the cost of electricity.[84] Tuition, room, and board now cost more than $8,600 a year at the average public university. To pay these fees the average family in the United States would have to commit 17 percent of its total pretax income to this one expense.[85] A private education is even more prohibitive. Denise Robinson, a schoolteacher in central Texas, describes the cost of putting her older daughter through the local Catholic college: "You don't make enough that you're [rich], but you don't qualify for financial aid. We were probably out at least $100,000 at the end."

It should come as no surprise that six out of ten Americans also believe it is "*absolutely essential*" that university administrators keep tuition from rising.[86] But despite public opinion, costs continue to spiral upward. University officials typically blame tuition hikes on the inevitable consequences of rising costs. They point to the high costs of keeping up with scientific discoveries, the need to provide technology resources for students and faculty, and the growth in financial aid—all valuable endeavors.[87] Economist David Breneman gives voice to this view, claiming, "There is no problem for the federal government or the colleges and universities to solve other than the public relations task of explaining the economic facts of life to the populace."[88]

But not all the cost increases are just "facts of life," as Dr. Breneman suggests. For example, the American Association of University Professors blames spiraling administrative costs, which grew by 60 percent between 1980 and 1997.[89] The American Council on Education points to "student expectations" for "a high level and wide variety of services," which includes, among other things, "better food services."[90] Another study shows that the more prestigious colleges have decreased the teaching loads of their undergraduate professors, giving them more time for research and other pursuits.[91]

And then there are sports. In winning years a few of the big programs might break even thanks to sell-out crowds and television deals, but for most colleges the costs to field teams in every sport from football to water polo must come out of the general budget. Basketball powerhouse Duke University is a case in point. Every year it takes $4 million to $5 million out of the university's general revenues to pump into the athletic budget. Columbia University allocates even more, redirecting $7 million of its general revenue to make up the shortfall in athletics.[92] In the race to win the most games, universities are spending more every year, and the deficits are getting larger. According to the National Collegiate Athletic Association, the overwhelming majority of colleges lose money on their sports programs. During the 1990s the average deficit grew by more than 50 percent for all but the largest universities.[93]

We point out these expenditures not because we are scrooges who don't enjoy a good football game (one of us is a diehard University of Oklahoma football fan). Our aim is to expose the myth that college costs are like helium balloons that inevitably rise by the immutable laws of nature. We believe that colleges are charging more not because they must, but because they can. Like parents, institutions of higher learning have entered into a bidding war of their own—not the war to provide the best value to families, but the war to produce the best research, win the most basketball games, and serve the best food. According to the *Chronicle of Higher Education,* virtually every university in America "aspires to make it into the top 50, or top 20, or top 10."[94] As a result, colleges have engaged in an "arms race of expenditures triggered by the pursuit of prestige."[95] And parents are stuck paying the bill.

In the absence of rising demand, this arms race of prestige just wouldn't have been possible. If Americans had not come to view a college degree as equivalent to an "admission ticket to good jobs and a middle-class lifestyle," then demand for a university slot would have been much less intense.[96] As a result, parents would have been much freer to shop for a college on the basis of price or to forgo higher education altogether if the price seemed too high. All but the most elite universities would have felt far more pressure to keep costs down. Colleges might have been forced to make some painful cuts, but university tuition would have behaved more like any other rational marketplace, in which supply and demand are balanced and price holds relatively steady.

Time for a Tuition Freeze?

Whenever the problem of college costs are discussed, conservative policymakers typically focus on making more loans available to families. But is this really a solution? In 2001, over 5 million students had borrowed $34 billion in federal student loans—more than triple the amount borrowed just ten years earlier.[97] Student borrowing from private lenders has grown even faster, increasing *fivefold* in just six years.[98] Nor do college students bear the burden alone; parents are also going deep into debt to pay for their children's education. Every year, more than a million families take out a second mortgage on their homes just to pay for educational expenses.[99] Borrowing does not reduce the costs; it simply means that families can pay and pay and pay some more. At what point do we agree that families have taken on all the debt they can handle? The debt load tripled in the past ten years—do we intend to let it triple again over the next decade? Offering these families more debt is like throwing rocks to a drowning man—it won't help.

Liberals, for their part, regularly call on taxpayers to foot more of the bill. But taxpayers *are* paying more. Over the past two decades, states increased per-pupil appropriations to public universities by 13 percent (adjusted for inflation).[100] How much more are taxpayers supposed to pay? Are state governments supposed to write a blank check for higher education, allowing universities to increase costs with abandon? College administrators point out that a 13 percent increase in public funding fell far short of the 41 percent growth in university expenditures, which is why they were forced to raise tuition so much. That may be true, but that simply says, "We're spending more than the state will give us, so we pass the costs on to families." That is not a ringing endorsement of the frugality of the current system.

The more-taxes approach suffers from the same problem the more-debt approach engenders. It gives colleges more money to spend, without any attempt to control their spiraling costs. Perhaps it is time to shake things up with a hold on price increases. A multi-year freeze on tuition at all our state universities would prompt an intensive discussion of higher education priorities and some hard choices. Do they *all* want to offer expensive sports programs? Should some colleges concentrate on science and engineering, while others focus on the liberal arts? Should universities be asked to educate more students in exchange for additional tax dollars? This approach would certainly hit the supply-and-demand problem right between the eyes.

If *all* state-supported universities were committed to stopping tuition increases, the effects would reverberate throughout the educational system. Many public colleges might rededicate themselves to serving their local communities, dropping out of the arms race for ephemeral national prestige. The pressure would be on private colleges to follow suit, lest the gap between private and public tuitions grow even larger. The upward spiral of tuition and the resulting it's-not-our-fault-everyone-else-is-doing-it mentality would receive a serious thumping.

Colleges and universities are like any other organism in their desire for survival and growth. Their leaders are true believers in the research and scholarly missions of their schools, and their desire for excellence—however it is measured among universities—is genuine. It is no wonder that they can always justify their rising costs and why they need every penny that comes their way—and more. There can *always* be more research, more athletic fields, more books for the library. To be sure, the issues are complex, and a spending freeze might force some universities to make some very tough choices. In the long run, however, it would refocus public universities on their mission—providing an education for all qualified members of the public, not just those who can come up with ten or twenty thousand dollars each year.

The Family Car

Not all of the extra income brought in by Mom's paycheck went to that house in the suburbs and preschool and college tuition. A lot of it went to another line item in the family budget, a favorite target of the over-consumption critics—that shiny, oversized, overgadgeted behemoth, the family car.

At first, we thought the family car might just shatter our case against the Over-Consumption Myth. Cars now come jam-packed with automatic gizmos that no one had even dreamed of a generation ago. And cars cost more than ever. The average family now spends an *additional* $4,000 (inflation adjusted) every year to buy, lease, and maintain the family automobiles.[101] In the words of a Toyota salesman quoted in *Affluenza,* "People's expectations are much higher. They want amenities—power steering, power brakes as standard, premium sound systems."[102] At last, a big-ticket item that that proves that Americans are indeed indulging themselves with lavish extravagances they can ill afford.

Not so fast. Families spend more, but not because they are upgrading to Corinthian leather and built-in seat warmers. Instead, the typical family with children spent its money on something a bit more prosaic—a second car.[103] Once an unheard-of luxury within the middle class, the second car has become a necessity. With Mom in the workforce and the family located ever further from the city's center, that second car became the only means for running errands, earning a second income, and getting by in the far-flung suburbs.[104]

What about the price tag on that second car? An average new car costs more than $22,000 today, compared with less than $16,000 in the late 1970s (inflation adjusted).[105] The critics might point a triumphant finger, but they would miss another important fact. Cars last longer than they used to. In the late 1970s, the average car on the road was just five and a half years old. Now the average family is driving a car that is more than eight years old.[106] Today's families pay more for that shiny new vehicle than their parents did, but they hold on to it longer too. In fact, when we analyzed unpublished data from the Bureau of Labor Statistics, we found that the average amount a family of four spends *per car* (car payments, insurance, maintenance and so forth) is 20 percent *less* than it was a generation ago.[107] For all the griping about those overpriced SUVs, there is little evidence that sunroofs and power windows are sending families to the poorhouse.

Leather interiors may not be responsible for the rise in bankruptcies, but the over-consumption camp might still argue that families could have saved by buying cheaper cars. After all, a family doesn't *need* a new SUV with a CD player, at least not in the same way that it needs decent day care or a home in a safe neighborhood. But we pause here to offer a bit of sympathy for the much-maligned buyer of the family car. The din from the car industry has changed pitch over the past generation. Glance at an advertisement from any maker of family cars, and there you'll see it: safety for sale. This testimonial is featured on the official Volvo Web site: "The driver of the truck lost control of his vehicle and hit me, and my wife, who was five months pregnant. . . . There was much talk that 'the Volvo had saved our lives' and I'm convinced it did. . . . I wish to thank the people at Volvo for the lives of my wife and my child. . . ."[108] Sure, maybe families could do without the twelve-speaker sound systems, but we wouldn't ask them to do without the automatic braking systems, the crash-resistant steel frames, or the dual airbags that they are spending all that money on.

But do the cars have to be so *big?* SUVs may drink gasoline with abandon, but families are also buying room for safety devices that didn't even exist in the early 1970s. Every time I (Elizabeth) strap my granddaughter into the car, I am reminded of what I did when Amelia was a baby. I tucked her in a wicker bassinet, which perched on the back seat of our Volkswagen Beetle. I was somewhat unusual—not because I failed to use so much as a seat belt to hold my seven-pound daughter in place—but because I opted not to hold her in my lap, where a simple fender bender would have transformed her into a free-flying projectile.

Safety standards have changed, with a real effect on the family pocketbook. I (Amelia) wouldn't even think of driving my toddler to the end of the block without strapping her into a plastic seat so enormous that she looks like an astronaut preparing to launch into outer space. We shelled out more than $100 for that seat, but the real expenditure was for our car. A few years ago I was driving a little two-door Mazda—more or less the modern equivalent of Elizabeth's Beetle. But when the baby came, the Mazda had to go, replaced by a four-door car big enough for two car seats (with the thought that our first-born may one day have a younger brother or sister to pick on). It gets particularly tough for families with more than two kids. Jane Stewart, a stay-at-home mom in Denver, describes the consequences of having three children under the age of five. According to most experts, the Stewarts should harness those three kids in the back seat—not just with a seat belt, but into a bulky car seat or "booster seat" designed especially for children—until they are at least *eight years old.*[109] Jane explains, "We have a Grand Cherokee and three car seats in the back. When the baby needs [the next-size car seat], we don't think all three will fit. Then it will be time for a Suburban or a minivan." A generation ago, the Stewarts could have fit their kids into the back seat of any sedan on the market, with room left over for the family dog. Today, even a Jeep Grand Cherokee—a car that weighs 4,000 pounds—is not big enough. The critics may be right that families don't need all those gizmos in their cars, but we would certainly take sides with the Stewarts against anyone who argued that they didn't need all that *room.*

By and large, families have spent prudently on their automobiles, or at least as prudently as they did a generation ago. And the money they are spending is paying off: The rate of child auto fatalities has declined steadily since the mid-1970s, thanks at least in part to safer cars and better car seats.[110] For all the criticism hurled at car manufacturers (and car buyers), it is important to note that families drive stronger, safer cars that last a lot longer than they used to.

Families Then, Families Now: The Two-Income Trap

It's time now to add it all up. Families are working harder and, thanks to Mom's income, they are making more money than ever before. And yet, they are spending more, too. So where does that leave the typical working family?

We offer two examples. We begin with Tom and Susan, representatives of the average middle-class family of a generation ago. (Once again, to make the comparisons easy, all figures are adjusted for inflation, reported in 2000 dollars throughout this discussion.) Tom works full-time, earning $38,700, the median income for a fully employed man in 1973, while Susan stays at home to care for the house and children.[111] Tom and Susan have the typical two children, one in grade school and a three-year-old who stays home with Susan. The family buys health insurance through Tom's job, to which they contribute $1,030 a year—the average amount spent by an insured family that made at least some contribution to the cost of a private insurance policy.[112] They own an average home in an average family neighborhood—costing them $5,310 a year in mortgage payments.[113] Shopping is within walking distance, so the family owns just one car, on which it spends $5,140 a year for car payments, maintenance, gas, and repairs.[114] And, like all good citizens, they pay their taxes, which claim about 24 percent of Tom's income.[115] Once all the taxes, mortgage payments, and other fixed expenses are paid, Tom and Susan are left with $17,834 in discretionary income (inflation adjusted), or about 46 percent of Tom's pretax paycheck. They aren't rich, but they have nearly $1,500 a month to cover food, clothing, utilities, and anything else they might need.

So how does our 1973 couple compare with Justin and Kimberly, the modern-day version of the traditional family? Like Tom, Justin is an average earner, bringing home $39,000 in 2000—not even 1 percent more than his counterpart of a generation ago. But there is one big difference: Thanks to Kimberly's full-time salary, the family's combined income is $67,800—a whopping 75 percent higher than the household income for Tom and Susan.[116] A quick look at their income statement shows how the modern dual-income couple has sailed past their single-income counterpart of a generation ago.

So where did all that money go? Like Tom and Susan, Justin and Kimberly bought an average home, but today that three-bedroom-two-bath ranch costs a lot more. Their annual mortgage payments are nearly $9,000.[117] The older child still goes to the public elementary

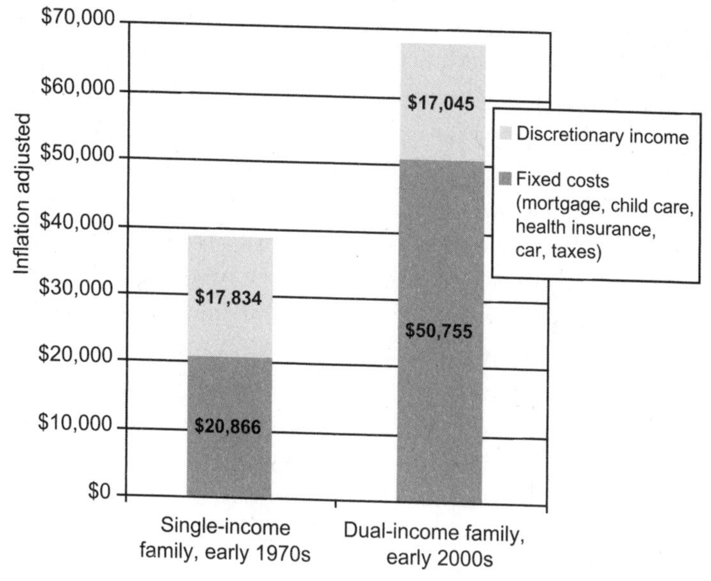

FIGURE 2.1 Fixed costs as a share of family income

school, but after school and during summer vacations he goes to day care, at an average yearly cost of $4,350. The younger child attends a full-time preschool/day care program, which costs the family $5,320 a year.[118] With Kimberly at work, the second car is a must, so the family spends more than $8,000 a year on its two vehicles. Health insurance is another must, and even with Justin's employer picking up a big share of the cost, insurance takes $1,650 from the couple's paychecks.[119] Taxes also take their toll. Thanks in part to Kimberly's extra income, the family has been bumped into a higher bracket, and the government takes 33 percent of the family's money.[120] So where does that leave Justin and Kimberly after these basic expenses are deducted? With $17,045—about $800 *less* than Tom and Susan, who were getting by on just one income.

This bears repeating. Today, after an average two-income family makes its house payments, car payments, insurance payments, and child care payments, they have *less* money left over, *even though they have a second, full-time earner in the workplace*.[121]

If Justin and Kimberly have less money left over than Tom and Susan did, what happens to a family that tries to get by on a single income in today's economy? Their expenses would be a little lower than Justin and Kimberly's. They can save on after-school care for the older child, their taxes will be lower, and, if they are lucky enough to live close to shopping and other services, perhaps they can get by without a second car. But if they tried to live a normal, middle-class life in other ways—buy an average home, send their younger child to preschool, purchase health insurance, and so forth—they would be left with only $6,720 a year to cover all their other expenses. They would have to find a way to buy food, clothing, utilities, life insurance, furniture, appliances, and so on with less than $600 a month. The modern single-earner family that tries to keep up an average lifestyle faces a *60 percent* drop in discretionary income compared with its one-income counterpart of a generation ago.

To all those critics who are calling for selfish mothers to return home, we have to ask—are you kidding? Do the math. And for all the advocates of "downshifting," we ask just how far down these families are supposed to shift.

We should point out that the expenses we have laid out are averages, and plenty of families manage to pay less (or more). But the alternatives families have pursued in an effort to make ends meet bear some scrutiny. Consider child care. Government statistics show that the average amount a family of four spends on after-school care is lower than the $4,350 we cited above. We calculated this figure from data on families who pay for child care, but the government "average" includes children who have a grandmother or an older sibling who watches them for free. That's a great way for those lucky families to save some money, but it doesn't do a bit of good for the typical family that has to rely on paid child care. For them, paying less money means getting less quality, such as an unlicensed neighbor who parks several children in front of her television or an over-crowded center with barely passable facilities.

There are other ways families could save money. Families could also cut their health insurance expenses. They could drop those costs to zero by following the model of millions of other middle-class families who simply live without health insurance and pray for the best. Or they could give up the house and move into an apartment in a marginal neighborhood. There are always options, but for families with children, these options signal that their middle-class lives are slipping away.

Even if they are able to trim around the edges, families are faced with a sobering truth: Every one of those expensive items we identified—mortgage, car payments, insurance, tuition—is a fixed cost. Families must pay them each and every month, through good times and bad times, no matter what. Unlike clothing or food, there is no way to cut back from one month to the next. Short of moving out of the house, withdrawing their daughter from preschool, or canceling the insurance policy altogether, Justin and Kimberly are stuck. Fully 75 percent of their income is earmarked for recurrent monthly expenses.

If all goes well, Justin and Kimberly may squeak by. They will even get a breather in another five years or so, when the children are old enough to be left alone after school. But the spending hiatus will last for just a few years, until the older child heads off to college. At that point, the family's budget will be squeezed harder than ever as they search for an extra $9,000 a year to cover room, board, and tuition for the local state university. If they are lucky, they will have set something aside during the intervening years, and they'll find a way to put their kids through college. And when they hit their mid- to late fifties, Justin and Kimberly might begin to think about putting something away for their retirement (about thirty years later than a financial planner would recommend).[122]

This projection assumes, of course, that nothing goes wrong. With 75 percent of income earmarked for fixed expenses, today's family has no margin for error. There is no leeway to cut back if Justin's hours are cut or if Kimberly gets laid off. There is no room in the budget if Kimberly needs to take a few months off work to care for Grandma, or if Justin hurts his back and can't work. The modern American family is walking on a high wire without a net; they pray there won't be any wind. If all goes well, they will make it across safely, their children will grow up and finish college, and they will move on to retirement. But if anything—anything at all—goes wrong, then today's two-income family is in big, big trouble.

In the next chapter, we explore just how much can go wrong.

3

Mom: The All-Purpose Safety Net

Carmen's third pregnancy was difficult. When she was thirty weeks along, she started hemorrhaging, and her obstetrician performed an emergency cesarean section. Little Gabe weighed just under two pounds at birth, and the doctors predicted a lifetime of severely impaired physical and cognitive ability for him. Many would have considered Gabe's fate a tragedy, but Carmen Ramirez saw it differently. "This was God's gift. He is my miracle baby. He came when my sister suddenly passed away. I could not believe I was pregnant. I felt so blessed."

Months later, Gabe still needed the support of a machine to breathe. He was a quiet baby who rarely fussed, but Carmen checked on him constantly. One evening, after putting Gabe to bed, Carmen started to fix dinner for her two older children. The macaroni had just started boiling when she left the kitchen abruptly and ran to the baby's room. "I don't know why, but I just needed to check again." She was confronted by a terrifying silence. Her heart began to race. "He aspirated. I had to do CPR on him."

Gabe survived, and over the next three years, he made some advances, but his progress was slow. Carmen explains that at age three, "He can't really walk or talk yet. . . . He's still on the bottle, [and] he's just now starting to eat table food. We have to make sure it's chopped up real fine. He could choke." Gabe is less passive now.

He screams incessantly when he is anxious, which presents a particular challenge because he still needs so much medical attention. "He's traumatized by doctors. He's traumatized by nurses, because of being stuck and probed. He knows the uniforms."

She had gone back to her job as a lab technician shortly after the birth of each of their other two children, but it didn't occur to either Carmen or her husband, Mike, that she could leave Gabe. "People are afraid to keep him, because of him being delicate," which made child care impossible to arrange. Even family members were reluctant to look after Gabe: "My mother-in-law was afraid to take him because of his condition. If I had her to watch him, I had to be back in an hour."

When Gabe was first born, Carmen had arranged a leave of absence from her job. But when the leave ran out, "I just resigned," explains Carmen. She pauses, adding hopefully, "But just until he's better."

Like many of the couples we interviewed for this book, Carmen and Mike ultimately filed for bankruptcy. The reason? Not the one their friends might guess: the staggering expense of tending to Gabe's medical needs. That is not to say that Gabe's care was inexpensive. He had undergone four surgeries by the time he was three years old, and, as Carmen explains, "His diaper bag comes along with a lot of medication." Then there are the specialists, the lab tests, the breathing machine, the special supplies. Gabe is well on his way to becoming a "million-dollar baby."

But Carmen and Mike were also very lucky: Nearly all of Gabe's expenses were covered by Mike's health insurance. Carmen reflects, "Thank God we had insurance. . . . We only paid for a few medications from time to time, the rest are copays." Three years after Gabe's birth, the family had paid less than $2,000 in medical bills—a tiny fraction of the debts they owed when they entered into bankruptcy.

So how did Carmen and Mike end up in so much trouble?

The All-Purpose Safety Net

When trouble strikes, the family falls back on its safety net. They seek out extra resources—more medical care, extra cash, someone to lend a hand—hoping they can regain their stability at some future time.

Liberals (and many moderates) are quick to point out that America's safety net has frayed. Welfare has been slashed, hospitals no longer offer free care to the poor, public housing has been shuttered, Medicaid funding has been cut, and so on throughout the pages of the *New York Times*.

There is something beyond the obvious hardship implied in this litany that is important to notice. The "safety net" provided by each of these programs serves only one segment of the population: the poor. Nearly all these programs involve a stringent means test, making them available only to those near or below the poverty line. They are designed to keep hunger, disease, and destitution at bay for the poorest members of society, at least for a while.

But what about the middle class? What is their safety net? Where do they turn in the case of a calamity? Unemployment insurance offers modest protection, and Social Security protects against penury in old age. But there is little more. For most families to qualify for any other form of government assistance, they would have to forgo everything that makes them middle-class—their homes, their jobs, their places in their communities.

There is little discussion about the safety net for middle-income families, no wise folks expounding about it on the Sunday talk shows, no long articles about it in the newspapers. The reason may be that the middle-class safety net isn't built with taxpayers' dollars. It is a private safety net, built family by family, home by home, far from the spotlight of media attention. The first lines of defense are the insurance policies, offering at least some financial protection against accident, illness, and death. Next is cash in the bank that can be tapped when the family has sudden needs. But there is another line of defense for families with children, another type of insurance that has been widely overlooked.

For middle-class families, the most important part of the safety net for generations has been the stay-at-home mother.

Today's wisdom holds that a couple that sends both spouses into the workforce is better off economically. They may be stressed out, they may feel guilty about sending their kids to day care, and they may have too little time for each other, but the one piece of good news that the family can count on is that they are more financially secure. The view is familiar, repeated with comforting regularity. "Jason's company isn't doing well. But if something happens to his job, at least Melinda is working." Or "The new house will be a stretch, but at least there are two of us to manage it." A recent book entitled *She Works/He Works: How Two-Income Families Are Happier, Healthier, and Better-Off* sums up this perspective:

> Because they have two full incomes that help buffer them against the terrible wrenches of a changing economy, they do not feel the gut-wrenching vulnerability of standing at the edge of a precipice, ready at any second to topple off the cliff if a company downsizes or relocates. . . . The dual earner family offers economic stability, protection against financial disaster.[1]

Stability and protection—delicious ideas for the modern family—and exactly what everyone knows a second income provides.

But what if it doesn't? What if the modern two-earner couple is actually *more vulnerable* than the traditional single-breadwinner family?

A generation or so ago (and even today), the typical one-earner family usually described the father as responsible for the economic health of the family, with the mother assigned to roles such as homemaker or helpmate. To the extent that she had an economic role, it was seen as one of careful spending; it was her job to ensure that Dad's salary went as far as possible, and so she mended torn shirts, packed bag lunches, and counted the family's pennies. Her economic contribution, in effect, was that of careful guardian of what her husband brought home.

But this traditional view was far too narrow. It conjures up an image of the stay-at-home mother who was forever confined to the home, unable or unwilling to make a financial contribution even when her family faced disaster. If her husband lost his job, she could do little more than stand by helplessly and wring her hands, or maybe clip a few more coupons and dilute the soup with more water. In reality, the stay-at-home mother was never such a cartoon figure. She has always worn many hats, changing roles as circumstances demanded. When her husband was working steadily, she would forgo a paycheck to spend her days at home taking care of the children and keeping house, but if circumstances changed, so did she. If her husband was laid off, fired, or otherwise left without a paycheck, the stay-at-home mother didn't simply stand helplessly on the sidelines as her family toppled off an economic cliff; she looked for a job to make up some of that lost income. Similarly, if her husband had a heart attack and was expected to stay home for a while, she could find work and add a new income source to help the family stay afloat financially. A stay-at-home mother served as the family's ultimate insurance against unemployment or disability—insurance that had a very real economic value even when it wasn't drawn on.

Consider Tom and Susan, the typical one-earner family from the 1970s we introduced in chapter 2. If Tom, who earned $38,700 a year (inflation-adjusted to 2000 dollars), was laid off from his job, he could dip into the public safety net and draw unemployment. But his unemployment check would cover only half of his previous salary, leaving a huge shortfall for basic expenses. Without half of his income, the family might face imminent disaster. But if Susan then entered the workforce to help her family through this rough patch, she could bring in much-needed income at just the right time. She wouldn't earn nearly as much as Tom did, but on average she would bring in nearly $22,000 a year.[2] Assuming it took Susan a couple of months to find work, the family would just about break even. If Tom could find another job within six months (the limit imposed by most states on how long someone can collect unemployment benefits),[3] the family should be able to weather the storm without any serious injury to their financial health.

What if Tom never made it back to his original income? Susan's new paycheck could still make the difference between their long-term survival and collapse. If Tom were able to return to work at a lower-paying job, or if he could find only a part-time job, even with his income cut in half, the now-two-earner family might approximate its earlier lifestyle—and its long-term economic prospects. Susan might need to remain in the workforce permanently, and the family would have no reserves to meet any future setbacks, but they could weather one hard economic blow—the permanent reduction of the primary breadwinner's income—intact.

Of course, Tom and Susan are merely an illustration; the realities of a father losing his job are far more varied and complex.[4] Researchers have found, for example, that a woman whose husband loses his job is more likely to enter the workforce if her children are older, perhaps because the higher cost of day care for small children can make a young mother's return to work too costly.[5] Some longtime stay-at-home mothers may find that they lack marketable skills; others may be frustrated that only low-wage jobs are available to them. In addition, a stay-at-home wife may have difficulty finding work when layoffs, such as the one that caught her husband, are making jobs scarce in their locale.[6] Notwithstanding these difficulties, there is considerable evidence that as a family's economic position deteriorates, stay-at-home wives do exactly what one might predict: They look for a job. Sociologists have found that a woman is far more likely to enter the workforce if her husband takes a permanent wage reduction, if he faces an extended period of unemployment, or if he receives little or no unemployment compensation.[7] This squares with common sense: If Tom found a well-paying job just a few weeks after being laid off, there would be little need for Susan to begin a job search. If, on the other hand, Tom couldn't find a job, or if the only jobs he could find paid considerably less than his previous position, then there would be far more pressure on Susan to find a way to bring home some additional money. Researchers have found that the effect of wives' added income is not trivial; for the average married man who loses his job, his wife's new income offsets more than 25 percent of his lost wages.[8] Indeed, that all-purpose insurance policy provided by the stay-at-home mother has paid off for millions of families.

One of us [Elizabeth] lived this story back in the 1960s in Oklahoma. I was thirteen when my father had a heart attack. Daddy had been working on our car, lying on the driveway on a cold November weekend, when his chest began to hurt. He put off going to the doctor until the next morning, when he was immediately hospitalized. Forty years later, the snatches of conversation I overheard remain as vivid as if someone had just spoken the words: "the possibility of more attacks," "not sure if he can ever work again," "have you made arrangements?" Daddy came home, gray and shaking, and he sat around the house for weeks. My mother had been at home for more than thirty years bringing up my three older brothers and me. She looked for a job for the first time since she was a nineteen-year-old girl with a part-time job singing the latest hits at a Tulsa radio station. After a few weeks of searching, she took a job in the catalog order department at Sears.

Eventually, Daddy went back to work, but to a job that paid about half what he had been earning. We lost the car, and there was more talk about what groceries cost and how expensive winter coats and dental visits had become, but no one went hungry and we stayed in our home. My mother continued with her job, and life settled back down. When I was a senior in high school, she talked about quitting, but she decided to keep working so that she and my father could help with the cost of my college tuition. When I left for college, they sold the house and moved into an apartment. The year I graduated, Mother quit her job.

Not only did stay-at-home wives like my mother function as backup workers, insuring against their husbands' loss of income, they were also available when the family had unexpected expenses. If there was an illness in the family, a stay-at-home mother could go to work to cover the deductibles, copayments, and other medical expenses not covered by insurance. If the family was uninsured, a stay-at-home mother could join the estimated 4 to 5 million women who now stay in full-time jobs just so that they can provide health insurance for their families.[9]

Divorce, which we will discuss in depth in chapter 5, is the single most common trigger for stay-at-home wives to enter the workforce. During the 1970s, when fewer than half of all married women were in the labor force, 83 percent of divorced women were working within two years of separation from their husbands.[10] A sudden need for cash can arise from all sorts of causes, encompassing both good news ("Cynthia got into Yale") and bad news ("Termites have eaten away the foundation of your house"). Either way, the key point remains the same: Families with a stay-at-home mother have a backup earner, someone who can add a jolt of income to the household—a jolt that can make the difference between covering the kids' tuition and keeping up with the doctors' bills rather than giving up health insurance or taking on a second mortgage.

In addition to playing the role of backup earner, the stay-at-home mother plays another critical *economic* role: backup caregiver. The full-time homemaker does more than change diapers and check homework; she is available to provide extra care for *anyone*—child or adult—who needs it. She is on hand to care for an elderly relative who can no longer take care of himself. Three out of four caregivers to the disabled elderly (excluding husbands and wives) are daughters, daughters-in-law, or other female relatives and friends (such as nieces or granddaughters). A generation ago the majority of these women did not work outside the home.[11] If Granddad has become too frail to manage on his own, the stay-at-home mother is available for the myriad tasks not covered by Medicare. She can help him dress every morning, drive him to the doctor's office, balance his checkbook, or just keep him company. And because she is at home full-time, she can perform these tasks without taking time off from her own job or forcing her family to live without a paycheck they had been counting on.

A mother who has gone into the workplace brings home a paycheck, but she forfeits the economic value of her backup role. So long as nothing goes wrong, the tradeoff is a simple choice between two viable alternatives. Some families prefer to have Mom at home and are willing to live with less money; others accommodate a working mother and enjoy a richer lifestyle. When trouble strikes, however, the family learns that the two choices may not have been as equivalent as they had seemed. Only one leaves the family with a safety net.

No New Money

Not long after Gabe was born, Carmen was back in the hospital, this time for an infection. She was run down, worried about how her family would care for Gabe, and frantic over the family's bills. "My fever was spiking and all I was thinking about was what bills I had to pay. I managed to get them to let me out of the hospital."

Eight months after Gabe was born, the Ramirez family was behind on the utilities bills. "I got one of those pink notices to disconnect [the power]. I was so scared—I need that electricity to pump the air into my kid's lungs." In the early spring of 2001, a creditor showed up at the police station where Mike is assigned, threatening to repossess the family minivan. The room fell quiet as the other police officers determinedly looked away, trying to give Mike some privacy as he pleaded with the man to give him a little more time to pay. The next day, Mike and Carmen went to see a lawyer. After twenty minutes with the paralegal, they signed the papers to file for bankruptcy.

Not every two-income family will face the financial crisis that hit Mike and Carmen. Whether they do depends in large part on how they spend the second salary. The single-breadwinner family, by definition, plans its financial commitments geared to a single income. A stay-at-home mother is a contingent worker, called on only in an emergency; in ordinary times, the family lives on one paycheck. In theory, the two-income family could take the same approach. They could spend one paycheck and keep the second one in reserve. If disaster strikes, they will have ample savings to cushion any blow.

The two-income family has another budgeting alternative. They can do exactly what the over-consumption camp claims they do—blow that second paycheck on expensive vacations, gadgets for the house, brand-name clothes, and dozens of other things they "don't really need." While this strategy might make the finger-waggers sputter with indignation, these families would actually be just as prepared for an emergency as their one-income counterparts. If something goes wrong, they can simply stop purchasing the extras without any serious harm to the family's standard of living, while Mom returns to her role as backup earner or caregiver. If Dad loses his job, Mom's income will be reallocated to cover the family's living expenses while her husband looks for a job.

Over the past 25 years, mothers poured into the workplace, but they did not fritter away their paychecks on buying sprees that could be abandoned at the first sign of trouble. Nor did they lock that money in the bank. Millions of two-income families used that second income to purchase opportunities for their children—a home in a safe neighborhood with good schools, a comprehensive health insurance policy, two reliable cars, preschool, and college tuition. They made long-term commitments to ongoing expenses—and they counted on both incomes to make ends meet.

Justin and Kimberly, the modern two-earner family we introduced in chapter 2, illustrate the point. If Justin lost his $39,000-a-year job, Kimberly would still be working. She would be earning $28,800 on average, which is considerably more than her counterpart Susan would have earned a generation earlier. With Justin's unemployment check, the couple's annual earnings would be $48,300, which would put them well ahead of Tom and Susan's post-layoff situation. But there is one critical difference: Tom and Susan were accustomed to living on less than $39,000 a year, whereas Justin and Kimberly had built their lives around an income of nearly $68,000 a year. The shortfall for Justin and Kimberly is much more severe.

Compared with a one-income couple, Justin and Kimberly are very poorly positioned to absorb a drop in income. As we showed in the previous chapter, their fixed monthly expenses are two and a half times

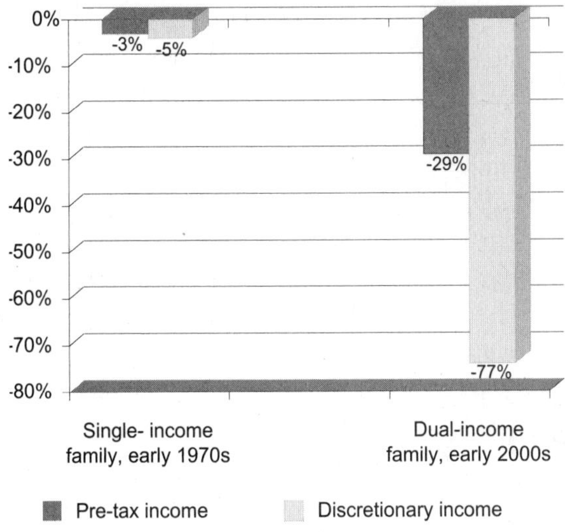

Note: Assumes stay-at-home wife finds job within two months, and husbands receive 50 percent of former income in unemployment benefits.
Source: Analysis of Consumer Expenditure Survey. For further discussion of the calculation of discretionary income for a one-income family in the 1970s and a two-income family in the 2000s, see chapter 2.

FIGURE 3.1 Income drop when husband loses job

higher than Tom and Susan's were back in 1973 (once again, all numbers are adjusted for inflation), so they have less discretionary money left over even when they are both fully employed. Without Justin's paycheck, the modern couple doesn't have a prayer of making ends meet.

Even if Justin finds a job within a few months, the family will continue to operate from a deficit, since there will be no *extra* income available to pay off the debts that mounted up while his paycheck was gone. This is in sharp contrast to Tom and Susan: If the former stay-at-home mother stays in the workforce temporarily, the couple should regain its financial footing within a few months of Tom's reemployment.

Proponents of the Over-Consumption Myth would be quick to point out that Justin and Kimberly don't actually *need* $68,000 a year and that their family *should* be able to get by on $48,000 a year. After all, Tom and Susan seemed to be getting along just fine—and holding on to their spot in the middle class—on $38,700 a generation ago. Be that as it may, Justin and Kimberly have signed binding contracts and long-term mortgages, made commitments and promises that depended on all $68,000 of income. They could (and in all likelihood would) cut back around the edges. They might cancel cable or eliminate take-out dinners; they could postpone replacing the stained carpet and cross beer and soda off the shopping list.[12] But the effect of such belt-tightening would be modest at best. They cannot make up for the almost $20,000 hole in the family's budget by eating less or forgoing a new pair of sneakers. In order to pull back to a $48,000 budget, Justin and Kimberly would need to sell their home, trade in their car, pull their younger child out of preschool, and enroll their older son in a lower-cost after-school day-care center—a process that would take months to accomplish. Moreover, they would be unlikely to take such draconian measures until they were already deep in financial trouble and forced to admit that the lives they once lived were gone forever.

The finger-waggers might not be willing to exonerate Justin and Kimberly, but it is important to notice something about their expenditures that turns the standard financial analysis on its head. Justin and Kimberly are vulnerable precisely because they did *not* overconsume on trinkets. They are vulnerable because they made long-term commitments to what most would consider sensible family purchases: housing, education, health insurance. They probably don't want to hear it right now, but Justin and Kimberly would be more secure financially if they had whooped off her entire salary on big-screen TVs and trips to the Bahamas, because those purchases do not require an ongoing financial commitment.

Should Justin and Kimberly have saved one income, locking it in the bank for a rainy day? Maybe, but even here the picture must be etched in shades of gray, rather than black and white. Money in the bank is great, but so are college degrees, decent medical care, and homes in good school districts. Indeed, Kimberly might ask the over-consumption critics and the financial planners what would be the point of working if she couldn't spend the money to buy better lives for her children? She wasn't sending her kids to day care every day just so she could go on a cruise or plan some glorious retirement for herself and her husband. Cash savings, money for retirement, treats, and vacations could come later. This couple decided that their children needed a good home *now*, good day care *now*, and good health insurance *now*. Many parents—and even a fair number of financial analysts—would agree with them.

Good Intentions

So how did families get sucked into the Two-Income Trap? The answer is unexpectedly simple: *No one saw it coming.*

The politics that surrounded women's collective decision to migrate into the workforce are a study in misdirection. On the left, the women's movement was battling for equal pay and equal opportunity, and any suggestion that the family might be better off with Mother at home was discounted as reactionary chauvinism. On the right, conservative commentators accused working mothers of everything from child abandonment to defying the laws of nature. The atmosphere was far too charged for any rational assessment of the financial consequences of sending both spouses into the workforce.

The massive miscalculation ensued because *both* sides of the political spectrum discounted the financial value of the stay-at-home mother. Feminist leader Betty Friedan scoffed at the economic role of the homemaker: "[T]he really important role that women serve as housewives is to buy more things for the house. . . . Somehow, somewhere, someone must have figured out that women will buy more things if they are kept in the underused, nameless-yearning, energy-to-get-rid-of state of being housewives."[13]

Feminists assumed that women's entry into the workforce entailed no real costs—only benefits. Conservatives, for their part, slavishly touted the emotional benefits that a stay-at-home mother provides to her children and fretted over "who will rock the cradle" when mothers abandon their homes.[14] There was no room in *either* worldview for the capable, resourceful mother who might spend her days devoted to the roles of wife and mother, but who could, if necessary, rise to the occasion and dive headlong into the workforce to support her family. No one saw the stay-at-home mom as the family's safety net.

Moreover, it was easy for each family to see income going up, but it was very hard to foresee what would happen if something went wrong. When most families plan their futures and pencil in their budgets, they concentrate on what is most immediate. They look at the paychecks coming in, the mortgage going out, the month-to-month fluctuations in the checking account. Except for those disquieting moments when they take out a life insurance policy or learn that a friend has lost his job, most don't notice the growing vulnerability that has seeped into their lives and stolen their security.

Turn Back the Clock?

Must mothers give up their jobs and head back home if they are to escape the Two-Income Trap? We suspect that at least a few conservative commentators will draw exactly that conclusion from these pages. But as two working mothers, we confess to deep resistance to calling for such a move. We remain dedicated to the best part of the feminist movement—the rock-solid belief that women who want to work should have every opportunity to do so. But personal politics aren't the point here. Such a mass exodus from workplace to home is about as likely as the revival of the horse-drawn buggy. Social and political forces have changed the shape of women's expectations and their role within the family. New information about the macroeconomic implications of their entry into the workforce is unlikely to change much.

Even if women listened hard to those admonishing them to remain at home, most could not do it. Such advice ignores the fact that families are caught in a trap. Any individual family that chooses to drop down to one income will be immediately penalized, while those who keep both parents in the workforce will gain a strategic advantage. Sure, they may understand that living on two incomes increases their risk of economic collapse, but risks dwell in the future—and the kids have needs that must be met today. Besides, in many families, it is far too late to contemplate pulling Mom out of the workforce. For the millions of parents who have already committed Mom's income to the mortgage and car payments, the time for such second thoughts is long past. If she leaves her job, these families stand to lose everything.

There is a better path out of the Two-Income Trap. Give families some breathing room. As befits a society in which the safety net must be built one family at a time, money in the bank is still the first line of defense against any economic bump in the road. Any program that helps families save money is a program that helps keep the middle class secure. At the moment, the federal government offers a handful of programs that give tax breaks to families who put money aside for specific expenses such as retirement, medical care, or college tuition.[15] These programs certainly sound promising, but they ask families to do something that is almost impossible in a capricious world: They ask them to predict the unpredictable. To take advantage of these programs, families need to know in advance which expenses will hit them and when they will need extra cash.

What happens when an unforeseen disaster strikes—when Dad loses his job or when Mom asks for a divorce? Families face events that elude all that careful planning. The first line of defense is their all-purpose passbook savings account, an account that is tax disadvantaged. If things get really bad, many families find that the only way to survive is to cash out their retirement accounts. The huge penalty associated with that withdrawal—set in place as a disincentive to withdraw early—doubles the pain. Not only has the family just wiped out any chance for a comfortable retirement, the government just took a hunk of their only savings—at a time when the family was already under extreme financial stress.

If the standard government policies were turned sideways, instead of asking each family to carve its nest egg into separate little tax-advantaged slices, middle-class families could be rewarded for *all* savings. All savings—not just savings specifically designated for retirement or education—should be exempt from taxes. Many liberals have opposed such a change for fear that it would disproportionately benefit the wealthy, who are the only ones with ample savings.[16] But this concern could easily be remedied. The tax change could be implemented on a sliding scale, so that those with modest means could save tax free, while the wealthy continued to be taxed. Or the government could compensate for the lost tax revenues by increasing other taxes on well-to-do households.

The fear of letting the rich off too easy should not overshadow the fact that middle-class families desperately need to build their own safety nets. America's personal savings rate has plummeted in the past thirty years, so that it now stands effectively at zero.[17] Encouraging savings shouldn't be about token programs for one or two specified uses. It should be a concerted government policy aimed at helping families build safety nets strong enough to see them through good times and bad.

Over the past generation, the Two-Income Trap has left the modern family in a position that is thick with irony. Today's parents are working harder than ever—far harder than their single-income counterparts of a generation ago—holding down full-time paying jobs and still covering all their obligations at home. Yet, paradoxically, without the safety net once provided by the stay-at-home mother, they are *more* vulnerable to financial disaster. They have little money left to build their own safety nets, and government policies tax most of their efforts to provide for themselves. They are caught: can't afford to work, can't afford to quit, and can't survive if something goes wrong.

If the risks of the world had remained exactly the same over the past generation—the same risk of getting laid off, the same odds of getting divorced, the same chance that Grandmother would grow too frail to live without assistance—then the Two-Income Trap would have imposed a moderate dose of hardship on American families as they struggled to survive in hard times. But, as we will show in the next chapter, the risks of the world did not stay the same. Families lost the stay-at-home mother just when they needed her most.

4

The Myth of the Immoral Debtor

There is a second myth about financial failure. This one is not about how families spend their money—in fact, it is not about dollars at all. This myth is about good and evil, ethics and righteousness. The Myth of the Immoral Debtor tells a story that begins in the past. In the good old days, goes the story, people paid their bills No Matter What. Not because they had more money, but because they had more honor. They paid their bills because it was the *right* thing to do; they would have died of shame rather than default. But today, the myth declares, the old morality is dead. We live in a time of easy virtue and decaying standards. To quote Republican Senator Orrin Hatch from Utah, large numbers of our fellow citizens "abuse the system" in order to "get around debts for which they are very capable of paying."[1]

The myth doesn't really require any proof, just a pugnacious assertion that our neighbors are cheating the system and the rest of us are paying for it. The Immoral Debtor Myth trades on an easy cynicism that passes for sophistication. Only chumps believe that everyone else is playing by the rules. People who are in the know understand that cheating is rampant, that millions of Americans are bankrupt or near-bankrupt because, according to Senator Hatch, "they run up huge bills and then expect society to pay for them."[2] When the creditors come calling, they stall, lie, and, sooner or later, declare bankruptcy so they can walk out on their debts.

Is there any truth to this claim? Have Americans gone from an age of honor and decency to a state of moral squalor? One problem with the Golden Age of Bill Paying is that no one can agree on when it actually occurred. Republican Congressman Henry Hyde recently complained, "Bankruptcy no longer carries with it the social stigma that it did twenty years ago. . . . Bankruptcy is becoming a first stop for some rather than a last resort."[3] Congressman Hyde wasn't the first to make this claim. He put the decline in the early 1980s, but he joined a long line of those who complained about declining standards. In the 1930s, Thomas D. Thacher, then solicitor general of the United States, expressed the often-repeated claim that numerous industrial workers were "running up bills without intention or ability to pay, and then filing a petition in bankruptcy."[4] Mr. Thacher, in turn, was preceded by nineteenth-century arbiters of public morality with similar complaints, who themselves were preceded by eighteenth-century critics, led by the venerable preacher Cotton Mather, who, in 1716, used his pulpit to decry the early American colonists who could not pay their debts, "for which they are to be Indicted, as Not Having the Fear of God before their Eyes."[5] It seems that the Golden Age of Bill Paying was always in the past, and that previous generations always had higher standards and greater integrity.[6] Indeed, if we listened to the public moralists, we would be left with the impression that America's moral fortitude has been rapidly disintegrating for at least 300 years!

What about today? Have Americans become cunning financial manipulators, ready to walk out on their debts without a moment's hesitation? Has the failure to repay or the decision to file for bankruptcy lost its sting? Once again, we turn to the numbers.

No Shame in Failure

The conviction that filing for bankruptcy no longer carries the stigma it once did is so widespread that it requires no proof. Whenever a commentator tries to verify the argument, the logic is usually circular. People would not file for bankruptcy if they felt stigmatized by it; therefore, if bankruptcies are up, stigma must be down. Impossible to disprove, and it sounds pretty good if no one pushes too hard on the logic.

A few economists have written about stigma, but the results are pretty much the same. They focus on a few economic measures—the unemployment rate, the GDP level, the inflation rate, and so forth—without ever actually talking to families, either those who file for bankruptcy or those who do not. These researchers then declare that a decline in stigma accounts for anything and everything that the bare numbers don't explain.[7] For example, if bankruptcy goes up while inflation goes down, it *must* be that stigma diminished because no other explanation presents itself. By this logic, the rise in bankruptcy filings might as well have been attributed to the number of SUVs on the roads or the number of burritos consumed—with exactly the same result.

Despite all the harrumphing, there is plenty of evidence that stigma is alive and well among families in financial trouble. One long-term study of family economics found that fully *half* of bankrupt families were unwilling to admit—even in an anonymous survey—that they had filed for bankruptcy.[8] Economists have calculated that there are millions of families who, after they took account of the legal fees and other costs, would be better off financially if they sought the protection of the bankruptcy courts. According to one estimate, about 17 percent of *all* households in the United States would see a significant improvement in their balance sheets if only they were willing to sign a bankruptcy petition.[9] That's 18 million households that would profit from a bankruptcy filing, compared with the 1.5 million that actually filed, suggesting that at least 16.5 million families are still trying to pay their debts for some reason that has nothing to do with the legal rules. It would seem that bankruptcy may look like just another "financial planning tool" to the economists who study it, but it is very different for the families who actually have to file the petitions and show up in court.[10]

Many commentators seem concerned that the families who file for bankruptcy are not sufficiently contrite. Democratic Senator Patricia

Murray from Washington argues that the Senate should make it a priority "to recapture the stigma associated with a bankruptcy filing."[11] The idea that they do not feel bad enough about their bankruptcy filings would have come as a shock to most of the families who filed. In her discussion of the psychology of bankruptcy, Constance Kilmark describes the people she has counseled to file for bankruptcy: "The anguish, shame, and embarrassment they experience over their situation is real and compelling."[12] In our own research, several mothers were willing to talk with us only on the condition that we not use the word "bankruptcy" during the telephone interview for fear that a child might pick up the extension phone and hear the dreaded word. Some said that just hearing the word still makes them cry, and they asked us to refer simply to "the event." More than 80 percent of the families we interviewed reported that they would be "embarrassed" or "very embarrassed" if their families, friends, or neighbors learned of their bankruptcy.[13]

So why would families file for bankruptcy even if they felt ashamed? *Because they believed they had no other choice.* By way of analogy, consider the stigma against nudity. Pretty much anyone over the age of three feels extremely embarrassed about getting naked in front of a stranger. But when people come down with a serious illness, when they are frightened by odd lumps or unexpected pains, they willingly shed their clothes in front of a bevy of medical professionals. They don't bare their bodies because they feel no stigma about nudity; they take off their clothes because it is the only way to get some help.

So it is for more than a million families each year. When given the choice between losing their homes or filing for bankruptcy, they chose bankruptcy. When faced with a choice between *never* paying off credit card debts and getting a chance to start fresh, they chose bankruptcy. It was embarrassing, it was humiliating, and they tried to hide it from their friends and families—but they did it. One California woman filed for bankruptcy after she lost her job and was on the brink of losing her home. She got her second chance, but the blow to her sense of self-worth was deeply painful. "I will *never* file for bankruptcy again. I will let them take my home or I will go without health care and food, and die and stand before Jesus before I do it again. It's a matter of self-worth and pride."

The Easy Way Out

The Myth of the Immoral Debtor has its variations. Some critics claim that families have gotten sneakier. Federal Judge Edith Jones, rumored to be a potential Bush appointee to the Supreme Court, asserts that "[b]ankruptcy is increasingly seen as a big 'game,' with the losers being those who live within their means, while the bankrupts pursue more interesting and carefree lives."[14] In the good old days, families would work their fingers to the bone to pay off their debts. But today, according to Judge Jones, "bankruptcy more and more is looked at as an option of 'first,' rather than 'last' resort." Families *could* pay their bills, but would rather take the easy way out.

Before we evaluate this claim, we should fill in a few basic facts about what it means to file for bankruptcy. Bankruptcy offers a one-time get-out-of-jail-free card. Although the specifics vary, the basic ideas are the same for both corporate and personal bankruptcies. When someone has gotten into serious financial trouble, he may seek protection from his creditors by filing for bankruptcy. The bankruptcy judge will supervise the case to ensure that creditors are repaid to the extent possible, while the debtor gets a chance to recover from disaster and make a fresh start.[15] For a business that is failing, the court takes legal jurisdiction over the company's assets and makes every effort to treat the various creditors equitably, which usually means only partial repayment of the outstanding debts.[16] In some cases, such as the high-profile dot-com failures of the early 2000s, the business is shuttered and the assets are sold off piecemeal, with all proceeds parceled out to the various creditors. In other cases, such as K-Mart and United Airlines, a portion of the debt is written off, and a leaner, "restructured" company is allowed to continue its operations.

For an individual who files bankruptcy, the process is similar. The courts take legal control over all his assets—the bank accounts, the house, the car—everything right down to Fluffy the cat and the old bike with a flat tire.[17] The judge orders those assets to be liquidated and used to repay creditors to the extent possible. So, for example, bank accounts must be emptied and stock portfolios must be sold; the judge might also order that jewelry or newer appliances be auctioned off to repay past debts. There are a few exceptions. Families are typically permitted to keep some clothes, furniture, and a few household goods. Home equity—the value of the home that exceeds the mortgage—creates a thorny problem. A few states, such as Florida and Texas, permit families to keep all their equity safe from other creditors, no matter how valuable the home; other states, such as Delaware and Maryland, force families to give up any equity in their homes, no matter how small.[18] But in all states, the creditors who have security interests—the home mortgage company and the car lender, for example—must be paid if the family wants to hold on to the asset. And some debts are never forgiven, no matter what. Taxes, student loans, alimony, and child support must be paid in full, regardless of how long it takes; bankruptcy offers no relief whatsoever.[19] But the rest of the debts—the credit cards, the hospital bills, the electric and gas bills—are paid proportionately from whatever property was sold off. At the end of the bankruptcy process, the family, like the corporation, gets to start with a clean slate. Most of their assets have been wiped out, but so have their debts—or at least some of them.

There are some important wrinkles in the consumer bankruptcy code. Unlike corporations, individuals must wait until the seventh year after filing for bankruptcy before they will be permitted to file again (a period drawn from biblical references).[20] Another wrinkle is that families have a choice about which form of bankruptcy to use. The first option, Chapter 7, permits a debtor to wipe out his debts in just a few months. In Chapter 13, the debtor files for bankruptcy in order to buy some time to pay what he owes, rather than to get rid of his debts altogether. The family works out a repayment plan, under which it commits to living on a sharply restricted budget for the next three to five years, handing over the remainder of each paycheck to a trustee who distributes it among the creditors.[21] Only after the payments are complete can the family discharge any debts that remain unpaid.[22]

In order to escape their debts, families must publicly disclose all their financial dealings, show their personal budgets to their creditors, and submit to supervision by a court-appointed trustee. For ten years, their credit reports will document their bankruptcy, making everything from car insurance to house payments more expensive. In some parts of the country, their names will be published in the newspaper. With online searches, the fact of their bankruptcy may pop up whenever someone tries to find them via the Internet. Future employers will discover the bankruptcy if they run a credit check (now a routine screening process for many jobs), which can lead to embarrassing explanations or, worse, a lost chance for a much-needed job. Most important, the family will still owe a large chunk of its debts—the home mortgage, the car loan, the taxes, the student loans, and so forth—even after filing for bankruptcy. But if a family is willing to go through all that, it can have at least some of its debts erased, no questions asked.

So is it possible that Judge Jones is right and today's families are using the bankruptcy courts more liberally than they used to? Once again, the data just don't support that argument. If a growing number of people were looking for the easy way out, then we would expect to find that families in bankruptcy today are in relatively better shape than those who filed a generation ago. For example, we might find that they have smaller debt loads relative to their incomes, with the clear implication that at least some of those folks could pay off the debts if they tried a little harder. Instead, just the opposite has happened. Today's bankrupt families are deeper in debt than their counterparts just twenty years earlier, and their overall financial picture—assets and debts—is worse.[23] In 1981, the median family filing for bankruptcy owed 80 percent of total annual income in credit card and other nonmortgage debts; by 2001, that figure had nearly doubled to *150 percent* of annual income. Even the credit industry, which has the most to gain from prying a few more dollars out of bankrupt families, estimates that only about 10 percent of families who file for bankruptcy could actually afford to repay even a portion of their discharged debts (although independent academics put that number closer to 1–2 percent). The remaining 90 percent are tapped out, too broke for even their creditors to bother with.[24]

There are other signs that families are not rushing headlong into bankruptcy at the first sign of trouble. The average person who filed for bankruptcy reports spending more than a year struggling with his debts before filing. Before they finally gave up and filed for bankruptcy, 50 percent of the families had their utilities or telephone shut off for nonpayment and nearly 60 percent did without needed medical care in order to save money. Indeed, one in five of these college-educated, home-owning families in bankruptcy said they had done without food at some point before filing because they simply couldn't afford it. By the time they sought refuge in the bankruptcy courts, the average family owed more than *an entire year's income* in nonmortgage debt.

Besides, the bankruptcy statistics are not the only signs of financial distress. The number of home foreclosures has more than tripled in the past 25 years, and car repossessions have doubled in just five years.[25] Judge Jones may think that bankruptcy filings are just a "big game," but for a family who no longer has a roof over their heads, we doubt that financial failure is much fun.

Fraud and Abuse

The Myth of the Immoral Debtor has one other variation: Today's families are more willing to lie, cheat, and file for bankruptcy under false pretenses. Everyone from Senator Orrin Hatch to the American Bankers Association contends that massive numbers of families filing for bankruptcy are engaged in "fraud and abuse."[26] Could they be right?

No one knows for certain how much fraud there is, although the courts go to great lengths to try to prevent it. If a person wanted to commit fraud in a bankruptcy petition, he would usually try to hide his assets from his creditors, perhaps in an offshore account, a bogus trust, or through transfer to a separate corporation or another person. In order to prevent this, every single personal bankruptcy filing is accompanied by detailed financial disclosures, filed under penalty of perjury, reviewed by a court-appointed trustee, and made public for any creditor or other interested party to scrutinize. Every debtor seeking bankruptcy relief must come to court in person, swear to "tell the truth, the whole truth, and nothing but the truth," and submit to cross-examination both by the trustee and any creditors who appear. If anything suspicious emerges, the debtor will be ordered back into court by a judge and examined further—under oath. Anyone who files a fraudulent bankruptcy petition or misrepresents his circumstances violates federal law and risks prosecution by the Department of Justice. A guilty verdict can result in jail time.[27] Any creditor who can show that a debtor lied on a credit application or otherwise committed fraud can have that debt exempted from discharge in bankruptcy; the creditor is also entitled to file criminal charges.

Even if they had evil in their hearts, it would be extremely difficult for the average family in bankruptcy to commit serious fraud. The overwhelming majority of people who file for personal bankruptcy aren't the financial sophisticates one usually associates with Swiss bank accounts and dummy corporations. They are ordinary, middle-class families whose total assets consist of a home, a car, and maybe a checking account. In our study of more than 2,000 bankrupt families, only one owned a second home—a small rental house that produced income, not a vacation place—and no one had an offshore account or a self-settled trust. Nor did these families have a personal attorney on retainer or a longtime accountant who might be persuaded to do a little finagling on the side. Just the opposite. Most people who filed for bankruptcy never even met a lawyer until the mortgage company sent a foreclosure notice, at which point they hired someone whose ad appeared in the yellow pages or on late-night television.[28] Typically the attorney spent less than half an hour giving them advice before passing them on to a paralegal who completed the paperwork necessary for the bankruptcy filing.[29]

The number of families committing fraud may have inched up over the years, although there is no evidence to support that claim. But if fraud alone accounted for the increase in the number of bankruptcies over the past generation, then eight out of every ten families filing for bankruptcy today would have to be committing fraud.[30] It seems pretty absurd to suggest that over the past decade roughly *10 million* families independently decided that they would commit a felony that could land them in jail—and that no one else heard about it.

The Myth of the Immoral Debtor might make for good headlines, but, like the Over-Consumption Myth, it won't hold up to hard analysis. Are there some families who are cheating? Of course. Just like there are some families who are over-consuming. Being in financial trouble confers no special state of grace that eliminates all the sharp operators and crafty manipulators who travel among us. But the stark numbers—bankruptcy filings that have quintupled, mortgage foreclosures that have tripled, car repossessions that have doubled—cannot be explained away so easily.

What Went Wrong

If the bankruptcy system isn't packed with frauds and cheats, then why are so many families in trouble? With a million and a half families declaring bankruptcy each year, one might expect innumerable explanations for all that financial mayhem. During our interviews we heard a wide variety of reasons. Some were victims of crime, some had made bad investments, some had problems with alcohol or gambling, and some had lost their homes in a flood or an earthquake. A few interviewees had actually done just what the "over-consumption" camp had accused them of—they had bought too many goodies on their credit cards. Perhaps the stand-out story was the man who filed for bankruptcy after he was shot while trying to foil a robbery at a nearby hardware store, and the resulting hospital bills and time off from work destroyed him financially.

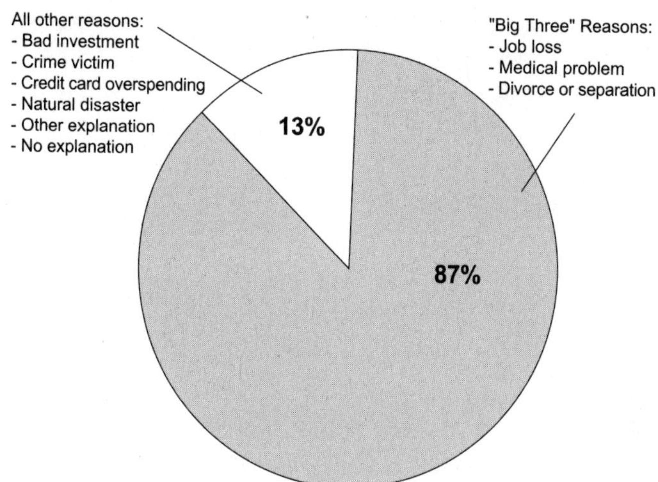

FIGURE 4.1 Reasons for filing for bankruptcy: families with children

While many of the stories are memorable for their odd details, the statistics reveal a much simpler picture. The overwhelming majority of financial failures are surprising not for their uniqueness, but for their sameness. Nearly nine out of ten families with children cite just three reasons for their bankruptcies: job loss, family breakup, and medical problems.[31] All the other reasons combined—acts of God, called up for military service, personal profligacy, and so on—account for just 13 percent of families in bankruptcy.

Two-Income Trap, Part Two

There's nothing new or exotic about the problems faced by American families today. Jobs have come and gone, couples have broken up, and illnesses and injuries have been facts of life since the first caveman kissed the first cavewoman good-bye and headed off to the hunt. But the Two-Income Trap compounded the ordinary risks of daily life. With Mom in the workplace and the family's safety net forfeited, a short-term job loss or a medium-sized illness now poses a far greater menace to a family that has no reserves. It takes less to sink these families; as a result, more of them go under.

But the two-income family didn't just lose its safety net. By sending both adults into the labor force, these families actually *increased* the chances that they would need that safety net. In fact, they doubled the risk. With two adults in the workforce, the dual-income family has *double* the odds that someone could get laid off, downsized, or otherwise left without a paycheck. Mom *or* Dad could suddenly lose a job.

The basic math may seem obvious, but the consequences are surprising. Consider Tom and Susan, the typical 1970s single-income family introduced in chapter 2. Statistically speaking, Tom faced a 2.5 percent chance of losing his job in any given year.[32] Had Justin and Kimberly, our present-day two-earner couple,[33] been around back then, they would have had a 4.9 percent chance of a major drop in income—almost double the chances of a single-income family.[34] The odds aren't doubled to exactly 5.0 (2.5 + 2.5) because in some of the families both the husband *and* the wife will be laid off, so the total number of families who experience a layoff is slightly less than 5.0 percent. (Of course, that also means some families get hit with two layoffs, a double catastrophe.) No matter how the odds are calculated, the principle is straightforward: two workers, two chances to lose a job.

This situation would be tough enough for the two-income family if the working world had stayed the same over the past generation. But, as anyone who watches the nightly news or reads the newspapers knows, the world did not stay the same. In the past twenty-five years, the chances that a worker will be laid off, downsized, or restructured out of a paycheck have increased substantially. One team of researchers calculated that the odds that a worker would suffer an involuntary job loss have increased by 28 percent since the 1970s.[35]

Growing job insecurity has been hard on single-income families, who now face a 28 percent higher chance that the breadwinner will lose his job. But for today's dual-income family, the numbers are doubly grim, as each spouse faces a higher likelihood of a job layoff. We estimate that in a single year, roughly 6.3 percent of dual-income

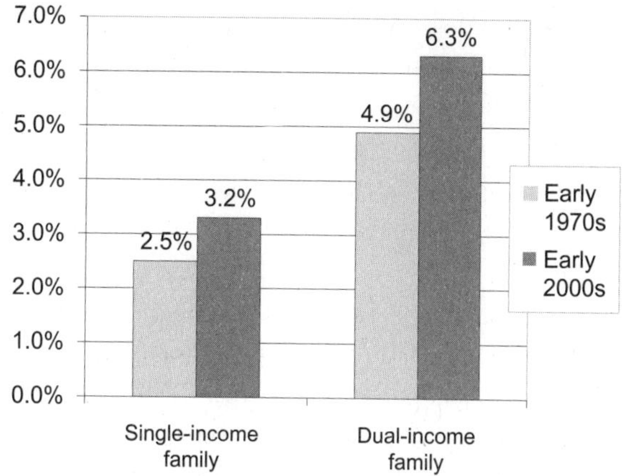

Annual risk that married couples will face an involuntary job loss.
Source: Analysis of data in Boisjoly, Duncan, and Smeeding.

FIGURE 4.2 How risk has grown: involuntary job loss

families—one out of every sixteen—will receive a pink slip.[36] That means that a family today with both husband and wife in the workforce is approximately *two and a half times* more likely to face a job loss than a single-income family of a generation ago.

Layoffs aren't the only way a family can lose a paycheck. Illness, accident, or disability can have the same effect. Once again, the dual-income family has doubled its risks. Two workers, two chances for a heart attack, a bad fall, or any other medical calamity that can leave a family without income.

This statistical analysis runs contrary to most families' assessment of the risks they face. With two incomes, most parents believe that they have built in some self-insurance against layoffs or medical problems. But they would be wrong. Two-income families are *more* likely to file for bankruptcy than their one-income counterparts.[37] Moreover, dual-income families who have filed for bankruptcy are also *more* likely to cite job loss or injury as the reason for their financial collapse.[38] The risks add up: In 2001, more than one million families will file for bankruptcy in the wake of a job loss, business failure, disability, or other form of income interruption.[39]

There is a painful irony to this. The family that sends both workers into the workforce in order to, as other researchers have claimed, "buffer them[selves] against the terrible wrenches of a changing economy"[40] have just made themselves *more* vulnerable to those very wrenches. Twice as likely, as a matter of fact.

Bad Timing

What about the other reasons for bankruptcy, such as family breakup and huge medical bills? At first glance, those problems don't appear to have anything to do with the Two-Income Trap. But those risks went up too, which proved to be very, very bad timing for the middle-class family that had let go of its safety net.

Consider medical bills. The ranks of the uninsured are swelling, and the problem has seeped into the middle class. In 2001, 1.4 million Americans lost their health insurance. Of the newly uninsured, 800,000 earned more than $75,000.[41] Experts calculate that an individual is now 49 percent more likely to be without health insurance than a generation ago.[42] Medical costs are escalating, and—surprise, surprise—a growing number of families are filing for bankruptcy in the wake of a catastrophic medical bill. Over the past twenty years, the number of families declaring bankruptcy in the wake of a serious illness has multiplied more than twentyfold, or *2,000 percent*.[43]

Demographics also pinched the family, as the number of Americans aged 85 and older (those most likely to need daily assistance) grew at a rate more than *six times* faster than that of the under-65 population.[44] A declining birth rate and a higher divorce rate compounded the problem. Today's elderly have fewer children to share the burden, and more are alone after a divorce. As a result, families with minor children are now almost twice as likely to be providing assistance to elderly parents than receiving it.[45]

At the same time, hospitals and insurance companies conspired to cut costs by dismissing patients "quicker and sicker." Today, one in three individuals require at-home care after being discharged from the hospital. That means that roughly 12 million families must step in to take care of a sick relative every year.[46] If all the adults in the family are already committed to the workplace, well, that's just too bad. Once again, the bankruptcy statistics confirm the story: Dual-earner couples are nearly twice as likely as single-breadwinner families to file for bankruptcy because of work lost as a result of an illness in the family.[47]

Divorce is another calamity that hits today's two-income families with greater frequency. Pretty much everyone knows that newlyweds now face a high chance of splitting up (although the risk is slightly less than the 50/50 number that circulates as conventional wisdom).[48] But there is a wrinkle to the statistics that hasn't made the news reports: The Two-Income Trap has wormed its way into the sanctity of marriage.

Many commentators have held out the hope that the divorce explosion will prove temporary and that marriages may actually become more stable as the sexes stride toward equality. *She Works/He Works* offers this bit of optimism:

> The era of the two-earner couple may in fact create more closeness in families, not less. . . . Divorces may decline as marriages become once again economic partnerships more like the ones they were before the industrial revolution. . . . fewer people will be able to waltz easily out of marriage, as they might have in the days when a thriving economy made good jobs easy to come by.[49]

This theory *sounds* good, and we wish we could share in the hopefulness.

Unfortunately, the data show otherwise. During the 1970s, a single-earner couple had about the same chances of splitting up as a dual-income couple. By the 1990s, however, a working wife was 40 percent more likely to divorce than her stay-at-home counterpart.[50] No one really knows why the difference has emerged, although sociologists have offered a number of competing theories. Perhaps the combination of working and bringing up the kids makes for a more stressful home life and leaves the two-earner couple with less time for each other. Or it may be that today's stay-at-home wives embrace more traditional gender roles, which can make for a smoother relationship. Feminist scholars offer their own explanation, arguing that working wives see themselves as less dependent on their husbands for financial support and are therefore freer to leave a bad relationship.[51] Whatever the reason, the grim fact remains: The modern two-income family faces a greater likelihood of divorce than the one-income family from a generation ago.

There is yet another wrinkle to the family-breakup statistics that often escapes attention—the couples who never marry. A quick glance at the census figures tells the story: Over the past twenty-five years the number of children whose mothers have never married increased more than 400 percent.[52] Many of these women are not really single, as the "never married" box on the census form might imply. Instead, they live for many years with a male partner. Since the 1970s the number of unmarried couples rearing children has increased *eightfold*. Today, cohabiting men and women represent more than 6 percent of all couples raising children, compared with less than 1 percent a generation ago.[53] Although 6 percent may sound like a modest proportion, the odds that a child will live with a cohabiting parent add up over time. According to one estimate, approximately four in ten children will spend some time in a cohabiting family before they turn sixteen.[54]

What does this have to do with the rising divorce rate? Cohabiting relationships share many of the financial characteristics of marriage since there are two adults to share the expenses and responsibilities of running a single household. When the cohabiting couple breaks up, the consequences are much like those when a married couple divorces. Someone has to find separate housing, and any joint obligations, such as a lease or a mortgage they both signed, must be resolved. If both partners are the children's biological parents, custody decisions must be settled, and arrangements for visitation and child support must be worked out. But here's the twist: The logistical consequences of splitting up may be the same, but the odds of breaking up are not. Cohabiting couples with children are more than twice as likely to split up as their married counterparts.[55] Once again, the frailty of families with children comes to the fore. As these unmarried parents go their separate ways, the number of families left without a second adult to share the burden continues to multiply.

Adding It Up

The list of ills—job loss, family breakup, and medical problems—is brutal, but it may also appear a bit eclectic and disjointed. After all, the divorce rate has nothing much to do with health insurance coverage; a corporate restructuring has no effect on the number of elderly folks who need help from their families.

When a family disaster makes the evening news, only one problem is in the spotlight at any given time. The *New York Times* carries a column about the terrible problems of the uninsured, or *60 Minutes* runs a story on divorce trends. Academics and other experts tend to reinforce this approach: Most of them have one highly focused area of expertise, and they usually write articles and hold forth on the talk shows about one specific category of calamity.

But families don't experience risks in neatly segmented boxes. Whether they give it much thought or not, they all live under the shadow of multiple dangers. A woman could lose her job, she could be struck with a devastating illness, her marriage could turn sour, *and* her parents could grow too feeble to care for themselves—and it could all happen at the same time. There is no law requiring that these disasters be polite enough to wait until the previous one is resolved and the family has recovered before a new one wreaks additional havoc.

Risk	*Change since 1970s*
Involuntary job loss	⇑ 150%
Wage-earner misses work due to illness or disability	⇑ 100%
Divorce[1]	⇑ 40%
Lack health insurance	⇑ 49%
Wage-earner misses work to care for sick child or elderly family member	⇑ 1,000+%

[1] Because of the limitations of the data, this figure represents the gap between the risk of divorce facing a modern one-earner and a modern two-earner couple, rather than a historical comparison.

FIGURE 4.3 How risks have grown: a comparison of one-income families in the 1970s and two-income families in the 2000s

Moreover, one disaster often triggers another. A layoff may leave a family without health insurance, increasing the exposure to an exorbitant medical bill. Similarly, a job loss may actually lead to divorce; sociologists have shown that as finances deteriorate, couples tend to fight more, increasing the chances that they will split up.[56] Among families in bankruptcy, nearly half report two of three problems—job loss, medical problems, or a family breakup—and about one in thirteen were hit by all three.[57] We have no statistical proof of the old wives' tale that bad things happen in threes, but there is ample evidence that disasters really do follow disasters.

There But for the Grace of God

If there is so little evidence that morals are declining, and so much evidence that slam-the-family risks are increasing, why does the Myth of the Immoral Debtor persist? Why don't we collectively agree once and for all that in most cases financial misfortune is simply a matter of bad luck, and that declining morals have nothing to do with the long lines at the bankruptcy courts? Perhaps the myth survives because it provides much-needed comfort in a dangerous world.

There is nothing glamorous or mysterious about the events that conspire to drive families into financial ruin. They are remarkably common, ordinary—and painful. For many people, reading about this litany of disasters will evoke memories that are disturbing, sometimes bitter, and sometimes very personal: That embarrassing morning when a friend was escorted out of the office during the latest round of company layoffs. The terrifying moment when the call came from the hospital emergency room. The sad day that Michelle told her husband that she wanted him to move out. For others, the list vibrates in harmony with the worries that keep them awake at night. What will happen if Grandma's forgetfulness is actually Alzheimer's? What if my husband's company goes under?

The possibility that a family—*our* family—faces a rapidly growing chance of disaster is too painful to think about, especially if there seems to be little way to avoid it. The Myth of the Immoral Debtor nourishes the unspoken idea that families who have lost their financial footing are a tainted group, some "other" who are different from the rest of us. If we can believe that those in serious trouble are morally suspect, then it is easier to glance away from the harsh dangers of everyday life. The myth supports a comforting illusion that the rest of us are safely distanced from financial collapse, making it possible to avoid that terrifying moment of connection with someone caught in a financial disaster, that frightening there-but-for-the-grace-of-God-go-I realization.

One Survivor's Story

Of course, not every job loss, divorce, or illness ends in the bankruptcy courts. Some families collapse under the weight of too many bills and not enough income, but many families do not. They may find themselves torn and battered, but they make it through.

Consider the Duprees. Jamal Dupree just turned forty, but he could be mistaken for a much older man. His face is deeply lined, and his hands shake when he lifts a cup of coffee. The trouble started with chest pains. Not the maybe-it's-heartburn sort of discomfort, but the real thing: "It felt like someone had my chest in his fist and was just squeezing all the breath out of me. I never hurt like that in all my life. I thought for sure my time was up."

Thanks to a quick-witted coworker who spirited Jamal to a hospital in nearby Nashville, Jamal's time was not up. Three months after his open-heart surgery, Jamal was able to climb a flight of stairs again. Five months later he returned to his job as a technician at the electric company.

But five months was a long time for Jamal to take off from work. His wife, Trish, lost a lot of time at her job as an airline ticket agent, spending days outside the intensive care unit and weeks caring for Jamal after he went home. As the medical bills arrived in the mail, the Duprees were confronted by exclusions and deductions they hadn't even known were written into their health insurance policy. "My medication costs me out of pocket over $200 per month. I don't know what I'd do if I didn't have health insurance, but really, it doesn't keep the wolf away from the door. They still want us to pay so much." Jamal had another scare a few weeks after he returned to work: "I had blackout spells because of a medication I was taking. I fell in the shower and hurt my rotator cuff in my shoulder. I need surgery, but I am putting it off because I can't afford the extra cost now. I would have a big bill at the end of the surgery."

But Jamal and Trish were lucky in other ways. Because Jamal has always been a worrier, he had signed up for every form of insurance his employer offered. Hefty deductions chewed a hole out of his paycheck each month, but when he had his heart attack, it paid off. Once his vacation time was used up, the disability insurance kicked in, giving the Duprees 60 percent of Jamal's former income. Jamal reflects, "It wasn't really enough, but I don't know what we would have done without that money."

The Duprees inevitably fell behind on their credit card bills, and they missed a mortgage payment. "Norwest [Mortgage, Inc.] called me a bunch of times. They said, 'We see you're having trouble paying your mortgage. Come to our office and get a second mortgage and pay off your other bills.'" Jamal held firm; he didn't want to risk losing the house that their three children were growing up in. But the calls scared him. He and Trish talked it through and decided that from now on, they would make the mortgage payment first—no matter what. Twice the gas was shut off, so they lived without hot water until the next check arrived, and the phone was disconnected for nearly a month. But Jamal kept making those house payments.

Four months after he returned to work, Jamal took a second job working the evening shift at 7-Eleven. Trish, meanwhile, had already requested all the overtime hours she could get. Their oldest son, Jared, got a job delivering pizzas on the weekends; most weeks he slips a few twenties to his mom. When his sister made the cheerleading squad, Jared quietly paid for her uniform. The Duprees have drained their kids' college funds, emptied their retirement accounts, and they haven't eaten in a restaurant in more than a year. They still have several thousand dollars in credit card bills, and Jamal is praying that he can avoid another surgery. But, with a little luck, they just may make it.

An Ounce of Prevention

What makes the Duprees' story different? Why did they endure, when so many others failed? Some of the answer was luck. Jamal was lucky to have a job to return to. (He was out too long for the Family and Medical Leave Act to safeguard his job.) Trish was lucky to get the overtime pay she badly needed. Most of all, they were lucky that no other disasters hit them while they were vulnerable.

But some part of their survival should be credited to planning, the ounce of prevention that policymakers and anxious families could learn from. Sensible planning starts with insurance. This is the classic prescription from any economist. Whenever a family (or a business) confronts the possibility of a potentially devastating danger, it is time to buy an insurance policy.

The Duprees' health insurance policy didn't cover everything; the deductibles are high enough to prevent Jamal from getting the rotator cuff surgery he badly needs. Many families have discovered that the exclusions, copayments, and caps on health insurance mean that they are on the hook for far more than they anticipated, while others have learned that much-needed services such as physical therapy or mental health treatment are scarcely covered at all. Health insurance is no guarantee that a catastrophic illness won't send a family into a financial tailspin. Approximately 240,000 families *with* continuous medical insurance file for bankruptcy every year at least in part because of outstanding medical bills.[58]

But without that insurance policy, the Duprees wouldn't have had a prayer. Ever since President Clinton promised to expand health insurance coverage to all Americans, coverage for the uninsured has remained a prominent political issue. And for a good reason: A lack of health insurance coverage sends as many as 150,000 families to the bankruptcy courts each year.[59]

But another form of insurance may be even more critical for preserving families' financial health in the wake of illness: disability coverage. The liberal policy wonks may stop us right here. What do we mean expansion of health insurance isn't the most important initiative since The New Deal? Reducing the number of uninsured ranks high on the agenda of both major political parties, whereas disability coverage is virtually nonexistent on the national agenda.

In the age of the Two-Income Trap, when families have sacrificed their own personal safety nets, disability insurance can be all that stands between them and financial ruin. Unfortunately, a majority of workers do not have any private long-term disability insurance, and only a handful of states provide coverage for their residents.[60] Unemployment insurance offers no relief, since most states require that an individual be "able" to work in order to qualify for benefits.[61] Fortunately, there is some good news here. Fixing the disability coverage problem may be easier than solving the health insurance crisis, because the apparatus already exists. Virtually every worker in America has long-term disability coverage through the Social Security Disability Insurance (SSDI) program. All that remains is to close the holes in the SSDI safety net, many of which are big enough to drive a truck through.

SSDI disability benefits are available only to those whose condition is expected to result in death or to last at least twelve months. In addition, there is a five-month waiting period after the onset of permanent illness. This means that anyone who, like Jamal Dupree, is seriously ill but is expected to recover within a year is out of luck. If the program were amended so that all serious illnesses were covered (even those not likely to result in death) and the waiting period were dropped to a few weeks (more like the unemployment insurance program), SSDI would save far more families from financial ruin. Disability benefits would still be reserved for those with a serious illness, but families would acquire an urgently needed safety net.

In addition, under the current SSDI guidelines, the disability must be so severe that the individual is unable to perform *any* job anywhere in the entire country, not just the job for which the worker is trained and has spent a lifetime building skills and qualifications. This means that someone who had worked for decades as an electrician or as a surgeon, but who developed a disability that prevented him from performing those duties, would not receive a single dime if he were deemed well enough to work as a telemarketer or a toll collector. The SSDI program could be modified to provide a sliding benefit depending on the level of disability (akin to many private disability policies), and temporary benefits could be offered while the worker undergoes retraining.

Universal, state-sponsored disability benefits would be ideal to fill the gap in the safety net. But families don't have to sit back and wait for the government to take action; they can purchase insurance in the private market, either through their employers or on their own. Expanded coverage won't protect families against every danger. A disability policy wouldn't have saved Carmen and Mike (from chapter 3), because it covers only workers who fall ill, not those who must take time off to care for other family members. But it could make a very big dent in the risks facing many families. We estimate that universal, comprehensive disability coverage could help as many as 300,000 families avoid the bankruptcy courts *every year*—and hundreds of thousands more who are on the brink of collapse.[62]

Similarly, a couple can purchase a long-term-care insurance policy for themselves—or for their aging parents—that covers both home health and nursing home care. Today, fewer than 10 percent of the nation's elderly have purchased private insurance to protect themselves against the risk that they will someday need long-term care, and even fewer working-age adults are covered.[63] Once again, these policies don't provide coverage against every possible contingency, but they offer another way for a family to mitigate one of life's dangers.

The solutions we propose here wouldn't be free to taxpayers, and the private market for insurance is far from perfect. On the other hand, these proposals aren't all that radical either. We haven't suggested a complete overhaul of the tax structure, and we haven't demanded that businesses cease and desist from ever closing another plant or firing another worker. Nor have we suggested that the United States should build a quasi-socialist safety net to rival the European model. All of the solutions we have proposed thus far—creating tax incentives for saving, expanding state-funded disability coverage, and encouraging families to insure themselves against an uncertain future—can be implemented within America's current blend of public and private systems without drastic changes or massive tax increases.

The Myth

When Orrin Hatch claims that the real change needed in America is for individuals to "take personal responsibility for their debts,"[64] we are left to wonder exactly what he has in mind. Should people take more responsibility for losing their jobs or for having heart attacks? Or does he mean that "responsible" families should sell their homes and move into the street as soon as they are laid off so they run no risk of falling behind on the mortgage or owing money to a landlord? Many of the families we studied lead lives that are already thick with personal responsibility—time lost from work to take care of an elderly parent, thousands of dollars of debts to provide medical care for a loved one. Perhaps if these families let go of some of that "personal responsibility" they would be in better financial shape—but we don't think they would be better people.

The Myth of the Immoral Debtor may be little more than an ugly fairy tale, but it has the power to maroon families—both emotionally and financially—just when they most need support. The changes needed to increase the safety of the middle class aren't radical, and they are not exorbitantly expensive. But they require a consensus that change is essential. So long as Americans can be persuaded that families in financial trouble have only themselves to blame, there will be no demand to change anything. In order to get on with the difficult business of making America once again safe for families to raise children, the Myth of the Immoral Debtor must be laid to rest for good.

5

Going It Alone in a Two-Income World

Gayle Pritchard taps nervously on the table as she talks about twelve years of marriage to Brad. The litany of complaints comes easily to her lips; she's told this story before. Brad drank too much. He didn't pick up after himself. He always forgot birthdays. But after a few more jabs, Gayle exhausts herself, and her face softens. "Brad loves his kids. On weekends he would lie on the couch for hours, with little Kaitlyn sound asleep across his lap, the drool just sliding all over his shirt and he never even minded. How could you hate a man like that?"

After more than a decade of marriage, their life together began to unravel. "They outsourced Brad's job at the distribution center. No severance. Nothing." Gayle was working hard, too tired to be very supportive. She dismissed Brad's mood swings as nothing more than "a male ego type thing." But then Brad started disappearing, spending his days and then nights away from home. The anger bubbles up again as Gayle recalls, "Money that was allotted for day care started disappearing."

After a few months, Brad found a new job and his dark moods lifted, but the damage was done. Gayle learned the reason for Brad's disappearances; he had been seeing another woman. Today Gayle looks back reflectively. "He felt like I didn't need him. . . . He lost confidence in himself. He found somebody to cater to that lack of self-confidence." She says it doesn't matter so much now, but at the time all she could think was that he had found some other woman beautiful, had put his hands on someone else. "I swear I could smell her on him. It made me crazy." She screamed, threw his clothes in the yard, and broke his baseball trophy. Brad didn't hang around for more. He found a new apartment and invited his girlfriend to move in.

Gayle was worried about making it on her own with three children, but she figured that she was pretty well situated to make a go of it. Brad let her keep the house, and he didn't intend to fight her in court over anything else they owned. He was hoping to keep the legal bills to a minimum. Gayle says with an embarrassed laugh, "We got one of those TV Guide divorces, the 'We agree on everything' kind."

Besides, Gayle was a good provider in her own right. She had a degree in communications and nine years in the Human Resources department at Exxon. By the time Brad moved out, she had been promoted to manager, and, thanks to "an awesome raise," she was earning $46,000 a year. In short, Gayle had about as much going for her as any modern middle-class mother starting her newly single life could hope for. She figured that she and her kids could make it.

The Best of Times . . .

Up to now, we have scrutinized, analyzed, poked, prodded, and otherwise expounded on nearly every aspect of the financial life of the modern middle-class family, but we haven't addressed *all* middle-class families. Indeed, we have been silent about the families who are most often in the news for their financial woes, those who first come to mind when the phrase "parents in financial trouble" comes up. We refer, of course, to the single mother.

Conventional wisdom holds that the single mother has a tough time making ends meet. (There are some single fathers, of course, but the overwhelming majority of custodial single parents are women, so we begin this discussion with them; we will return to the fathers later in this chapter.) Generations before America had even dreamed of a government-sponsored welfare program, charitable foundations offered their assistance to "Widows and Orphans," based on the widespread understanding that a woman with children would have a tough time getting by on her own. During the divorce explosion of the 1970s, the spotlight turned from the widow to the divorced mother, but the concept was basically the same: Without a man around, a woman with children was in big trouble. In the 1980s, sociologist Lenore Weitzman made headlines with her claim that in the immediate wake of divorce, a woman's standard of living drops by 73 percent from her married state.[1] Several scholars later showed that Weitzman overstated the extent of the decline, but there is widespread agreement about her basic conclusion: Most mothers tumble down the economic ladder after they divorce.[2] Nor is the postdivorce financial tumble a phenomenon confined solely to poor women. In fact, the drop is hardest for women in the middle and upper classes, since they have farther to fall.[3]

A generation ago, flush with the emerging power of the feminist movement, women's groups began to push what seemed like an obvious solution to the economic woes facing divorced mothers: Help women get more money. According to this logic, single mothers would be safe only if they earned more money in the workplace and if the laws were changed to squeeze more out of their ex-husbands. The first item on the agenda fit neatly with advancing the cause for all women, regardless of marital status. Women should get more job training, better educations, and stronger legal protection in the workplace, which should all translate into one thing—bigger paychecks for *all* women, single and married alike. The second objective focused directly on the rules of divorce. Women's paychecks should be supplemented by generous child support awards from their ex-husbands, which should be rigorously enforced by every sheriff's department in the country. The double prescription—make more and collect more—promised to lift the single mother from a precarious state of dependence and bring her the financial security she so desperately needed.

Was the women's movement right? This is one of those rare social theories that we don't have to debate in the abstract. The past generation has been a giant laboratory for testing exactly the get-a-job-get-child-support-and-be-safe prescription; all we have to do is look at the evidence.

Over the past generation, millions of married women have embraced the protect-yourself strategy. Going to college, getting a good job, and staying in the workforce have come to be seen as the only sensible way for a married mother to protect herself in this age of rampant divorce. Conservative social critic Danielle Crittenden observes:

> I don't believe placing a baby in day care is either easily or thoughtlessly done by most mothers. No, the fundamental reason why mothers of small children feel they cannot afford to stay home today, when a generation ago they didn't, is the greater prospect of divorce. The modern woman expects to support herself, and knows the danger of being unable to do so. The fear a woman has of having to fend for herself and her children at some point underlies why even happily married women often feel obliged to work when there's no immediate financial reason for them to do so.[4]

This attitude reflects our collective common sense. If a woman stays in the workforce, she will gain experience and make more money. And, if she makes more money, she will be better off if her husband leaves her—or so the argument goes.

Once again, we focus on the circumstances of the middle-class family. There has been a great deal of news (much of it bad) about the plight of the low-income single mother. Trapped in poverty without a husband, with a limited education and dismal career prospects, garnering little support from the state, the community, or from the child's father, chronically poor mothers have become the living symbols of the rough underside of the economy. But what about middle-class single mothers, women like Gayle Pritchard who have a good education, substantial work experience, a decent income, and, in most cases, an ex-husband solidly on the hook for child support? These women have followed the go-to-work prescription faithfully, making astounding gains in nearly every arena over the past generation—gains that should have translated into rising fortunes for the postdivorce family.

What happened when millions of middle-class mothers headed into the workplace? The media tends to focus on the bad news—the shocking sexual harassment of a female employee at Mitsubishi or antiquated policies that keep women out of prestigious military colleges and off fancy golf courses. The bad news makes for good headlines, but it shouldn't be allowed to overshadow one very important fact: American women have come a very long way in a very short time.

Consider, for example, women's enhanced legal protection. The mantra of equal opportunity in the workplace has become so ingrained in our collective consciousness that it can be easy to forget the (not so distant) days when the playing field wasn't nearly so level. When I (Elizabeth) was an elementary school teacher fresh out of college in 1970, the public school district didn't even bother to hide the fact that there were two separate pay scales—one for men and one for women. The differential was a matter of public record, and it produced little concern among either the public or my fellow teachers. Indeed, the policy was widely viewed as a normal feature of almost every "family-friendly" workplace. After all, men needed those higher wages to support a family at home. Today public schools, along with virtually every other employer in the country, have dismantled their separate pay structures, thanks largely to sweeping reforms in federal and state laws. Moreover, nearly every major employer in the United States has adopted a formal policy of equal opportunity for women. The battle for full legal equality may not be entirely won, but during the past generation women have made phenomenal strides—progress that has translated into material gains on the job.

Bolstered with protection from the courts, today's women are better prepared for the workforce than any other generation in history. Not only are they better educated than any previous cohort of women, but by some measures they are now even better educated than men. Today's young women are more likely to finish high school than young men—reversing the situation of a generation ago. They are also more likely to pursue higher education. In 1970, six out of ten college students were men; today that figure is exactly inverted—nearly six out of ten college students are women.[5] Armed with better educations, women have seen their professional opportunities mushroom. In the early years of my [Elizabeth's] career, it seemed that at nearly every step along the way, my compatriots and I were the "first" women to achieve something or other. In 1975, at a prestigious law firm on Wall Street, my friend Valerie and I were the first women ever offered summer internships. (Over the course of that summer I was mistaken for a waitress, a secretary, a cleaning person, and "Harry's daughter," despite the obligatory suit and floppy bow tie I donned every day.) Today, women account for nearly one-third of practicing attorneys nationwide, and women are almost as likely as men to be managers or supervisors. Women also account for 41 percent of university professors, and they now hold at least one seat on the board of directors of nearly three out of four major corporations in America.[6]

All that progress has translated into just what the feminists and politicians had hoped for—more money for women. Since 1960, women's wages have grown *ten times* faster than men's.[7] Women with children were not left behind. Today, employed women with children earn just 4 percent less than their childless sisters.[8] Women also face a much lower risk of unemployment than they did a generation ago, they are more likely to own their own businesses, and a growing number earn more than their husbands.[9] Women haven't yet caught up with men, but they are gaining fast.

So women are making more money. But what about the other half of the prescription—child support? The "deadbeat dad" makes a prominent appearance in nearly every conversation about single mothers. There is some truth to those headlines, but there is another truth that gets lost in all the hoopla over the shiftless father: Women have made enormous strides in collecting from their ex-husbands. A generation ago there was little government support for a woman whose ex was delinquent on his child support payments. In the late 1970s, as a young lawyer, I [Elizabeth] tried to help my friend Marcie garnish her ex-husband's wages to enforce a child support order. The fellow was an international importer from a wealthy family. He had a high-paying job, but he hadn't paid a cent of his court-ordered support since he had walked out two years earlier—a classic deadbeat if ever there was one. Meanwhile, Marcie and her toddler were supplementing her income as a teacher's aide with food stamps. Despite my legal training and young-lawyer zeal, I could not find a single person in the any of the county or state offices to help Marcie. When I finally initiated a lawsuit on her behalf (something she could never have afforded on her own), the local district attorney told me that enforcing child support orders "just isn't in my job description."

It wasn't until the 1980s that this system changed. Congress passed a series of laws that guaranteed women all around the country the opportunity to garnish their ex-husband's paychecks.[10] Congress also ordered uniform support guidelines in 1984; until then, each woman was at the mercy of whatever whims and prejudices influenced the judge who decided her particular case.[11] The penalties for nonpayment have also been stiffened. In some states a man who falls behind on his child support payments stands to lose his driver's license or his work permit (such as a contractor's license). He may even be thrown in jail. Today, federal and state governments spend more than $3 billion on child support enforcement, compared with less than $400 million (inflation adjusted) in the mid-1970s.[12] The system is still far from perfect, but these improvements have helped millions of women. Since 1976, the proportion of women receiving child support has increased 17 percent for divorced mothers and *300 percent* for never-married mothers.[13]

The numbers show that the feminist prescription has been followed to the letter. Today's middle-class mothers embark on single life with better educations, better job training, better legal support, and bigger paychecks than any women in history. They are backed up by more effective state-sponsored child support enforcement than ever before. In a single generation, their gains have been nothing short of extraordinary. With all that progress, we should confidently predict that while single mothers may still have a tougher time than married parents, their situation must be improving. Right?

. . . The Worst of Times

Wrong. Despite all the progress, middle-class single mothers are no more financially secure today than they were a generation ago. Indeed, our data show that despite their amazing advancements at work, in school, and in the courts, these women are actually *less* secure than they were just twenty-five years ago.

In chapter 1, we described our astonishment when we first saw the bankruptcy data for single mothers. That first look told us that something is amiss. Badly so. Single mothers are now more likely than any other group to file for bankruptcy—more likely than the elderly, more likely than divorced men, more likely than minorities, and more likely than people living in poor neighborhoods. Indeed, single mothers are 50 percent more likely than married parents to go bankrupt, and three times more likely than childless people—married or single.[14]

Motherhood is now the single best indicator that an unmarried middle-class woman will end up bankrupt. In the world of financial devastation, there are two groups of people: single mothers and others.

And the lines at the bankruptcy courts are not the only sign of distress. Federal Reserve data revealed that *one in eleven* single parents are more than 60 days past due on their bills (compared with one in thirty married couples without children).[15] Single mothers are also more likely to lose their homes. When we analyzed unpublished data from the Department of Housing and Urban Development, we found that among single parents who had purchased a home in the 1980s with a mortgage backed by the Federal Housing Administration (FHA), more than *one in ten* had lost their home by 2002 because of foreclosure.[16]

The difficulties facing single mothers are not the inevitable consequence of bringing up children without a father around. The bankruptcy courts weren't always flooded with single mothers; quite the opposite. In the early 1980s, about 69,000 unmarried women filed for bankruptcy in a single year.[17] Unfortunately, we don't know how many of them had children. (Our current research project is the first to gather this information on a national scale.) But suppose that 45 percent of these women had children—the same proportion as today. (In all likelihood, this assumption overstates the number of single mothers in bankruptcy in the early 1980s because there were relatively fewer women raising children on their own back then than there are today.[18]) Even with that assumption, the data would suggest that in 1981 there were (at most) 31,000 single mothers at the end of their financial ropes. That would have been about one in every 200 single mothers filing for bankruptcy in a single year, implying that single mothers may have been somewhat more likely to go bankrupt than married couples or single men—but only somewhat (see Figure 5.1).[19] This means that, for the most part, single mothers a generation ago were swimming in more or less the same financial pool as everyone else, and they had about the same chances of staying afloat.

But the economics shifted powerfully in just twenty years. Today, more than 200,000 single mothers go bankrupt each year. That translates into one in every 38 single mothers filing for bankruptcy in a single year.[20] At a time when women are advancing on multiple fronts—economic, political, educational, legal—the number of single mothers going broke has increased by more than 600 percent, and the gap between single mothers and everyone else continues to widen. If current trends persist, *more than one of every six single mothers will go bankrupt by the end of the decade.*[21]

Perhaps these women are the unlucky ones the women's revolution left behind? Could they be the teen mothers and welfare dependents

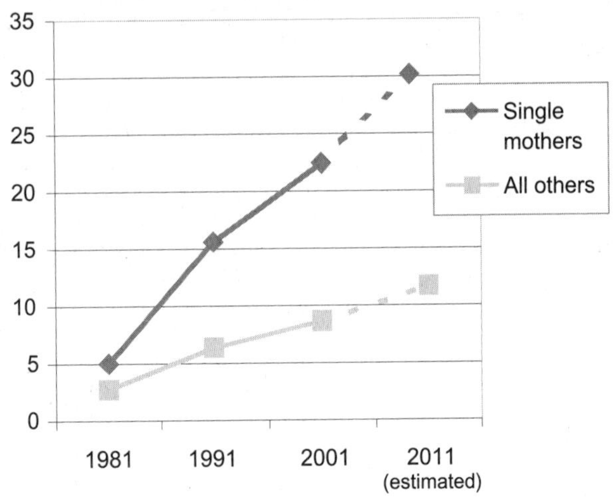

Bankruptcy Filing rates per 1,000 population

Source: 2001 Consumer Bankruptcy Project; Sullivan, Warren, and Westbrook, 1989 and 2000.

FIGURE 5.1 Single mothers and others: bankruptcy filing rates

the media usually associates with poor-single-mothers? No. The women represented in this graph are predominantly middle class—exactly the women who were supposed to have benefited from all those advances made by the women's movement. Like Gayle Pritchard, these women took advantage of improved educational opportunities. In fact, single mothers who have been to college are actually *more* likely to end up bankrupt than their less educated sisters—nearly 60 percent more likely.[22]

They are also more likely to have a good job. While few of the single mothers who crowd the bankruptcy courts are doctors or lawyers, most of these women have decent jobs. They are scattered throughout the employment spectrum, but there are more teachers, managers, and administrative assistants in the bankruptcy courts, and fewer fast-food workers and cleaning women, than there are in the general population.[23] Single mothers in bankruptcy are also *more* likely to have achieved that cornerstone of the American dream, home ownership. Fully 52 percent of these women owned their own homes, compared with just 36 percent of single parents in the general population.[24] Nor are they especially young. Nearly 80 percent of these women have already passed their thirtieth birthday.

The single mothers who file for bankruptcy are not some distant group imprisoned in a far-away ghetto. By every social measure we can assemble, these women are a solid part of the middle class. They are not strangers; they are our neighbors. They have flown higher than any earlier generation of women, only to discover that they fall farther.

Continuing Fallout from the Two-Income Trap

Although Gayle Pritchard had almost everything else going for her on the day her husband moved out, there was one big black mark against her: her family's balance sheet. In 1999, the Pritchards had cashed out their savings, sinking it all into what the couple hoped would prove to be a wise investment, their first home. At $105,000, the three-bedroom ranch in suburban Houston would undoubtedly make the family "house poor," but Gayle was determined. "I wanted my children to have a place to call their own, to have a yard, to know their neighbors. . . . I grew up in a house, and I wanted my kids to have the same experience."

The Pritchards had a simple financial plan. Brad's salary was to "maintain the family" and Gayle's was to pay the mortgage. Now that Brad's paycheck was gone, Gayle was stuck. Her paycheck maintained the family, but there was nothing left to pay the mortgage. "I got three months behind on the mortgage because I was just trying to keep my family fed. It was just so damn hard." When the foreclosure notice arrived, she filed for bankruptcy and worked out a repayment plan with the mortgage lender. Gayle reflects, "I knew that I was at the lowest point in my life. . . . I went ahead and filed but it was done very, very reluctantly. I mean, I couldn't keep asking people like my mom to bail me out again."

The relief provided by the bankruptcy courts was only partial. The monthly payments for her home actually increased when she filed. Gayle now had to pay off an additional $10,750 in late fees and past-due interest that her lender had tacked on—and that extra money had to be paid within three years, not over the thirty-year life of her mortgage. At the time we spoke with her, Gayle's expenditures on property taxes, mortgage payments, and utilities claimed nearly *three-quarters* of her take-home pay.[25] She couldn't expect much help from child support, either. Brad still owed child support to his first wife, so he was due to pay Gayle only $350 a month, less than one-quarter of the family's housing expenses.

Gayle often thinks about giving up her home, but she is deeply reluctant to do so. "My kids had already gone through so much instability with the way that their dad left. I needed them to feel some stability. . . . My oldest son said, 'Mama, if I have to get a job to help you, I will. I don't want to move again.' . . . He was only ten." Gayle pauses while she thinks about her oldest child. Barely past bed-wetting, still sleeping with a night-light, he has taken on the solemn worries of adulthood. Gayle added quietly, "I felt I owed it to him to hold on to this house as long as I can."

If we took the typical approach to analyzing the economic difficulties facing single mothers like Gayle Pritchard, we would start our investigation on the day her husband walked out. We would pose the usual set of queries: Did the divorce court treat this woman fairly? Did the judge order enough child support and alimony? Did the ex-husband follow through on his legal obligations?

The problem with the usual approach is that it focuses attention far too late in the story. Like so many single mothers, Gayle's financial problems started back when she was married, when she and her husband stumbled into the Two-Income Trap by committing both of their paychecks to cover their monthly expenses. The family no longer had a stay-at-home mother who could take a job after her husband moved out—that is, there was no way to bring in *new* dollars to cover the costs of divorce.[26]

And those costs add up. There are the lawyers, one for him and one for her. Court costs. Document preparation fees. Charges for photocopying the legal and financial records. The costs are substantial if the parties can agree on everything; if they fight, the lawyers just get richer. And legal fees are only the beginning. Someone has to move out, and that means cash for first and last month's rent, phone installation charges, a separate checking account. Some furniture? Dishes? A shower curtain? Then there are the unexpected costs, which tend to creep higher when there are no longer two adults to divide the chores and help each other with life's little emergencies. Will he send out his laundry and eat out more often? Will she hire someone to change the oil in the car and clean out the gutters? Without Dad to share the burden, will she miss work more often when the kids get sick? Will he give up overtime on Saturdays because that is his only day with the kids? With the savings account drained by the legal bills and the costs piling up, the credit card may be the only way to fill in the gaps.

After divorce, they still have to meet their regular financial commitments—those that are the hardest kind to cut back. The biggest item in the family budget is the home, which would make it the most logical place to try to downsize. But mothers like Gayle Pritchard are guided by more than a steely eye on the balance sheet. They strongly resist pulling their children out of familiar schools and neighborhoods at the same moment that their family life is disintegrating. Moreover, many women fear that without their husband's income, they will never get approval to buy another home, even one with a smaller price tag. They are haunted by the nameless dread that if they relinquish that precious bit of real estate, they will be letting go of the middle-class aspirations they hold for their children.

Where else can they cut? Should they sell Mom's car—the one she drives to work every day? Should they pull Junior out of day care or tell their son to quit college? Should they drop the health insurance policy? This isn't a matter of living more frugally. These are the costs that families incur to keep their children safe and hold them securely in the middle class, even when there is no longer a father in the home. To give these up is to admit more than financial failure; it means failing as parents.

So where does that leave the newly single mother? She is living the feminist dream, better educated and earning far more than her sisters of a generation ago. And yet, in the wake of divorce, she will learn just how far she can fall. In chapter 2 we showed that Tom and Susan, the typical one-earner family in the 1970s, had 46 percent of Tom's income left over once the housing, health insurance, and other fixed expenses had been paid. If Tom and Susan split up, Susan's discretionary income, once she collected child support payments and found a new job, would fall to just 19 percent of the family's predivorce income.[27] That is a staggering drop, making it tough for the newly formed fatherless household to survive a generation ago. But things are *worse* for today's working mothers. Today, the two-earner *married* family starts out just slightly better off than the *divorced* woman of a generation ago, with only 25 percent of income available for food, utilities, clothing, and all other discretionary purchases. But if today's two-parent family is squeezed, the postdivorce mother is crushed. If Justin and Kimberly (the typical two-earner family in the 2000s) divorce, Kimberly's discretionary income would drop to a mere *4 percent* of the family's predivorce income, even after she collects child support.[28] (See Figure 5.2.) The middle-class life she and her husband once provided for their children would vanish.

The bad news isn't over. The public face of divorce implies that the biggest struggle facing a divorcing couple is the fight over who-gets-what. Think of Donald and Ivanna Trump, or former General Electric CEO Jack Welch and the ex-wife who broadcast his lavish compensation package to an eager public. Long, protracted battles, plenty of he-said-she-said drama, and a debate in the local newspapers over who-deserved-what makes for juicy stories. But today's

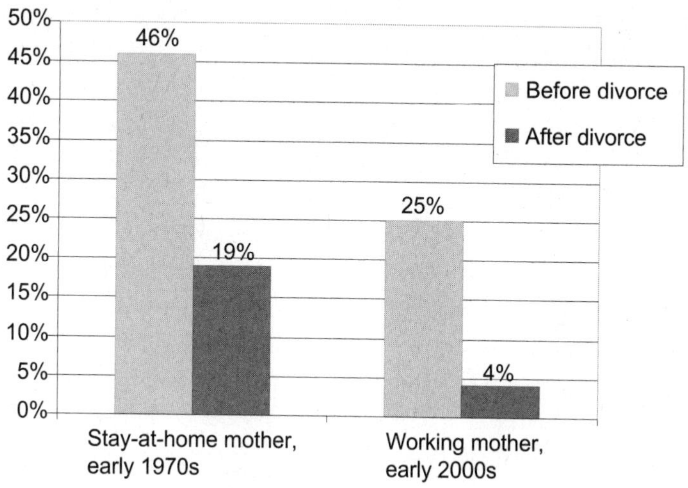

Discretionary income as a percent of total predivorce family income, after expenditures on taxes, mortgage, child care, health insurance, and automobile for typical family with two children. Assumes stay-at-home mother enters the workforce after the divorce, and that both mothers receive child support. *Source:* Analysis of Consumer Expenditure Survey. For more information on calculation of discretionary income, see above and see chapter 2.

FIGURE 5.2 Discretionary income, before and after divorce

middle-class families don't just split up the home, the bank accounts, and the kids. They must also split up the *debt*. And unlike the bank accounts, they don't get just 50 percent apiece. They each face *100 percent* responsibility for any debts they both signed their names to.

When a husband and wife file for divorce, they may tear up the contract between themselves, but they cannot tear up their obligations to the rest of the world. Kenesha Brooks, a California mother of two, got a very expensive lesson in the law of legal liability. She discovered that her ex-husband had been keeping his business afloat on the couple's credit cards: "I didn't work in the business and didn't have anything to do with what happened." The family court judge agreed with Kenesha, ordering her ex to pay child support and to pay off all of the couple's debt. But his business failed, and Kenesha's ex-husband could not find a high-paying job. Instead, he drifted into odd jobs at minimum wage. He never paid back any of the credit card or utility bills, so the interest, penalties, and late charges compounded month after month—while Kenesha thought they were all being paid. Eventually, the balance swelled to more than $50,000, a sum that was more than double her ex's annual salary. So the creditors went after Kenesha, who soon discovered that in the eyes of the law that governs debtors and creditors, it doesn't matter who ran the family business or what agreement the couple has worked out between them. If both names are on the original loan documents, and if one spouse misses a payment, the creditors have every legal right (and every incentive) to go after the other one—and that holds true regardless of what the divorce court orders. The couple may decide not to share their lives any longer, but their economic fortunes will remain united for many years.

A generation ago, when the average family didn't even have a credit card, postdivorce debt splitting wasn't all that important.[29] But today, a family begins divorce proceedings deep in a financial hole, so that negotiating who pays which debts can be a matter of survival. Sometimes the judge will simply split the debt down the middle, ordering each to pay half. In other cases the judge will order lower child-support payments in return for a father's commitment to take on the whole load of debt. One way or another, both parents pay for the fact that they face divorce already awash in red ink. Over the past generation, average savings has dropped from 11 percent of income to negative 1 percent, while credit card debt has climbed from 4 percent of income to 12 percent (see Figure 5.3).[30] As a consequence, the modern mother starts out her postdivorce life with higher fixed costs, more debt, and less money in the bank—a recipe for financial disaster.

Trying to Compete in a Two-Income World

The single mother is under enormous pressure to scale back, but scaling back is now harder than ever. A generation ago she had to compete with male-breadwinner families for a house in the suburbs.

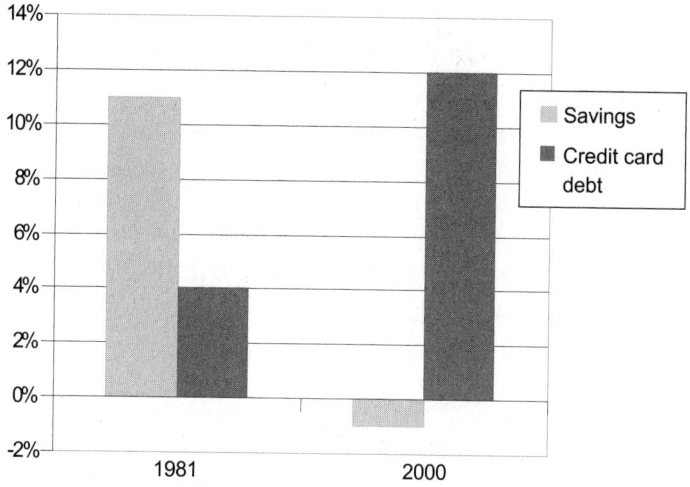

Savings and debt as a percent of personal income.

Source: Analysis of data in SMR Research Corporation, *The New Bankruptcy Epidemic.*

FIGURE 5.3 Less savings, more debt

Everything that defined a middle-class life for children in her community—decent schools, a safe car, health insurance—was typically purchased with the income of a higher-earning male, which made it tough for a divorced mother to keep up. The women's movement promised to make things easier for these women, since a bigger paycheck was supposed to translate into financial security for single mothers. But this formula missed one important fact. Single mothers weren't the only ones to enter the workforce; married mothers went to work too.

For every increase in the paycheck of a single mother, there is now a corresponding increase in a married couple's income as well. As a growing number of married mothers enter the workforce, the income gap between single and married parents is growing, notwithstanding rising wages for single mothers. In the mid-1970s, a typical married couple with children earned $29,800 (inflation adjusted) more than the average single mother; today that gap is more than $41,000.[31] No matter how hard she works, how many extra hours she puts in or training sessions she attends, the modern single mother will never catch up.

The irony is palpable. Lured by the promise of financial security for themselves and their children, millions of women marched into the workforce. And yet, if their husbands leave, they discover that despite their growing paychecks, they are in no position to compete in a two-income world. Moreover, the postdivorce woman must deal with the fact that she and her ex had built a middle-class life that depended on two incomes, and now she must cope without that second paycheck. By all predictions, the middle-class single mother should be better off than her counterpart of any generation before her. Yet despite her education, her work experience, and the support of the courts, the modern single mother is more likely to face financial failure than ever before.

The Facts of Marriage

Some women take an alternate path to survive the economic blows raining down on their families: They remarry. Sure, we know that marriage—even second marriage—is supposed to be about chemistry and companionship, but getting a foreclosure notice can make anyone rethink what she really needs from a relationship. Even now, a generation after the Women's Revolution, the surest way for a woman to regain her financial footing after a divorce is to find a husband—and to do it quickly.[32] Like many single mothers, Gayle dreams about a quick way out of her economic hole: "If I was to get married again, and he only had a part-time salary, I could make it." In a world of economic hurt, even a guy with half a job looks good.

What about the mother who was never married to begin with? The majority of single mothers in bankruptcy are divorced or separated, but there are some who never had a husband.[33] Divorced women got into trouble when they lost one of the incomes they were counting on. But how did mothers who never married end up in trouble? For some, the answer is pretty much the same as for their divorced sisters: A man moved out. Although they weren't legally married, many were in long-term relationships. When the couple broke up, these women went through an economic—if not a legal—divorce, and they were sent into the same kind of economic tailspin as their previously married sisters.[34] Other unmarried mothers never had a partner to begin with, but they learned that with only one adult in the household, even a short period of unemployment or a medium-sized medical bill could send them from survival to collapse in a few months.

Out of the Trap: Make Dad Pay More?

After the Pritchards split up, Brad rented an efficiency apartment on the north side of Houston, near his new job. His girlfriend moved in, but she drifted off just a few months later. It seems that Brad was not much fun any more.

Brad landed a job as an assistant supervisor at an oil refinery, earning $27,000 a year. "I guess the money's not that bad. It's just they take so much out of my check. Seems like all I get are the leftovers." Between his payments to his first wife and to Gayle and the kids, his employer withholds almost $1,200 a month. This means that 60 percent of Brad's take-home pay goes to child support—the legal limit.[35]

Technically, Brad lives above the poverty line, but just barely. He lost his health insurance when his earlier job was outsourced, and his attorney wants $1,000 for the divorce paperwork. His apartment is an empty shell, with nothing but a television perched on a box, an old couch that folds out into a bed, and a card table in the kitchen. Usually an easygoing man who liked to go out on the town, Brad has begun to wake up sweating in the middle of the night. He has two failed marriages, five kids he sees only sporadically, and not enough money left to fill up the tank in his van.

So how can a single-parent family get out of the trap? We begin with the solution put forth by nearly every politician, women's group, and angry mother: Make Dad pay more.

The argument has plenty of emotional appeal. It resonates with some of our most basic values: equity between men and women, following through on commitments, protecting our children. It also fits with our common sense. After all, everyone knows some unfortunate woman who is having a dreadful time making ends meet since she got stiffed by her ex. And we have all heard news reports about the men who are absconding without making their payments.

The experts of a generation ago (and even today) predicted with such confidence that better child support enforcement would ensure financial security for single mothers. But does increasing child support really hold the key to survival for millions of middle-class single mothers? Do ex-husbands hold the untapped wealth that single mothers need for financial security, and all that remains is to seek it out?

America has spent a generation hunting down the devious deadbeat dad, but single mothers are in more trouble than ever. It doesn't come through in most news reports, but the overwhelming majority of middle-class fathers today are like Brad Pritchard. They pay the support they owe. According to one survey, nonresident fathers who earned more than $30,000 a year reported that they were paying more than 95 percent of their court-ordered child support.[36] This statistic may be somewhat distorted by men who overestimate their own payments. (Single mothers usually report receiving less than fathers report paying.) But another survey of single mothers found similar results. Among fathers who were steadily employed (which includes a number of men who work for low wages), 80 percent of their ex-wives reported receiving full payment.[37] These numbers stand as a reminder that there is not much left to collect. Additional enforcement of child support can provide only limited help to struggling middle-class women and their children.

And what about the dads who don't pay? About two-thirds of these men do not pay because they are not legally required to pay; they have not had paternity established or they are separated but not yet divorced.[38] What about those who have child support orders in place but don't pay what they owe, the infamous "deadbeat dads"? It turns out that the nonpayers are far more likely to have low incomes and to live in poverty.[39] According to one estimate, six out of ten nonresident fathers who fail to pay child support either have low incomes, are substance abusers, or have outstanding obligations to support new children.[40] Another study found that most nonpayers had recently been unemployed.[41] These guys may be down on their luck, irresponsible, or just plain mean, but the stone-cold reality is that unemployment, poverty-level wages, drug addiction, and additional kids to provide for make it far more difficult for these men to come up with regular support payments. And no amount of legal pressure will change that.

Share the Pain?

Some activists argue that women like Gayle Pritchard are in financial trouble because, as Lenore Weitzman observed: "Current child support awards are too low . . . and place a disproportionate financial burden on mothers."[42] According to this line of thinking, judges should demand more money from men in the beginning, making child support awards substantially larger. Again, the arguments are highly charged. Women's groups point to the fact that custodial mothers are far more likely to end up in poverty than their ex-husbands, and increasing child support awards is one way to ensure more equitable living standards for kids.[43] Fathers' groups, for their part, argue that child support guidelines are already too rigid because they ignore a man's obligations (such as those to support a new family) and changes in his ex-wife's income (such as the earnings of her new husband). Support orders also disregard changes to a father's income. According to one study of men who experienced a sharp drop in earnings, only 4 percent were able to persuade the courts to lower their child support payments.[44]

In either case, activists on behalf of single mothers are probably right in their basic conclusion: Privation could be spread more evenly between men and women. Child support guidelines could be changed to ensure that no man would have a penny more discretionary income than his ex-wife does, and that if one ex-spouse suffers, so does the other. Several family law reformers have embraced what we call the Share-the-Pain model, whose "ultimate goal is for all family members to emerge from a marital breakdown with roughly equal standards of living, so that no one, specifically children and those who care for them, suffers disproportionately from the failure of a marriage."[45] According to this approach, if the mother and children live at twice the poverty rate, then so should the ex-husband.

Fair enough. But the critical question is, how far would these changes get today's single mother? Would the Share-the-Pain model lift single mothers and their children out of their financial hole? Brad is already paying *more* than the Share-the-Pain model would call for: Gayle lives at 2.8 times the poverty level, whereas Brad, after paying child support to both his ex-wives, scrapes by at just 1.4 times the poverty level. By this measure, Gayle and her kids are doing much better than her ex-husband, yet she is still bankrupt.

Of course, Brad's situation is particularly bad because he has two ex-wives to support. What would happen to a more typical dual-income couple if they divorced? If Justin and Kimberly (the typical two-earner couple we met in previous chapters) split up, and the courts followed the Share-the-Pain approach, Justin would be required to pay Kimberly roughly $12,400 a year—close to half his take-home pay.[46] Kimberly's situation would be undeniably better than under current guidelines, since her support checks would increase considerably. But if she wanted to keep the home, the car, the day care, and the health insurance, she would still face a *54 percent* drop in discretionary income, even if Justin paid every penny. To be sure, this is better than the 86 percent drop she would experience under the current system.[47] The Share-the-Pain model might appeal to our sense of fairness, and it might even be the right response to a bad situation. But even such a drastic change to the child support guidelines is no panacea for the middle-class single mother—and no guarantee of her financial survival.

What if Dad shares custody of the kids? This is an increasingly likely outcome. Approximately one out of six divorcing couples are awarded joint custody.[48] Many fathers' rights groups support the trend, arguing that joint custody is "in the best interest of children [and fosters] a meaningful relationship with both of their parents."[49] But what about the financial impact of these arrangements? Joint custody would free Mom from the overwhelming burden of bearing sole responsibility for all the day-to-day child care requirements, but the overall impact on her financial well-being is more complex. Consider housing. When the Pritchards split up, the only way Brad avoided the bankruptcy courts was to live in the cheapest efficiency apartment he could find. If he had needed to find a home suitable for his three children (preferably near their school), he wouldn't have had a prayer of making ends meet—or of making support payments to either of his ex-wives. Joint custody effectively doubles the family's housing expenses without creating any new income to cover the costs. Cars, furniture, clothing, utilities—there are no savings, but substantial opportunities to increase costs when both parents provide half-time homes for their children.

Joint custody can have another serious financial side effect on a woman: She may end up with less child support. With both parents providing a home for their children, courts are less inclined to order that child support flow in a single predetermined direction, from Dad to Mom. One study found that judges are three times more likely to order no child support under a joint custody case than a case where the mother is awarded sole custody.[50] Joint custody may be the best way to involve fathers in their children's lives, but it is no financial promised land for either single parent.

Tapped Out

Divorced fathers have become a kind of mythic solution. Anyone concerned about the financial distress of single mothers simply joins in the rallying cry to "Make dads pay more." Once again, we offer sobering data. There is substantial evidence that millions of fathers are already struggling to make their current payments and may not be able to pay more, regardless of what the courts order. Only 46 percent of divorced fathers own their own homes, a rate that is about half that of married fathers generally. Divorced fathers are also less likely to own a car.[51] Indeed, one out of three unmarried, nonresident fathers cannot even maintain their own household and live with their parents or other extended family.[52]

Even more tellingly, our data indicate that unmarried mothers aren't the only ones filing for bankruptcy in record numbers. Divorced dads are in just about as much trouble. We estimate that more than 160,000 men with child support and alimony obligations will end up in bankruptcy this year alone. This means that fathers who owe child support are more than three times more likely to file for bankruptcy than single men who don't owe support.[53] Indeed, nonresident fathers with child support obligations are the only group that approaches single mothers in their extraordinarily high levels of financial distress.

These men are caught in the same financial maelstrom as their ex-wives. They must come up with money for an apartment and all the accoutrements of their newly single lives, not to mention thousands of dollars in legal fees, but they too have nothing in savings to cover these costs. Like their soon-to-be ex-wives, many turn to debt to get through the months following the divorce. Brad Pritchard is already a few thousand dollars in the hole, and bankruptcy may be just around the corner. "I was brought up that you sign your name, you pay your bills. Period. But if things keep on this way, I just don't know. . . ."

Men like Brad Pritchard do not file for bankruptcy as a way of ducking out of their support obligations. Bankruptcy law is quite firm on this point. All child support and alimony orders survive a bankruptcy filing *100 percent intact*. These men may escape their credit card debts and outstanding medical bills, and they may slide out from underneath some business debts or drop their car loans (if they give up their cars), but they cannot reduce their current or past-due child support obligations by a single penny. So why do they file? Many of them are in the bankruptcy courts to shake off Citibank and Ford Motor Credit so they can free up the money they need to fulfill their obligations to their children. Congressman Henry Hyde and his cronies may charge that these men suffer "an absence of personal responsibility," but for many, filing for bankruptcy may be the most responsible thing these divorced fathers can do for their children.[54]

A Lesson from the Two-Parent Family

The illusion that dads can pay enough to stabilize the broken family is born partly of hope and partly of despair. If Dad can't pay more, how does the single mother ever escape the Two-Income Trap? For that matter, how does the divorced father break free? They do it the same way the dual-income family does.

The predicament of divorced mothers has worsened not because divorce itself is any harder, but because couples today are in worse shape before they split up. Solutions that improve the financial footing of married couples will help divorcing parents by putting them in a stronger position as they embark on their newly separated lives. So, for example, if decent public schools were made available to *all* children, regardless of the child's zip code, then the bidding wars for suburban housing would let up and the newly single mother could start off divorced life with a more modest mortgage. She also might be less reluctant to give up the family home and move into a cheaper house if a school choice policy ensured that she wouldn't be forced to transfer the kids to an unfamiliar—and often inferior—public school. Similarly, if publicly funded preschool were made available to *all* children, a single mother with young children would have more leeway in her budget.

In addition, policies that encourage personal savings (see chapter 3) and discourage debt (which we'll discuss in chapter 6) would help *both* spouses survive the economic aftermath of divorce. If a woman started her divorced life with no credit card debt and some money in the bank, she would have a better chance of holding on to her house and staying out of the bankruptcy courts. And if a father left his marriage on more secure financial footing, he would stand a better chance of making his child support payments and keeping himself and his ex-wife out of bankruptcy. Likewise, policies that expand health insurance and disability coverage would particularly benefit single parents because they are most vulnerable when disaster strikes.

Are there any policies that should single out the single mother? There might be one. As we noted in chapter 2, universal publicly funded day care might have unintended financial consequences, some of which would be particularly negative for the traditional single-breadwinner two-parent family. But the government could play another role in taking care of youngsters: free (or subsidized) child care for the children of single parents. This would give the newly single mother an immediate, much-needed financial leg up, improving her chances of competing in a two-income world. And it would do so without increasing the pressure on two-parent families to send both adults to work.

During the past generation, the single mother has come into her own politically. Nearly 10 million strong, these women are no longer shunned by politicians and religious leaders. They star in sitcoms, they are featured in congressional debates, and they help swing elections. But their economic fortunes—or misfortunes—are treated as something that begin the day their marriages end. Politicians build up political capital by loudly proclaiming their support for these women, while their ex-husbands either disappear from the story or are vilified as deadbeats who don't care about their children. In our view, all that noise just diverts attention from any meaningful changes that could actually improve the lot of middle-class mothers and fathers.

Current views of the economics of divorce accomplish little more than stoking a tired old battle between the sexes. The laws have been changed, and child support orders, while not perfect, are now reasonably well enforced for millions of middle-class families. It is time for a fresh approach to improving the circumstances of *all* middle-class parents, married and single alike.

6

The Cement Life Raft

In May 1998, First Lady Hillary Clinton was the star attraction at a Boston fund-raiser for candidates who supported women's issues. The lineup was impressive: she stood shoulder to shoulder with a half dozen congresswomen, including Nancy Pelosi and Sheila Jackson Lee, arguably among the most powerful female politicians in America at the time. Mrs. Clinton was in her element, vibrant and hard-hitting in front of an almost all-woman audience that applauded her every sentence. Her speech was part policy (federal subsidies for day care and access to health insurance) and part pep rally (help send more Democrats to Congress). She swept out of the ballroom as the crowd jumped to its feet to cheer her on.

I (Elizabeth) stood waiting in the darkened hallway in a service entrance. I had been invited to meet with Mrs. Clinton, and there I stood, not knowing a single person either in the ballroom or among the entourage that trailed along with her. I listened as young women—presumably Mrs. Clinton's aides—chatted quietly about who were the "major players" in the room and whether that neon-red jacket made one of the congresswomen look too pasty. Behind me, two beefy men in overcoats stood silently, continuously scanning in all directions.

Mrs. Clinton thrust her hand forward. "You must be Professor Warren. I read your op-ed in the *New York Times* about women and bankruptcy, and I want to talk with you." A few weeks earlier I had written a column that sharply criticized a bill making its way through Congress that proposed to undercut bankruptcy protections for middle-class families in financial trouble.[1] Before I could respond, Mrs. Clinton snapped her head sharply to the side and called to no one in particular, "Where's lunch? I'm hungry."

We were ushered to a small office with cracked leatherette chairs, carefully set out with lunch for the First Lady—half a hamburger, French fries, Diet Coke—and an iced tea for me. The small army of aides and security agents were left behind in the hallway; there were just the two of us in the tiny room.

Before she had taken a single bite of her hamburger, Mrs. Clinton tore into the business at hand: "I have two questions for you: How are women affected by the bankruptcy laws, and how did a woman get to be a chaired professor at Harvard Law School?"

For the next twenty-five minutes, I pounded Mrs. Clinton with graphs, charts, and projections. She ate fast and asked questions even faster. I have taught bankruptcy law to thousands of students—some of them among the brightest in the country—but I never saw one like Mrs. Clinton. Impatient, lightning-quick, and interested in all the nuances. In just half an hour, she went from knowing almost nothing about the bankruptcy system to grasping the counterintuitive twist that single mothers were *helped* when their ex-husbands filed bankruptcy because these men could discharge credit card debts and use the money to catch up on their child support. I explained to Mrs. Clinton how the pending bankruptcy bill would effectively dismantle bankruptcy protections for families, forcing single mothers to compete with legions of credit card bill collectors for an ex-husband's income and making it more difficult for families to hold on to their homes.

At the end of our discussion, Mrs. Clinton stood up and said, "Well, I'm convinced. It is our job to stop *that awful bill*. You help me, and I'll help you." We talked university politics for a bit, then walked outside. As we stepped through the door, she grabbed me by the shoulder, turned me around for the obligatory photograph, shook my hand again, and headed off with her people.

Mrs. Clinton's newfound opposition to the bankruptcy bill surprised me. Given her legal training and her devotion to women's causes, I had certainly expected her to grasp the importance of the issue. But President Clinton's staff had been quietly supporting the bankruptcy bill for several months. Bill Clinton wanted to show that he and other "New Democrats" could play ball with business interests, and the major banks were lobbying hard for changes in the bankruptcy laws. I had expected that it would take a lot more than thirty minutes to convince Hillary Clinton to depart from the position widely rumored to be supported by her husband.

But Mrs. Clinton stayed firm in her fight against "that awful bill." She was convinced that the bill was "unfair to women and children," and she intended to stand by her principles, even if it cost some Democratic party candidates campaign contributions.[2] Over the ensuing months, she was true to her word. With her strong support, the Democrats slowed the bill's passage through Congress.[3] When Congress finally passed the bill in October 2000, President Clinton vetoed it. The following summer, an aide explained to me the abrupt about-face: "A couple of days after Mrs. Clinton met with you, we changed sides [on the bankruptcy bill] so fast that you could see skid marks in the hallways of the White House." Thanks to Mrs. Clinton, families still had one financial refuge left—at least for the moment.

But the story doesn't end there. The banking lobbyists were persistent. President Clinton was on his way out, and credit card giant MBNA emerged as the single biggest contributors to President Bush's campaign.[4] In the spring of 2001, the bankruptcy bill was reintroduced in the Senate, essentially unchanged from the version President Clinton had vetoed the previous year.

This time freshman Senator Hillary Clinton voted in favor of the bill.

Had the bill been transformed to get rid of all those awful provisions that had so concerned First Lady Hillary Clinton? No.[5] The bill was essentially the same, but Hillary Rodham Clinton was not. As First Lady, Mrs. Clinton had been persuaded that the bill was bad for families, and she was willing to fight for her beliefs. Her husband was a lame duck at the time he vetoed the bill; he could afford to forgo future campaign contributions. As New York's newest senator, however, it seems that Hillary Clinton could not afford such a principled position. Campaigns cost money, and that money wasn't coming from families in financial trouble. Senator Clinton received $140,000 in campaign contributions from banking industry executives in a single year, making her one of the top two recipients in the Senate.[6] Big banks were now part of Senator Clinton's constituency. She wanted their support, and they wanted hers—including a vote in favor of "that awful bill."

The Brave New (Unregulated) World

There is one final chapter in the story of how millions of seemingly ordinary, middle-class families found themselves falling off a financial cliff. Just at the time when parents got caught in a vicious bidding war for middle-class housing, just as the cost of college tuition and health insurance shot into the stratosphere, just as layoffs increased and the divorce rate jumped, a new player appeared on the scene. A newly deregulated lending industry emerged, eager to lend a few bucks whenever the family came up short.

Pick up almost any newspaper, and there will be a story about America's most widespread addiction: the insatiable hunger for debt. Every year for the past decade, mortgage debt has set a new record.[7] Home equity loans grew even faster, increasing by over 150 percent in just four years.[8] And no one would dare leave home without a fistful of those little plastic cards.

The news media rarely give any explanation for *why* all that debt piled up, leaving the reader to infer that the debt explosion is some sort of inevitable by-product of today's moral and economic climate. But Americans didn't wake up one morning and decide en masse that they needed stuff so much that they'd be delighted to take on a big fat second mortgage and that they'd be thrilled to skip a credit card payment or two, as the headlines might imply. Nor was there a sudden "national conspiracy of people who buy credit cards and then max them out," as one professor of finance claimed.[9] Those mountains of debt were made possible by one very important change that largely went unnoticed in all the discussions about Americans and debt—a seemingly small modification in the laws of consumer finance, a tiny change that transformed centuries of family economics in an instant.

Just a generation ago, the average family simply couldn't get into the kind of financial hole that has become so familiar today. The reason was straightforward: A middle-class family couldn't borrow very much money. High-limit, all-purpose credit cards did not exist for those with average means. There were no mortgages available for 125 percent of the home's value and no offers in the daily mail for second and third home equity loans. There were no "payday lenders," no "live checks," no "instant money," and certainly no offers to "consolidate" all that debt by moving it from one credit card to another. A generation ago, a family that wanted to borrow money had only a handful of options. Instead of running up debt anonymously, a prospective borrower was forced to meet a stern-looking banker, face-to-face. Families were asked to produce past tax returns and pay stubs, credit references, and projected budgets that showed how they planned to repay the money. If they wanted to take out a mortgage for a new home, they were typically required to come up with a 20 percent down payment from their own savings.[10] If they wanted money for any other purpose, they were required to give a detailed account of their spending plans, and the banker had a fairly narrow set of answers he wanted to hear: building an extra bedroom on the house, buying a new car, sending the twins off to college. Some retailers offered credit to move their merchandise, but cash loans and lines of credit for "making ends meet until John finds a new job" or "putting groceries on the table until the child support checks begin" were not in the lending lexicon.

The reason for the lenders' cautious approach was not that the bankers of yesteryear were thriftier or that Americans hadn't yet developed a taste for "unbridled consumption."[11] The reason was a far more powerful one, and it affected every lender and every borrower in the country: The law was different. In those days, the banking industry was highly regulated, and usury laws created ironclad limits on how much interest a bank could charge on a loan. As a result, banks' profit margins were modest, and families that wanted to borrow money had to prove they had a very high likelihood of repaying it.[12] The judgment was not moralistic; it was supported by stubborn financial reality. Unlike today, bank vaults were firmly closed to families already in financial trouble.

From the founding of the Republic through the late 1970s, interest rates had been a matter for states to determine, and the states had imposed limits on the amount of interest that could be charged on consumer loans.[13] The logic behind the laws was straightforward: State governments wanted to protect their citizens from back-alley loan sharks and aggressive lenders who would cost families their homes.

But the states' authority to regulate lending within their borders was wiped out by an obscure federal regulation. In 1978, a Supreme Court opinion interpreting some ambiguous language in a little-known federal statute opened the door for banks to "export" interest rates from one state to another.[14] This meant that a bank with lending operations in South Dakota—where the interest ceiling was 24 percent, at a time when the rates in most states were capped at 12 to 18 percent—would have a distinct advantage. A South Dakota bank could now issue loans at 24 percent interest to a family living in New York (where rates on most loans were capped at 12 percent), without worrying about the corporate officers ending up in a New York prison next to loan sharks who collected by breaking people's fingers until they paid. Under the new law of the land, South Dakota banks could collect their profits from New York families, and there wasn't a thing the New York legal system could do about it.[15]

The race was soon on. Local politicians across the country quickly figured out that all they had to do was raise the interest rate ceiling, and lending institutions would flock to their states. Suddenly there was a new way for states to attract clean, white-collar jobs, and even grab a share of corporate taxes in the process. Sure, there might be some hardship for families that stumbled into high-interest loans they really couldn't afford. But most of the hardship would be exported to the residents of other states, while the benefits—jobs and tax revenues—would stay local. By way of analogy, consider America's drug laws. Suppose that South Dakota passed a law (and the federal government permitted it) that made it legal to grow marijuana inside the state and to sell it anywhere in the country. South Dakota would bear only a tiny fraction of the total social costs of marijuana use, while reaping 100 percent of the profits for sales elsewhere. Suddenly the downside of marijuana use that once made legalization unthinkable—drug addiction, health problems, traffic accidents, and so forth—might start to look pretty insignificant next to all those dollars the state could rake in.

Lenders also began to see the possibilities opened up by the new laws. No longer would credit be a prized commodity, doled out parsimoniously. By the mid-1980s, credit had become a highly profitable consumer product, like running shoes or soft drinks, and the new game was to sell as much as possible.[16] How to manage the risk that some customers might default on the debt? Simple: move the lending operations to South Dakota—or Delaware, which quickly followed South Dakota's lead—and then raise the interest rates for customers across the country.[17] Banks would "lose" money on some credit card customers, but, thanks to higher interest rates, those losses would be more than offset by the profits on the rest. Over the past decade, bad debt losses and loan write-offs have soared, but profits have risen even faster.[18] In this new sky's-the-limit world, the stern-faced banker and the long application forms have been replaced by chirpy advertisements and "preapproved" credit offers. Banks can now lend to anyone and everyone (including those in financial trouble) and still make a handsome profit.

The Debt Explosion

In the new world of unregulated lending, families are barraged with advertisements and offers for a new product: all the debt they could ever want, and more. Now, in a single year, more than five *billion* preapproved credit card offers—totaling over $350,000 of credit *per family*—pour into mailboxes all across America.[19] Magazine ads, telephone calls during dinner, and flyers at the bottom of grocery store bags barrage families with even more offers of credit, while roving bands of credit card marketers haunt college campuses and shopping malls. Credit card debt has increased accordingly: from less than $10 billion in 1968 (inflation adjusted) to more than $600 billion in 2000, an increase of more than *6,000 percent*.[20] It would seem that once Americans got a first bite of the debt apple, they just couldn't get enough.

But what are families spending all that money on? Did they blow it on "vacations and luxury items," as one columnist claimed?[21] This explanation might gratify the self-righteous bill-payers, but it doesn't square with the facts. Undoubtedly, all that easy credit dangling under everyone's noses enticed a few more Americans into buying things they could have lived without. As we showed in chapter 2, today's families are spending more on some goods, such as computers, home electronics, and pet food, than they did a generation ago. But they are spending less on food, clothing, appliances, home furnishings, and tobacco—a lot less. There is no evidence of an increase in impulse buying or luxury acquisitions over the past thirty years—certainly nothing that could account for a 6,000 percent increase in credit card debt. Moreover, the expenditures that have shown the biggest increases—e.g., housing, health insurance, college tuition, preschool—are the purchases *least* likely to appear on a credit card bill.

If families aren't buying more goods, then what are they using all that debt for? They get into debt trying to buy their way out of the Two-Income Trap. The bidding war has inflated the cost of middle-class life to the point that once they have paid the mortgage and other fixed expenses, families have little discretionary income left—and even less margin for error. What to do when something goes wrong, as it increasingly does? Since the two-income family does not have a stay-at-home mom to call on to help make ends meet when emergency strikes, the family turns to debt to make it through to the next payday.

No advertisements trumpet, "When your husband leaves you, there's MasterCard." Nor do we hear: "American Express: Don't lose your job without it." But those slogans would be closer to the truth about how credit is used today. When corporate layoffs loom, workers apply for as many credit cards as possible to see them through until they can find a new job.[22] When health insurance lapses, the family hands a MasterCard to the doctor and prays for the best.[23] And when Dad walks out, that "E-Z check" stuffed in with the latest credit card bill looks like just the thing to tide Mom over until the child support checks arrive. Later, when the credit card payments become unmanageable, the family takes on a second mortgage to consolidate all that debt. No one would suspect it from looking at the ads, but for every family taking out a second mortgage to pay for a vacation, there are sixty-one more families taking on a second mortgage so they can pay down their credit card bills and medical debts.[24]

The bankruptcy court offers a peek at those in the most trouble with debt. The Myth of the Immoral Debtor would have us believe that these families consumed their way into bankruptcy, running up their credit cards to cover their "reckless spending."[25] They are at least half right; families in bankruptcy are choking on credit card debt. Ninety-one percent of the families in bankruptcy were carrying balances on their cards by the time they filed. A third of homeowners were carrying second or even third mortgages or had refinanced their mortgages to get some cash.[26] The amount of debt was truly staggering. Nearly one-third of bankruptcy filers—more than 400,000 families—owed *an entire year's salary* on their credit cards, a hole that was virtually impossible to dig a generation ago.[27]

But the critics are off the mark on one point—the role played by over-consumption or its ubiquitous cousin, "trouble managing money." By 2001, those two reasons combined to account for less than 6 percent of families in bankruptcy.[28] What about the rest? The overwhelming majority of bankrupt families faced far more serious problems. As we showed in chapter 4, nearly 90 percent had been felled by a job loss, a medical problem, or a family breakup, or by some combination of all three.

Potential Supreme Court nominee Judge Edith Jones asserts that "overspending and an unwillingness to live within one's means 'causes' debt."[29] She is probably right. These families certainly overspent, accepting medical care they could not afford and making child support payments that left them with too little to pay the rent. They also lived beyond their means, trying to hold on to their houses and cars even after they lost their jobs. But we are forced to wonder, what would Judge Jones suggest those families have done? Not gone to the emergency room when the chest pains started? Moved the kids into a shelter the day their father moved out? Paid MasterCard and Visa, even if it meant not feeding their children? It is doubtlessly satisfying to point the long finger of blame at personal irresponsibility and overspending. But only the willfully ignorant refuse to acknowledge the real reasons behind all that debt.

Mortgaging the Future

Interest rate deregulation dovetailed neatly with a seemingly unrelated phenomenon: the bidding war for suburban housing. The mortgage industry shook off its interest rate regulations just a few years after the credit card industry.[30] In the new world of unfettered mortgage lending, no longer would the middle-class family be restricted to a conventional 80 percent mortgage. The floodgates were opened, and families could get all the mortgage money they ever dreamed of to bid on that precious home in the suburbs—even if the price tag was more than they could realistically afford.

Competition for houses in good neighborhoods has always been stiff, and overloading on mortgage debt to purchase a better home has long posed a temptation for young families. A generation ago, however, it simply wasn't possible to give in to that temptation; mortgage lenders didn't allow it. But today the game is different. It has become routine for lenders to issue unmanageable mortgages. The best evidence comes from the mortgage industry itself. Fannie Mae, the quasi-governmental agency that underwrites a huge fraction of home mortgage lending in the United States, advises families that "monthly housing expenses should not represent more than 25 to 28 percent of gross monthly income."[31] Accordingly, anyone whose housing costs exceed 40 percent of their earnings would be considered "house poor," spending so much on housing that they jeopardize their overall financial security.[32] But the label is misleading. Many of the "house poor" are not poor at all. They are middle-class families that overextended themselves in a desperate effort to find a home in the midst of a fearsome bidding war. Over the past generation, at the same time that millions of households sent a second earner into the workforce, the proportion of *middle-class families* that would be classified as house poor or near-poor has quadrupled.[33]

The down payment—once a critical device for screening potential borrowers—has virtually disappeared. In the mid-1970s, first-time home buyers put down, on average, 18 percent of the purchase price in order to get a mortgage.[34] Today, that figure has shrunk to just *3 percent*.[35] While a small down payment may sound appealing to those of us who remember scrimping and saving before we could purchase our first home, it has a more ominous side. The family that can't come up with a down payment pays higher points and fees, and many are forced by their lenders to purchase additional credit insurance. These families get mortgages they couldn't have gotten a generation ago, but they pay a lot more for them. More important, families that don't make a down payment are more likely to lose their homes, which is why traditional lenders required the 20 percent down payment in the first place. According to one study, families that make a down payment of less than 5 percent of the purchase price are fifteen to twenty times more likely to default than those who put down 20 percent or more.[36] The obvious solution would be to reimpose some standards in the mortgage market, but deregulation continues to reign supreme. Even as defaults are rising, President Bush argues that the federal government should work to reduce families' down payments even further—with no thought about how those low down payments may cost millions of families their chance at staying in their homes.[37]

As regulatory control over interest rates collapsed, a new industry was born: the "subprime" mortgage lender. Subprime lenders specialize in issuing high-interest mortgages to families with spotty credit who are unlikely to qualify for traditional, low-cost "prime" mortgages. In the early days of deregulation, subprime mortgage lending was unheard of. But by the mid-1990s, banking giants such as Chase Manhattan and Citibank, fat with profits from credit card lending, were looking for new markets to tap.[38] They applied the same principles to home mortgage lending that had profited their credit card divisions so handsomely: Charge high interest rates and sell, sell, sell.

To give a sense of just how expensive subprime mortgages are, consider this: In 2001, when standard mortgage loans were in the 6.5 percent range, Citibank's *average* mortgage rate (which included both subprime and traditional mortgages) was 15.6 percent.[39] To put that in perspective, a family buying a $175,000 home with a subprime loan at 15.6 percent would pay *an extra $420,000* during the 30-year life of the mortgage—that is, over and above the payments due on a prime mortgage. Had the family gotten a traditional mortgage instead, they would have been able to put two children through college, purchase half a dozen new cars, *and* put enough aside for a comfortable retirement.

Citibank and other subprime lenders typically defend their business practices by arguing that they are helping more families own their own homes.[40] But this is little more than public relations hot air. In the overwhelming majority of cases, subprime lenders prey on families that *already* own their own homes, rather than expanding access to new homeowners. Fully 80 percent of subprime mortgages involve refinancing loans for families that already own their homes.[41] For these families, subprime lending does nothing more than increase the family's housing costs, taking resources away from other investments and increasing the chances that the family will lose its home if anything goes wrong.

Subprime lending has an even more pernicious effect. It ensnares people who, in a regulated market, would have had access to lower-cost mortgages. Lenders' own data show that many of the families that end up in the subprime market are middle-class families that would typically qualify for a traditional mortgage. At Citibank, for example, researchers have concluded that at least 40 percent of those who were sold ruinous subprime mortgages would have qualified for prime-rate loans.[42] Nor is Citibank an isolated case: A study by the Department of Housing and Urban Development revealed that *one in nine* middle-income families (and one in fourteen upper-income families) who refinanced a home mortgage ended up with a high-fee, high-interest subprime mortgage.[43] For many of these families there is no trade-off between access to credit and the cost of credit. They had their pockets picked, plain and simple.

Why would middle-class families take on high-interest mortgages if they could qualify for better deals? The answer, quite simply, is they didn't know they could do any better. Many unsuspecting families are steered to an overpriced mortgage by a broker or some other middleman who represents himself as acting in the borrower's best interests, but who is actually taking big fees and commissions from subprime lenders.[44] In some neighborhoods these brokers go door-to-door, acting as "bird dogs" for lenders, looking for unsuspecting homeowners who might be tempted by the promise of extra cash. Other families get broadsided by extra fees and hidden costs that don't show up until it is too late to go to another lender. One industry expert describes the phenomenon: "Mrs. Jones negotiates an 8 percent loan and the paperwork comes in at 10 percent. And the loan officer or the broker says, 'Don't worry, I'll take care of that, just sign here.'"[45]

Every now and then a case comes to the forefront that is particularly egregious. Citibank was recently caught in one of those cases. In 2002, Citibank's subprime lending subsidiary was prosecuted for deceptive marketing practices, and the company paid $240 million to settle the case (at the time, the largest settlement of its kind).[46] A former loan officer testified about how she marketed the mortgages: "If someone appeared uneducated, inarticulate, was a minority, or was particularly old or young, I would try to include all the [additional costs] CitiFinancial offered."[47] In other words, lending agents routinely steered families to higher-cost loans whenever they thought there was a chance they could get away with it.

Such steering hits minority homeowners with particular force. Several researchers have shown that minority families are far more likely than white families to get stuck with subprime mortgages, even when the data are controlled for income and credit rating.[48] According to one study, African-American borrowers are *450 percent* more likely than whites to end up with a subprime instead of a prime mortgage.[49] In fact, residents in high-income, predominantly black neighborhoods are actually *more* likely to get a subprime mortgage than residents in low-income white neighborhoods—more than twice as likely.[50]

In many cases, these lenders don't just want families' money; they also want to take people's homes. Banks have been caught deliberately issuing mortgages to families that could not afford them, with the ultimate aim of foreclosing on these homes. This practice is so common it has its own name in the industry: "Loan to Own."[51] These lenders have found that foreclosing can be more profitable than just simply collecting a mortgage payment every month, because the property can then be resold for more than the outstanding loan amount.[52] So the lender rakes in fees at closing and high monthly payments for a few years, then waits for the family to fall behind and sweeps in to take the property. The lender wins every possible way—high profits if the family manages to make all its payments, and higher profits if the family does not.

The results are in. After two decades of mortgage deregulation, today's homeowners are *three and a half times* more likely to lose their homes to foreclosure than their counterparts a generation ago.[53] This defies the economists' expectations. Today's record low interest rates and rising home prices should have translated into a *falling* rate of home foreclosure, not a rising one. The only explanation is a lending industry run amok. The rise in "loan-to-own" lending, the disappearance of the down payment, and the explosion in high-interest, subprime refinances have taken their toll, as a growing number of families learn the painful consequences of getting trapped by a mortgage industry that has been allowed to make up its own rules.

And so it was that family spending was transformed in a single generation. In the late 1970s and early 1980s, consumer lending was deregulated, launching a complicated, potentially dangerous product on an unsuspecting public. The timing could not have been worse. Just as corporations were downsizing across America, just when a bidding war for decent family housing was heating up, and just when families lost the all-purpose safety net once provided by the stay-at-home mother, easy credit flooded in, looking just like a life raft to the family that was drowning.

Where the Money Is

"Why do you rob banks?" The question was put to Willie Sutton, famed bank robber of the 1940s. He replied, "Because that's where the money is." That's how most businesses work: They make profits by dealing with customers who have money. And that is how the lending business used to work: Companies made loans to people who had the money (or soon would have the money) to repay them.

Much has been made about the changing nature of America's debtors. Americans don't have the same work ethic that they once did, people don't work hard to pay their bills as they once did, and on and on. Even my [Elizabeth's] elderly father agreed, telling me quiet stories of destitute families that labored for years to pay bills they had run up during the Great Depression. My father used to talk about Herring Hardware, a farm supply store that my grandfather had run in rural Oklahoma beginning back in 1904. When the Dust Bowl hit in the 1930s and families could no longer scratch a living out of their modest farms, many packed up and headed west, an exodus etched in the national memory by John Steinbeck's *Grapes of Wrath*. Some of those families never forgot the debts they left behind. Twenty years later, my grandfather would still get an occasional envelope with a few twenty-dollar bills and a handwritten note: "Grant, we finally got ahead a little. Put this on my account, and let me know if I owe you more. Aileen sends her best to Ethel." My father would lean back at the end of one of these stories and remark that these were "good people, good people who followed through on what they owed." Then he would pause and draw his mouth into a hard line. "Folks just aren't like that anymore."

But my father—and everyone else who talks about changing values—overlooks one very important fact: Borrowers aren't the only ones who changed. Lenders changed too, arguably far more than the people to whom they were lending. Most Americans guard their credit ratings jealously, living with a slightly prickly sensation that they could be cut off if they fell behind or forgot to pay a bill. What they don't realize is that when a borrower makes a partial payment, when he misses a bill, and when his credit rating drops, he actually gets *more* offers for credit.[54] He is not just down on his luck, behind on his bills, and short on cash; he has now joined the ranks of an elite group—The Lending Industry's Most Profitable Customers.

Consider the example set by Citibank, America's largest credit card issuer. In 1990, I [Elizabeth] was hired as a one-day consultant by Citibank to address a gathering of some forty senior lending executives. The task: use my research to suggest policies that would help Citibank cut its losses from cardholders in financial trouble. I arrived at Citibank's New York headquarters with dozens of graphs and charts tucked in my file folders. I was ushered into a large, brightly lit conference room where each chair was filled by someone outfitted in a starched shirt, silk tie, and dark suit. The executives stayed with me all day, eating lunch at the conference tables as we continued our discussions about the effects of unemployment on loan defaults and the rising number of bankruptcies among two-earner families. As the afternoon came to a close, I summarized my recommendations. The short version could be boiled down to a single, not very startling, idea: Stop lending money to families that are already in obvious financial trouble. This would have been quite easy to implement. Citibank had reams of data on most of its borrowers, particularly those who had black marks on their credit reports. I suggested that the policy could be put in place within a few short months, potentially cutting Citibank's bankruptcy-related losses by as much as 50 percent.[55]

There were interested murmurs around the room, and several hands eagerly shot up. But before I could call on anyone, one slightly older man spoke up. He had been silent throughout the long day, leaning back in his chair and giving me a faintly bemused smile. "Professor Warren," he began. The room hushed immediately, and I suddenly realized that I had been oblivious to the corporate pecking order; this was the guy who outranked everyone else in the room. "We appreciate your presentation. We really do. But we have no interest in cutting back on our lending to these people. They are the ones who provide most of our profits."[56] With that, he got up, and the meeting was over. I was ushered out, and I never heard from Citibank again—except to get my monthly credit card bills.

Citibank understood the new economics of consumer credit. Credit card issuers make their profits from lending lots of money and charging hefty fees to families that are financially strapped. More than 75 percent of credit card profits come from people who make those low, minimum monthly payments.[57] And who makes minimum monthly payments at 26 percent interest? Who pays late fees, overbalance charges, and cash advance premiums? Families that can barely make ends meet, households precariously balanced between financial survival and complete collapse. These are the families that are singled out by the lending industry, barraged with special offers, personalized advertisements, and home phone calls, all with one objective in mind: *get them to borrow more money.*

After he suffered a heart attack, missed several months' work, and fell behind on his mortgage, Jamal Dupree (from chapter 4) got the hard sell from his mortgage lender. When Jamal missed a payment, the mortgage company sent him dozens of personalized letters with a single goal—to persuade him to take out yet another mortgage. "They'd send out a notice, saying 'you need a vacation, take out this thousand dollars and pay it back in ninety days.' If you didn't pay it back in ninety days, they charged you 22 percent interest." When he didn't respond to the mailers, the mortgage company started calling Jamal at home, as often as four times a week. Again, the company wasn't calling to collect the payments he had already missed; it was calling to sign him up for even more debt. Jamal resisted, but his mortgage lender didn't let up. "When I turned them down, they called my wife [at work], trying to get her to talk me into it."

The strategy used by today's lenders exactly reverses the approach bankers used a generation ago when their main goal was to be repaid on time, not to string along the payments for as long as possible. Herring Hardware may have collected most of its debts—even during the Great Depression—but its lending policies were radically different from those embraced by today's major lenders. Unlike today's megabanks, Herring Hardware *stopped* making loans when a family got in trouble. Grandfather Herring would never have dreamed of sending a flyer in the mail cheerfully suggesting, "Fred, you're behind on your payments for the fertilizer. Can we lend you the money for a new cookstove?" Nor would the local bank have suggested a second mortgage to the family that had just missed a payment on its first mortgage.[58]

There is another important difference. When families arranged credit in my grandfather's store, he charged them a simple 1 percent per month. Neither he nor the bank had any penalty fees or shifting rates of interest. When someone missed a payment, the rate was still 1 percent a month. Today, that practice has disappeared. Like Jamal's mortgage lender, many banks routinely double or even triple the interest rate the moment someone is a few days late with a payment. Then there are the fees. This year credit card companies will charge more than *$7 billion* in late fees (quadruple what they charged less than ten years ago)—a penalty unheard of in my grandfather's day.[59] Moreover, when my grandfather got a check in the mail, he applied it to the principal balance on the loan; he wouldn't have dreamed of telling those families that with compounded interest at the new rates and special overbalance fees and late-payment penalties, they now owed $4,000 for their original $800 purchase.

Repo Man in the Suburbs

In an era when lenders routinely target the almost-bankrupt for extra loans, how do they ensure that they will get their money back? Corporate lenders don't have "Jimmy the finger-breaker" on retainer, but they do have thousands of trained professionals who do nothing but hound families for money.[60] Most of the time, these agents make their living by calling families at home, reminding them that they are late on their bills and pressing them to make a payment. (Or, in the case of Jamal Dupree, urging them to take on a second loan to pay off the first.) But when a simple request isn't enough, they, too, use tougher tactics.

Sears, America's fourth-largest retail chain, got caught threatening to nab a battery from a Massachusetts family's car unless the family promised to send Sears some money—money that the family no longer owed.[61] This was in clear violation of the law.[62] The family had filed for bankruptcy protection, so Sears was legally barred from further collection efforts. Aside from that, it is reasonable to wonder: What could Sears possibly want with a used car battery? Or with the used dehumidifiers, mattresses, and Walkmans the company had threatened to take back from thousands of other families?[63] Sears was not in the business of selling used household goods. And it would have cost the company several hundred dollars to hire a repo man and send a truck to someone's door—far more than a used Walkman or car battery would be worth.[64] Sears almost certainly didn't want those goods; the company wanted the money people would pay to keep the Sears repo man away. The company probably hoped that some families were unaware of their legal rights, and that if they were frightened enough, they just might keep making payments on old bills, even after those bills had been discharged in bankruptcy. FBI Special Agent in Charge Barry Mawn described the Sears case as an example of "Corporate America blindly [pursuing] profitability over its obligation to treat the consuming public with fairness and honesty."[65]

And Sears was not alone: AT&T, General Electric Credit, Federated Department Stores (owner of Macy's), J.C. Penney, Circuit City, Tandy (owner of Radio Shack), and General Motors also paid multimillion dollar fines for making collection threats against families whose debts had been forgiven in the bankruptcy courts.[66] But these companies were punished for pursuing families that were under the protection of the bankruptcy courts, not for aggressive collection tactics per se. Indeed, many aggressive collection tactics are perfectly legal. For example, Sears, unlike J.C. Penney, issues credit cards that add some special touches in the fine print. Whenever a customer purchases something on a Sears card, the goods become collateral against the loan. That means that Sears is within its legal rights to repossess (or to threaten to repossess) everything the family bought with the card if it falls behind on its bills. Even when those threats are patently absurd.

Consider, for example, a conversation we had with "Sally," a former Sears collection agent in the Boston area. Sally's job was to call families that had fallen behind and to pressure them to pay up. One incident particularly stood out in Sally's memory. When another Sears agent threatened to repossess a mattress from a woman who was delinquent on her payments, the customer in question stuck to her guns. "You will not. It isn't worth anything. Besides, you can't even sell a used mattress. It's not legal."[67] Sally's coworker was quick on her feet. "We'll come and get it because we can. And then, *we'll set it on fire and burn it up*. It won't give us anything, but you won't have it either." The woman caved in and sent Sears a check for $50. According to Sally, the story was widely told and retold in her department and praised by the department manager as an example of "real initiative." Since we only have Sally's word, we can't confirm the facts of her account, but it is a matter of public record that Sears has threatened to repossess used mattresses from other families.[68]

Sally's real expertise wasn't collecting from the living. She spent most of her days collecting from the dead—or at least the family members of the dead. When a person dies, only a cosigner on the account is liable for the bill. If no one has cosigned, the store can repossess the goods (if the original contract permitted this) or collect from the estate of the deceased, but they cannot hold other family members liable for the debt. The company is not, however, prohibited from *trying* to collect from the family. So Sally's job was to call the adult children or grieving widows of customers who had died leaving an outstanding bill. She typically started a call with something gentle and confidential. "Mabel was a longtime member of the Sears family, and we're sure she would have wanted her bills to be paid." Sally then read from a list of purchases Mabel had made on her Sears card, inserting some personal comments. "I see she bought eyeglasses. And some baby clothes—I love those sweet little sweaters and matching caps, don't you?" If the soft sell didn't work, Sally would turn up the heat, threatening to send a collection agent who would plow through the deceased's closets and drawers and "take back what belonged to Sears." If that wasn't enough, there was a final warning that must have sent many families running for the checkbook: She threatened to reclaim every gift ever purchased on the Sears card. Again, the claim seems ridiculous; how would a Sears agent ever figure out that Mabel had given the frilly dress to her grandniece in Detroit, while the Walkman had gone to a great-grandson in Denver? But these threats were put to grieving family members who had just lost a loved one, not to battle-hardened debt-dodgers who were primed to defend themselves. Not surprisingly, Sally said that most families paid.

We remind the reader that we have only Sally's word to go on. It is possible that she wasn't telling the whole truth or that she had an ax to grind. But a statement by former Sears CEO Arthur C. Martinez is certainly in keeping with Sally's story. He explained the company's aggressive debt collection practices this way: "We have an old-fashioned view. People should pay for what they take."[69] As he touted that "old-fashioned view" of debt, Mr. Martinez seemed oddly blind to the fact that Sears is no longer an "old-fashioned" merchant. At the time Mr. Martinez made his statement, Sears reportedly earned *more* money from the interest and late fees the company charged its credit cardholders than it earned from selling merchandise.[70] In other words, Sears kept all those stores open and sold all those Lady Kenmore washing machines and Craftsman tools in the hope that its customers would buy on credit and pay over time. Merchants like my grandfather used to offer credit as a way to increase store purchases. For stores like Sears, that formula has been turned upside-down: Store purchases have become a way to increase credit card debt. That's not "old-fashioned" at all; indeed, it is possible only in the new world of uncapped interest rates and deregulated lending.

A Problem That Can Be Solved

The problems posed by families deep in debt may seem intractable, or at least so deeply embedded that only a complex, expensive array of regulations and laws could turn things around. But this is one problem that isn't so hard to solve. The consumer-credit monster could be beaten back if Congress would enact a simple provision into law—a provision that wouldn't require the creation of vast new oversight committees or contentious battles in the Supreme Court. Congress could simply revive the usury laws that served this country since the American Revolution. Federal law could be amended to close the loopholes that let one state override the lending rules of another.[71] Alternatively, Congress could impose a uniform rate to apply across the country. Such a provision would enable the states or the federal government to reimpose meaningful limits on interest rates.

Consumer lenders balk at the notion of reregulation, immediately claiming that tighter limits on interest rates would put America at risk for another banking disaster like the Savings and Loan (S&L) crisis of the late 1970s. Hemmed in by high inflation rates and low limits on interest rates, the S&Ls (which issued most home mortgages) found themselves hemorrhaging money.[72] But the real problem was inflation, not usury rates per se, which had worked reasonably well for centuries. At the time, usury limits in most states were fixed at a specific number, and they hadn't been written with double-digit inflation in mind. But that would be an easy problem to solve. To avoid a repeat of the S&L crisis, all that is needed is to tie the limit on interest rates to the inflation rate or the prime rate (which changes with inflation) so that the two never get too far out of sync. (To keep a check on fees, points, and all the other hidden charges, these costs should be included in the interest calculations up front.) That way, mortgage and credit card interest rates would be higher when inflation is rampant, but they would come right back down when the inflation monster is tamed. The ceiling on interest rates would float up and down, but it would always be tethered to the lender's cost of funds. That way, banks would always be able to lend profitably, *and* consumers would always be protected from unreasonable rates.

The beauty of this approach is that it would help families get out of debt *without costing taxpayers a dime*. How would it work? By harnessing the energy of the marketplace. Lenders themselves would transform mortgage and credit card practices just by acting in their own best interest. Since they would no longer be allowed to charge exorbitant interest rates to families with marginal credit records, it would become unprofitable for lenders to pursue families in financial trouble. Instead, banks would once again have a reason to screen potential borrowers carefully, making loans only to those who really can afford to repay.

We hear the antiregulation camp clear their throats, ready to explain why regulating the credit industry (or any other industry, for that matter) is a bad idea. On the surface, their logic sounds convincing. A deregulated market reduces costs and provides more choices for home buyers and credit card holders, so consumers should win out—eventually. Besides, as federal judge Edith Jones wrote, "Nobody is holding a gun to consumers' heads and forcing them to send in credit card applications."[73] People always have the option of walking away from an overpriced mortgage offer or an outrageous credit card offer.

But this argument rests on one very important supposition—a well-functioning market for credit. Any honest economist will explain that markets work efficiently only when there is a level playing field, when consumers have full information about the costs and risks associated with whatever they are purchasing. The evidence is strong that the lending playing field is anything but level. After all, if the market were working properly, how could Citibank sell 40 percent of its high-priced subprime mortgages to families with good credit who would have qualified for low-cost mortgages? How could the company's loan officers get away with charging extra fees to anyone who "appeared uneducated"? And why would low-income whites get better terms on their mortgages than high-income African Americans? A perfect market free to operate without government interference certainly sounds good, but it is little more than a fantasy held up to distract policymakers while lenders rake in profits from those who never quite figure out the terms in fine print.

The argument for reregulation of consumer lending is a lot like the argument for regulating any other useful but potentially dangerous product. Consider the toaster. People buy toasters for home use. No one makes them buy toasters, and they could live without toasters. If they understood electrical engineering, they could evaluate the safety of each toaster under every possible scenario. But toasters are regulated. No toaster manufacturer may peddle toasters that have even a 1 percent chance of catching fire. Toaster makers (and conservative economists) could point out that riskier toasters could be made more cheaply, and that permitting their sale would expand the number of toaster owners in the country. Companies might put special disclaimers and instructions on their toasters, telling customers how to extinguish the fires themselves. But as a nation, we have collectively decided that the risks posed by an unregulated toaster industry are not acceptable.

The government regulates the sale of millions of products—everything from children's pajamas to aspirin to automobiles—to protect consumers from the risks of substantial injury. For most of America's history, loans to consumers fell squarely within that definition. Interest rates and other terms were carefully limited by state legislatures and patrolled, when necessary, by state attorneys general. Predatory loans may not set houses on fire the way a faulty toaster might, but they steal people's homes all the same. America has had more than twenty years to observe the effects of a deregulated lending industry, and the evidence is overwhelming. It is time to call the experiment a failure.

Reregulation would help solve a litany of evils. The most important is worth its own headline: Limiting interest rates would halt the rapid rise in home foreclosures. With a lower ceiling on interest rates, lenders would lead the charge to reestablish an appropriate match between family income and mortgage size, which would have the effect of reducing the mass of families that are sucked into mortgages they have no hope of paying. Minority communities would no longer find themselves stripped of wealth by predatory subprime lenders. And homeowners would no longer be suckered into second and third mortgages that promise to lower their monthly bills but that actually rob them of the family home.

Interest rate regulation would also take the ammunition out of the middle-class bidding war, helping to save families from the Two-Income Trap. Competition for the best neighborhoods would continue, but if *no one* could get a mortgage that ate up 40 or 50 percent of the family's entire income, then home prices would begin to settle down to Earth. To many economists, this is a scandalous notion, involving a reduction in Americans' "net worth." But that net worth isn't worth anything unless a family plans to sell its home and live in a cave, because the next house the family buys would carry a similarly outrageous price tag. Some families with weaker credit histories or more modest incomes might find themselves limited to smaller houses, but they would also be far less likely to end up in a home that drove them into the bankruptcy courts. Moreover, as housing prices leveled off, more families would be able to afford a home *without* having to resort to a subprime mortgage. Reregulation of interest rates would bring relief to *all* families, not just those already in serious trouble.

Families would also be far less likely to get into trouble with their credit cards. With appropriate limits on interest rates, banks would still be able to issue credit cards profitably, and consumers would still have access to those convenient plastic cards. But banks would have far greater incentive to screen cardholders, offering only as much credit as each family could repay. Moreover, there would be no incentive to single out families in financial trouble, tempting them at the moment when they are most vulnerable with special offers of extra credit at exorbitant rates. Banks would have no reason to scour credit records looking for homeowners in trouble, offering to "solve" their credit problems by putting their homes at risk through second or third mortgages.

Limits on interest rates would reverse another disturbing trend—the transfer of wealth away from lower- and middle-income families. Since 1970, banking profits (inflation-adjusted) have more than tripled, growing by more than *$50 billion*.[74] Those profits weren't the rewards for important innovations. Lenders didn't invent a faster computer, design a better car, or make a great new movie that everyone wanted to see. (Indeed, many would argue that the quality of banking service actually declined during this period.) No, they sold pretty much the same thing they always had—debt. The difference was that they sold more of it, and they charged higher prices.

A modest example illustrates what is happening to American families. Credit card companies basically have three costs: marketing costs, collection costs, and the cost to borrow the money they will re-lend to consumers. The Federal Reserve lowered interest rates nine times in 2001, which meant that credit card companies' cost of borrowing fell considerably. Even so, they held steady the rates they charged most of their cardholders. The result? A $10 billion windfall for credit card companies.[75] Nothing had changed in the way these companies did business; their marketing costs stayed the same, their collection costs stayed the same, and their products stayed the same. The only difference was that their already-high profits jumped by an *additional* $10 billion. That $10 billion was paid by families across the country—$10 billion that might have paid for medical bills or college tuition, school shoes or car repairs—or even paid down the balances on outstanding loans. In a single year, 10 billion extra dollars disappeared from families' wallets and reappeared on the balance sheets of a handful of corporate lenders. Families got nothing in return; they paid out dollars that, if interest rates had been regulated, would have belonged to them.

Regulation would also eliminate the worst abuses of a lending industry run amok. Payday lenders would no longer target minority neighborhoods with short-term loans at interest rates of 100, 500, and even 1,000 percent—rates that would make any mobster drool.[76] The more subtle forms of loan sharking would also disappear, so that when families managed to get into trouble with credit card debt, lenders would no longer be able to prey on their desperation by doubling the interest rates and piling on the late fees that turn their debts into financial quicksand.

What about families' access to credit? Deregulation of the mortgage lending industry was not a right-wing conspiracy; it was actually supported by most Democrats as well.[77] Many liberals got behind the move for traditionally liberal reasons: They wanted to defend lower-income families. They had been persuaded that the risks posed by overaggressive lenders might not be as dangerous as once was thought. A deregulated lending market could even prove to be a critical tool to help low-income and disadvantaged groups improve their lot. After all, working-class families needed credit to start businesses, to build homes, and to send their kids to college—things that upper-income families had long had plenty of opportunities to do.

Moreover, there was a growing body of evidence that even though it was illegal, overt discrimination and "redlining"—the practice by which mortgage lenders refused to lend in certain neighborhoods—

was crippling housing markets in minority neighborhoods and denying low- and moderate-income families the chance to build wealth through home ownership. The new solution was to "democratize credit"—make credit available to anyone and everyone, no matter how poor.[78] The prediction was for a more perfect world in which home ownership rates would go up, a sluggish economy would begin to boom, and cities would blossom—all thanks to the free flow of credit.

Obviously, that perfect world didn't come to pass. But politicians may still worry: If America turns back the clock on lending regulation, what will happen to the home-ownership rate? Every time anyone talks about putting restrictions on interest rates, the lending industry puts up one of those heart-warming advertisements that show a family with two kids and a dog moving into their first home. But the hard numbers belie those happy ads. Reregulation of interest rates would have very little effect on home-ownership rates.[79] Since the mortgage industry was deregulated in 1980, the proportion of families owning their own homes has increased by less than 3 percentage points.[80] Plenty of factors have contributed to these modest overall gains, such as a long-running economic boom, the aging of the population, and a falling inflation rate—and those factors won't be affected by changes to mortgage regulations. Moreover, since most high-interest subprime mortgages are used for refinancing, not for families trying to buy their first homes, outlawing those mortgages should have little effect on the number of first-time home buyers. In fact, if fewer families were pushed out of their homes by creditors intent on raking in profits through loan-to-own scams and predatory practices, the overall number of homeowners in America might be higher.

What about the "democratization of credit" for which activists fought so hard? If interest rates are regulated once again, will credit become undemocratic, available only to those with realistic prospects for repayment? To answer this, it is time to step back a moment. The original intent of the credit democratization movement was for credit to help more families become financially independent. Credit was not supposed to be an end in itself. But it seems that the original intent has been forgotten. Consider, for example, the motto of one prominent advocacy group: "Access to credit and capital is a basic civil right."[81] Is it a civil right to pay interest on a credit card balance for the rest of a person's natural life? A family that finances its home with a subprime mortgage can end up paying twice as much for that home as a family that gets the market rate. Is it really a basic civil right to pay double for a home? And foreclosure rates are skyrocketing. Is it a civil right to lose that home in a sheriff's auction? The dream of democratization of credit was to use credit as a vehicle to expand home ownership, to launch businesses, and ultimately to help build wealth in neighborhoods that are short on it. The point was not to bombard families with more credit than they could possibly afford or to flood the market with complicated loans that only a CPA could understand.

But the mantra of expanding access to credit has been hard for consumer activists and politicians to abandon. As a result, reform efforts have fragmented into a patchwork of measures intended to curb "predatory" lending practices. The problem is that no one can agree on how to define "predatory" lending.[82] As the *Economist* dryly observes: "As with pornography, consumer activists and legislators say they know predatory lending when they see it."[83] The National Housing Institute defines predatory lending as "any unfair credit practice that harms the borrower or supports a credit system that promotes inequality and poverty."[84] But what constitutes "unfair"? And who decides whether a system is promoting inequality or poverty?

Attempting to stamp out "predatory" and "unfair" practices is certainly better than ignoring them, but it puts legislators in the position of trying to uncover the latest shenanigans and redefine abuses, always two steps behind the lenders who keep changing their products to sidestep regulations.[85] It also gives far too much room for lenders to circumvent the intent of the law. For example, the New York State Banking Department recently banned "unaffordable loans," except "under compelling circumstances."[86] We suspect that any crafty loan marketer could dream up some "compelling circumstances" that would permit a lender to sell overpriced loans. The only way to stop predatory lending once and for all is to go directly to the heart of the loan—the interest rate. Limiting the amount of interest that creditors can charge avoids the hide-and-seek game over what is and what is not "predatory," offering instead a simple, effective means of regulation.

In order to achieve the real dream of "credit democratization," it is time to recognize, once and for all, that families are *not* better off getting credit at double, triple, or even ten times the market rate. If a family does not have the income to qualify for a loan at a reasonable rate, *then they should not get that loan*. It does no one any favors to impose a modern-day debtor's prison on hard-working families. They would be better off renting an apartment and putting whatever extra money they have into savings accounts rather than paying double the market rate for a mortgage. If the private market cannot meet the needs of all communities, then it may be necessary for the government to step in to provide alternative sources of credit.[87] The point worth emphasizing is that overpriced credit is no solution. Getting robbed to buy a home or to get a cash advance is still getting robbed, and it should be illegal.

Deafening Silence

If America's crippling addiction to debt could be shaken off with a simple regulatory change, what are the politicians doing about it? The answer, quite simply, is nothing.

As the number of mortgage foreclosures skyrockets, as credit card debt soars, as the lines at the bankruptcy courthouse stretch out into the street and around the block, all we hear from Washington is the sound of silence. There has been no serious progress on any proposal to rein in predatory lending: no measure to control credit card fees, no proposal to ban creditors from trying to collect from a dead person's brothers and sisters, and certainly no bill to bring back meaningful limits on interest rates. The national political parties have found time to take positions on the speed of the Internet, ergonomic standards in the workplace, and regional restrictions on dairy products, but they have claimed no position on the financial issues that profoundly affect millions of middle-class families.[88]

There is, however, one notable exception to all that inaction. Congress has paid attention to one troubling statistic—the rapidly growing number of families filing for bankruptcy. High interest rates and aggressive marketing of complicated debt products echo through the bankruptcy statistics, as record numbers of families seek refuge in the bankruptcy courts after getting in over their heads with too much easy credit at exorbitant interest rates.[89] In 1994, Congress created a bipartisan commission to study the issue. The group's charter was relatively straightforward: to investigate why so many families were in trouble and to develop recommendations to improve the situation. I [Elizabeth] was named senior adviser to the National Bankruptcy Review Commission.

Three years later, the commission delivered its report to Congress. The 1,100-page document detailed why so many families were in trouble (job losses, medical problems, and divorce) and identified certain lending practices that put families at particular risk. More important, it reaffirmed that the bankruptcy laws were, for the most part, working as Congress had originally intended: to offer families a fresh start in the wake of financial and personal disaster. It concluded with recommendations for modest legislative changes that were designed to curb abuses by both borrowers and lenders.[90]

But the Congressional bankruptcy commission was not to have the final world. While the commission was busy gathering facts, holding hearings, and analyzing current practices, another group also went to work, advancing a very different perspective. The "National Consumer Bankruptcy Coalition" (NCBC), the clever moniker of the banking industry lobby, was pushing its own agenda.[91] The major banks had hit on a new strategy to reduce their bankruptcy losses. Rather than stop lending to families in financial trouble (as Elizabeth had counseled Citibank), they had a simpler and more profitable solution—restrict the rights of consumers to file for bankruptcy.

If fewer people could turn to bankruptcy for relief, more families would be subject to collection efforts from banks—and every other creditor—forever. Those families might never pay off their bills in full, but they would continue to rack up the interest and penalties, and at least a few would make some small payment every month, effectively becoming lifelong profit wells for their creditors. For the rest—those who simply could not come up with the money, no matter how hard they were squeezed—the lenders might eventually write off some of those loans voluntarily. (Although one wouldn't guess it from all the fiery rhetoric, bankruptcy filings account for just a fraction of lending industry losses; in the large majority of cases, the bank simply gets tired of trying to collect.[92]) But if a family were not permitted to file for bankruptcy, it would be the lender, not the family in trouble, that would decide when the collection calls should stop.[93]

And so the banking lobby drafted a new bankruptcy law. To get all the lenders on board, the coalition added changes that would give better deals for car lenders, mortgage lenders, education loan servicers, landlords, credit unions—in short, better deals for everyone except families in trouble. The credit industry moved fast, persuading two friendly congressmen to introduce their bill in September 1997, a month before the official Bankruptcy Commission was scheduled to release its report.[94] From then on, all eyes were on what Hillary Clinton would eventually dub "that awful bill."

The "awful bill" was long and complex, couched in virtually unreadable prose.[95] But to a trained bankruptcy lawyer, the intent was unmistakable: to undercut virtually every protection in the bankruptcy laws. Under the proposed legislation, child support payments would no longer take precedence over all credit card debt. As a result, more single mothers would be forced to compete with professional collection agents when they needed money from their bankrupt ex-husbands. Homeowners who had fallen behind on their mortgages would be prevented from catching up on past-due house payments until they had also paid off their credit card debts, increasing the likelihood of foreclosure. Families would no longer be able to free themselves from certain unsecured debts, so they would be required to make payments (plus penalties, late fees, and interest) on some of those bills for the rest of their natural lives—even if those payments took up 100 percent of their paychecks.

To win over legislators, credit industry executives lobbied extensively and donated more than $60 million in political contributions.[96] This was followed by a public relations strategy that would make any spin doctor proud. Instead of telling the public that the bankruptcy reform bill would improve profits for credit card companies and giant banks (not exactly the most sympathetic group), the NCBC and its supporters in Congress announced that the bill would help the American family. To quote Democratic Representative Rick Boucher: "The typical American family pays a hidden tax of $550 each year because of . . . bankruptcies of mere convenience."[97] The implied promise, repeated so often that it has become an article of faith, was that changing the laws would put $550 a year in the pocket of every bill-paying American family.[98]

Well that certainly *sounds* good; after all, who wouldn't want some extra cash? But there are a few serious problems with this claim. First, the figure is a gross exaggeration. According to the NCBC, the same banking lobby group that generated the $550 promise, only 100,000 of the 1.5 million families who file for bankruptcy each year could afford to repay some of their debts. In other words, under the proposed bill, those 100,000 bankrupt families would be expected to generate $550 for every household in America, since the other 1.4 million are already tapped out.[99] So we did the math. Suppose the laws were changed, and those 100,000 families could no longer seek protection from the bankruptcy courts, and they were forced to repay as much as they possibly could. In order to return an amount that added up to $550 for every household in America, each one of those bankrupt families would have to repay more than $550,000 in a single year! In our sample of more than 2,000 bankrupt families, not one even *owed* $550,000, let alone earned enough money to repay that amount. But even if a magic fairy somehow gave all the bankrupt families every dollar they needed to repay their debts in full, what makes anyone think the banks would pass that money on to consumers? Recall that the credit card industry got a $10 billion windfall from falling interest rates in 2001 that they did not pass on to their customers. Why would this supposed $550 per family be any different?

Nevertheless, the combination of intense lobbying and a good cover story had its intended effect. Despite President Clinton's veto, the bankruptcy bill was reintroduced in the next session of Congress. This time, even Senator Hillary Clinton bowed to big business. She had been in office two months when she had her chance to vote on what she had called that "awful bill." Sure, the official Bankruptcy Commission had better credentials than the banking lobby. Yes, her husband had actually appointed the Chairman of the Commission and two of the commissioners. And she clearly understood that families in trouble would be hit hardest by the proposed changes. But the Bankruptcy Commission did not make campaign contributions or have its own lobbyists, and neither do families in financial trouble. Senator Clinton had taken $140,000 in campaign contributions from the banking industry, and she proved willing to overcome her "strong reservations about whether this bill is both balanced and responsible"[100] and voted in favor of "that awful bill."

Goliath Meets David

We could stop here. We could join the chorus of those who routinely bemoan the political clout of a few big businesses, and we could make the obligatory plea for effective campaign finance reform (which somehow never quite takes hold in a meaningful way, despite the clamor). But if we stopped now, we would be missing the best part of the story—the part that shows that although the banking industry may be powerful, it isn't the only voice that gets heard in Washington.

The cards were certainly stacked in favor of passing the banking industry's version of the bankruptcy bill in 2002. So who stopped the "awful bill" from becoming law? The answer may surprise the reader; it certainly surprised the credit industry and the congressional power brokers. An unlikely group of citizens organized without any help from big business, and they made sure Congress paid attention. Who were these citizens? Women.

What prompted them to organize was not the financial issues in the pro-creditor bankruptcy bill, which were numerous. Nor was it concern over single mothers or women homeowners, who would have been hit particularly hard if the bill had become law. No, the issue that riled up the women's groups was abortion.

What does bankruptcy have to do with abortion? In Washington, a great deal. Over the past several years, pro-choice groups had scored significant court victories against a few prominent abortion clinic protesters by obtaining money judgments against them, only to see those victories turn to dust when the protesters declared bankruptcy and discharged their debts.[101] In a strange twist of politics, the credit industry's version of the bankruptcy bill had been supported by Senator Charles Schumer, of New York, who had garnered strong support among women's groups for his pro-choice politics. Ever responsive to his constituents, Senator Schumer inserted a provision into the bankruptcy bill that would make it more difficult for abortion clinic protesters to discharge judgments entered against them if they were sued for their protest activities, much in the same way drunk drivers and embezzlers cannot use bankruptcy to discharge judgments against themselves. Eager to appeal to women voters, the Senate had accepted the amendment in 2001. But in 2002, when the bankruptcy bill went back to the House with the abortion amendment in it, a coalition of right-to-life representatives refused to go along. They brought the bill to a standstill.

Desperate to get the bill passed, the banking lobby went back to the Senate, pressuring Senator Schumer to remove the controversial abortion provision. The industry ran attack ads against him in his home state, demanding that he support the bankruptcy bill—and claiming that he was costing every American family $550 a year.[102] (The attack on Senator Schumer was particularly ironic, since he had received more campaign contributions from the credit industry than any other Senator, just nosing out fellow New Yorker Hillary Clinton.[103]) But by this point, the pro-choice women's groups were also mobilized, and they held firm, supporting Senator Schumer and threatening to withhold support from any elected official who moved to take the provision out of the bankruptcy bill. In one of those rare defining moments, Senator Schumer had to choose between big business and pro-choice women, both of whom had supported his campaign. He chose women, and the amendment remained in the bill.

Ultimately, two strange bedfellows—a small group of socially conservative Republicans and a handful of progressive Democrats—gathered enough momentum to defeat the bankruptcy bill against the best-financed lobbying campaign of the 107th Congress.

Reclaiming the Politics of the Family

The real victors on that strange day were the grassroots groups that successfully flexed their muscles against the most well-funded lobbying group in America, showing the world that even the credit industry can be defeated *if* key groups can be rallied against them. What was the key to action? It was not simply a matter of putting forth the facts. Congress had already impaneled a Bankruptcy Commission to write 1,100 pages of facts, which few even bothered to read. No, the real key was to match up the politics of financial distress with the interests of the rest of the country. The right-to-life organizations put a face on those who would be affected by the Schumer Amendment, showcasing stories of elderly grandmothers and churchgoing families who protest abortion as a matter of conscience. The pro-choice organizations put their own face on the issue, spotlighting violent abortion protesters who had found a loophole that let them get away with breaking the law.

There is a lesson here. To put sound economic policies on the political agenda, families also need to find a face. So long as they are "debtors" or "bankrupts," their needs can be dismissed. Instead, they need to be seen as members of powerful constituencies, members of groups that command the respect—and the fear—of the political elite. Families in financial trouble must be depicted as they really are: "parents of young children," "nonresident fathers paying child support," "suburban homeowners," "African-American middle-class families," "single mothers," "families sending a kid to college," "multigenerational Hispanic families." Most of all, the groups that defend these people need to organize against those who are picking their constituents' pockets.

The case is not hard to make. Consider the circumstances of African Americans. For decades, the National Association for the Advancement of Colored People (NAACP) and other minority rights groups have lobbied to expand African-American home ownership, and they have been at least somewhat successful in their efforts. Now predatory and subprime lenders threaten to unravel those hard-won gains. Every year, more than 300,000 black and Hispanic homeowners file for bankruptcy in a desperate attempt to hold on to their homes. Hispanic homeowners are nearly three times more likely than white homeowners to file for bankruptcy, and black homeowners are more than *six times* more likely.[104] The same signs of distress are evident outside the bankruptcy courts. When we analyzed unpublished data from the Department of Housing and Urban Development, we found that among families who had purchased a home with an FHA-backed mortgage, African Americans were twice as likely as white homeowners to lose their home in foreclosure.[105] Payday lenders and subprime mortgage companies deliberately target minority neighborhoods, confident that they can get away with fleecing these families.[106] Billions of dollars are flowing out of the communities that can least afford it, directly into the pockets of giant lenders and their shareholders.

We are not the first to document these problems; minority rights groups are well aware of the dangers of predatory lending. There is, however, an important question of how high economic issues should rank in their list of priorities. When Senator Trent Lott seemingly expressed his nostalgia for a segregated America, minority groups around the country barraged the talk shows and newspapers, and Lott was ultimately stripped of his powerful position as majority leader of the Senate. Similarly, when Texaco executives were accused of using racial slurs to refer to African Americans, the company was boycotted, sued for millions of dollars, and forced to adopt new practices to ensure that its black employees had better opportunities.[107] But when a Citibank official said in sworn affidavits that she regularly added extra fees to a home mortgage "[i]f someone . . . was a minority," there was little response. Citibank quietly agreed to a cash settlement with the FTC, and there were no press releases from the NAACP, no interviews on the evening news, no calls for Citibank's highly visible CEO, Sandy Weill, to resign.

Subprime lending, payday loans, and the host of predatory, high-interest loan products that target minority neighborhoods should be called by their true names: legally sanctioned corporate plans to steal from minorities. Many years ago, a host of community groups worked together to oppose discriminatory lending and to help pass the Community Reinvestment Act despite stiff opposition from the banking industry. It is time for these groups to come together again to eliminate the modern version of economic discrimination, which parades under different names but has the same devastating effects.

A Woman's Issue: Minority groups should not be asked to bear the burden on their own. Women's groups also need to pick up the mantle of economic reform. Middle-class financial distress may sound like a gender-neutral issue, but it is not. In just two decades, the number of single-filing women declaring bankruptcy has grown by more than 600 percent. Women with children are more likely to lose their homes and more likely to be late on their bills. And single women with children are now *three times* more likely to go bankrupt than men without children.[108]

The notion that women should fight for economic reform is hardly new. From the early days of the struggle for "Equal Pay for Equal Work," women's groups have protested for financial justice. But the issue of economic reform for middle-class women is often shunted aside by other priorities. For example, the NOW Legal Defense and Education Fund vigorously opposed the credit industry–backed bankruptcy bill, doing the painstaking legwork to convince nearly thirty other women's groups as disparate as Church Women United, Hadassah, and the YWCA to join the fight.[109] Yet NOW Legal Defense also offered its very public support to Senator Joseph Biden, featuring him as women's strongest ally in the Senate because he supported the Violence Against Women Act.[110] Apparently, his support of this bill trumped any concerns the group might have had over the fact that Senator Biden is "the leading Democratic proponent" and "one of the . . . strongest supporters" of the very bankruptcy bill against which NOW Legal Defense had fought so hard.[111]

Women's groups have too few dollars and too little (wo)man power to fight every injustice. But there is another lesson in the tale of the bankruptcy bill. Women's issues are not just about childbearing or domestic violence. If it were framed properly, middle-class economic reform just might become the issue that could galvanize millions of mainstream women to join the fight for women's issues. The numbers are certainly there. This year, more women will file bankruptcy papers than will receive college diplomas. More women with children will search for a bankruptcy lawyer than will seek subsidized day care. And in a statistic with special significance for Senator Biden, more women will be victimized by predatory lenders than will seek protection from an abusive husband or boyfriend.[112]

The point is not to discredit other worthy causes or to pit one disadvantaged group against another. Nor would we suggest that battered women deserve less help or that subsidized day care is unimportant. The point is simply that family economics should not be left to giant corporations and paid lobbyists, and senators like Joe Biden should not be allowed to sell out women in the morning and be heralded as their friend in the evening. Middle-class women need help, and right now no one is putting their economic interests first.

Political groups on the conservative end of the political spectrum should step up as well. Groups such as the Family Research Council and Focus on the Family organize their political and educational activities around the family. But economics are nestled at the core of family values. Any group that is serious about lowering divorce rates should focus on reducing the economic stress that strains a marriage. Any group that cares about children should be vitally interested in how home mortgages are marketed and how tens of thousands of kids are getting kicked out of their houses. And any group that thinks Mom ought to have the option to stay home with the kids should be powerfully concerned about the debt trap that chains millions of middle-class women to their offices.

A few religious leaders have involved themselves in family economics. In a recent letter to Congress, several faith-based organizations, including Catholics, Jews, and Unitarians, joined to argue that "[s]ocial justice for the socially and economically disadvantaged is part of the cherished moral tradition shared by all of our religions."[113] Citing a passage from the Bible about forgiveness of debts, the group called on Congress to abandon the proposed bankruptcy bill because the hardship it would impose on families was out of line with their religious beliefs. When they saw that the vitality of the family was at stake, these groups mobilized their moral authority against those who would rob families of their economic independence. Other faith-based organizations should heed the call and follow their lead.

Liberal or conservative, faith-based or secular, any group that sees its mission as *families* should have interest rate regulation and bankruptcy protection at the very top of its agenda. Predatory lending is a family issue. Usury is a family issue. Bankruptcy is a family issue. These laws affect families—people with children—more than anyone else. There is likely no other issue—divorce, welfare reform, child custody—that will directly touch more middle-class families than the mortgage and credit card interest rates that drain away their economic viability and sap the intimacy and joy from family life.

7

The Financial Fire Drill

How should a family protect itself from the Two-Income Trap? The deck is stacked against today's parents who struggle to solve financial problems on their own. A generation of bidding wars has launched an army of competing buyers against any family that tries to cut back on its spending. And a generation of layoffs, divorces, and spiraling medical costs has hit pretty much everyone. In the pages of this book we have offered suggestions for collective action—recommendations for Congress and state legislatures, political action groups and faith-based organizations, school districts and community institutions. We firmly believe that collective action is the most effective remedy and that it is essential for reestablishing the economic security middle-class parents so badly need.

But such changes take time, and families need to safeguard themselves now. So what should a family do? For starters, everyone raising a family should read a good book on financial planning. But be warned: The basic premise of most of these books can be misleading, even dangerous. They show how to draw up a budget or choose a mutual fund, but in most cases their advice is aimed only at those lucky families for whom work is steady, everyone is healthy, and there are no emergencies. Disaster—a lost job, a premature birth, a divorce—is the defining theme of the financial lives of millions of families, but it doesn't appear in most financial advice books—or in most families' financial plans.

Any firefighter will explain that the time to prepare for an emergency is *before* the house catches on fire. Install smoke detectors, get the oily rags out of the garage, run through a practice fire drill—and do it now, when there is no smoke in the air. The same advice should hold for financial protection. In the same spirit as a fire drill for home safety, the clever parent should run her own financial fire drill.

A financial fire drill should pose three questions:

1. Can your family survive without one income? If your family is like the average two-income family, then you face a one in sixteen chance that in any given year, at least one of you will lose your job.[1] If you are a single parent, you actually face smaller odds of a layoff (because there is only one person at work), but the consequence of a job loss can be even worse if that sole income disappears. In either case, the litmus test is the same: Can you survive for six months without one of the incomes that you currently rely on? If you are a married couple with only one earner, then the question is easier: Could the stay-at-home parent enter the job market if something happened to the primary breadwinner? Regardless of your group, if the answer is no, then it's time for some disaster planning.

2. Can you downshift the fixed expenses? If you are having trouble making ends meet, the average financial planning book advises you to "pass up those impulse purchases or another dinner out" so that you can save more and get out of debt.[2] But the experts have it exactly wrong. If you eliminate all the treats now, while times are good, then where will you cut back when a real financial crisis appears? Take another look at your budget. If you are feeling squeezed during ordinary times, it is likely that you have a much bigger problem than an occasional dinner at the Olive Garden. You have a problem with your fixed costs.

Now is the time to take a hard look at the necessities, not the frills. If you're having a difficult time making ends meet, think about lowering your fixed expenses. Can you manage a few more years without a new car? Can you sign up for the lower-cost HMO, even if that means shifting the kids to a different pediatrician? Would your toddler be all right in a less expensive preschool? And, toughest of all, should you move to a cheaper house, one you can manage on a smaller mortgage? These are obviously difficult decisions for any family. But it is better to confront them now, when you have time and flexibility to make reasonable choices, rather than later, when the creditors are calling and your back is to the wall.

Lurking in these words is a piece of corollary advice to the family shopping for a home: *Don't stretch yourself to buy a house you can't afford*. If the only way you can meet the mortgage payments for your dream home is to tighten your belt and commit both incomes, don't do it. The fact that you have been approved for a mortgage is no guarantee that you can actually afford it. As painful as it may be, it is wiser to rent for a few more years or to buy a smaller home. That oversized mortgage will leave you with no room for error, no cash for even minor emergencies—let alone a real disaster.

There is a silver lining to all this abstemious advice. *It is okay to splurge on extras*. Never mind the dour looks from the Over-Consumption camp. So long as you are staying out of debt and putting something away in savings, you should feel free to buy the kids a new pair of Nikes or treat yourself to a night on the town. If the tough times come, you can drop those expenditures in a heartbeat. As long as your fixed expenses are low enough that you can manage during a crisis, then you can count yourself secure enough to go ahead and have some fun.

3. What is your emergency backup plan? Now is the time for the painful game of "what-ifs." What if your husband loses his job? What if grandma's health fails? What if your own health fails? What if you and your spouse split up? The point of this litany is not to send you running for the aspirin bottle, but to help you be prepared if the unthinkable happens. As difficult as it may be, you need to make a plan and to consider what could be done now to make that plan feasible. Add a separate line to your budget for these just-in-case safety precautions.

The emergency backup plan may cause you to rethink some of your financial commitments. Pay particular attention to timing. In finances, long-term commitments are the most dangerous kind. Sometimes they are unavoidable, such as when you buy a home or go to college. But whenever possible, go for a shorter commitment, since that will give you what you most need in times of trouble—flexibility. So, for example, choose a 36-month car loan instead of a 60-month commitment. If that drives the payment up too high, then heed the warning: You cannot afford this car, and you should opt for something cheaper. Once you pay off this car, hang on to it for an extra year or two and keep making payments to yourself. After two or three times around, you can pay for your car in advance, giving yourself that much more flexibility in your budget. Details may vary on any loan, but think of every long-term commitment in terms of walking a tightrope—so long as your family is on the rope, there is a risk of disaster. Take the shortest walks you can.

You should also assess your insurance coverage. Should you purchase a disability insurance policy, just in case? Should you beef up your life insurance policy? Talk with your parents about their plans. Can you help them buy long-term care insurance? Perhaps your siblings could help out as well. Long-term care insurance can give several families—your own, your parents' and your siblings'—a better chance of surviving financially if your parents need daily assistance. When everyone is healthy, the thought of disability can seem like a remote possibility, a bad dream that strikes others, not busy families with young children. But the fact remains: Medical problems send three-quarters of a million families to the bankruptcy courts each year. So think about more insurance. If you never use it, then count yourself lucky.

Help that won't help. A growing number of credit card companies have begun to hawk "credit protection" insurance, urging you to "protect your family" in the event of a job loss, disability, or death in the family. This sounds like a perfect prescription, but buyer beware. Most of these policies do nothing more than make the minimum monthly payment on the balance you were carrying at the time you lost your job or developed a disability. Some policies also promise to discharge your debt in the event of your death, but this, too, is a flimsy benefit. Regardless of your insurance status, your heirs will not be required to pay your balance; in most cases the credit card company will write off your debts even if you never purchased the credit protection insurance.[3] Moreover, if you don't have an outstanding balance, credit insurance doesn't do a thing for you. Worst of all, this form of insurance is wildly expensive. If you carry a $3,000 balance, you'll pay over $300 a year for an average policy.[4] If you can scrape together some money, buy a real disability policy from a reputable insurance company or put your money in the bank. Credit insurance is a sucker's bet.

When the House Is Already on Fire

What about those families for whom the fire drill comes too late? They are the ones most often ignored by the advice peddlers, and they are the most likely to be victimized by unscrupulous creditors. These are also the families to whom this book is dedicated, so we offer them a few direct words of advice and (we hope) comfort.

Avoid the blame game. With the benefit of 20/20 hindsight, it is tempting to beat yourself up about the smarter choices you might have made. But if you are like nearly 90 percent of the families in financial trouble, you got that way because something lousy happened to you. Maybe your business went under, your husband left you, or you got too sick to work. If you made the decisions you did in order to take care of your family, then, at least in our opinion, you have nothing to feel guilty about. Go easy on yourself; your creditors certainly won't.

And go easy on your spouse. Your financial well-being isn't the only thing at risk right now; so is your marriage. Consider this: If your family is like most, your marriage may be more vulnerable right now than at any other time in your life. Myra, a dental hygienist in a small town in Pennsylvania, filed for bankruptcy after her husband lost his job. She sums up the problem neatly: "Except for the financial problems that almost destroyed our marriage, we have a perfect relationship. Money is the only thing that we argue about, but that's enough to ruin even the best friendship." Husbands may feel shamed by their inability to provide, and wives may feel overburdened by the demands of bill collectors, bosses, and children. Be kind. You are both under enormous strain right now, and taking it out on each other will only make things worse.

You should also know that you are not alone. There are several million families in situations not too different from your own. They worked hard, tried to provide for their families, and ended up in financial hell. You may not know it, but scattered among the folks in your grocery store, your PTA, your church or synagogue, and even your family, are men and women just like you—people who have done their best for their families and who are now in financial collapse. You are in good company.

Hold on to your treasures. The greatest danger for a family in financial distress is not bill collectors (although they can be the most annoying). The greatest danger is false optimism. We heard it over and over again in our interviews: "We thought Mark would be back at work right away." "I thought I could work things out with my husband after a little time apart." "We didn't think grandpa could go on like this much longer." These families knew they had been hit by a disaster, but they didn't respond fast enough because they thought it would pass quickly. That is the deadly trick about a financial crisis: It is nearly always impossible to predict when it will end. For families already in trouble, now is the time to plan for the worst, just in case the bad news doesn't get better. So turn off the phone, ignore the junk mail, and pop in a video for the kids. It is time for some cold, hard calculations.

A family facing a financial crisis should think like a family at war. You must concentrate on preserving what matters most, and you must let the other things go. When trouble comes, ask the central question: Which of your assets do you most want to hold on to? Maybe it's your car, your home, or your health insurance policy. Decide which things you value most, and *pay those bills first*. It doesn't matter who else is making demands on your resources or what they are threatening you with. Once you are in trouble, you will need to fight—and you should be fighting for the things you care about, not trying to satisfy the loudest or most aggressive creditor.

Most important, do not, under any circumstances, put those assets at risk. You will be bombarded by offers to "lower your monthly payments" by taking out a second mortgage or cashing out the equity from your home. *Don't do it.* Refinancing their homes to pay down other bills is the single biggest mistake made by families in trouble. The mortgage companies (and even some financial advisors) may tell you it is savvy to replace your high-interest credit card debt with low-interest mortgage debt. But if you are in financial trouble, you will probably be steered into a high-cost, subprime mortgage, making any gains illusory. Worst of all, you will be jeopardizing the roof over your family's head. Take a moment to consider. Do you honestly believe those "low monthly payments" are a free gift? Not a chance. If the mortgage lender gives you a lower rate than the credit card company, it is because the mortgage lender gets something in return—the right to push you into the street, seize your home, and sell it.

If your troubles get bad enough, you can file for bankruptcy to eliminate your high-interest credit card debts and cash advances, but bankruptcy cannot help with a home equity loan or a refinanced mortgage. You must pay the mortgage lender in full (plus all penalties, late fees, and interest) or face foreclosure. The chance to save a few dollars a month on your credit card bills is not worth running the risk that you won't have a place to live.

Plan strategically. If the bills keep piling up, take a realistic look at your overall situation. Can you pay off your debts in the next two years? If the answer is no, talk to an attorney, read a good book about your legal options, and look into filing for bankruptcy.[5] But be aware that bankruptcy is essentially a one-time option that will be unavailable again for six years. Once you file for bankruptcy, you must fly without any parachute.[6]

If at all possible, wait until the crisis has passed before declaring bankruptcy. If you are out of work, wait until you have found a new job. If you have a child who is seriously ill, wait until he is better and the health insurance has paid what it owes. It can be extremely tough to hold on that long, especially if collection notices are stacking up and creditors are calling you every night. But if you wait, you minimize the risk that you will once again find yourself buried in debt after you file for bankruptcy. The bankruptcy system gives a rare opportunity for a second chance. If you wait to file until the worst of your problems are over, you give yourself the best odds of getting exactly what you need from the bankruptcy judge—a fresh start.

Guilt-free default. What about all those bills you will never repay? Whatever you do, *don't* reassume any old debts that were discharged by the courts. One in four families signs on to pay off debts they no longer owe after filing for bankruptcy.[7] Why? Because they don't understand their rights. As the story about Sears showed (chapter 6), creditors routinely bully bankrupt families by threatening to repossess the family's possessions. Except for the house or the car, this is nearly always an empty threat. Creditors almost never repossess, because it is just not worth their time and money. It typically costs a creditor at least $350 to send a truck to your house and cart something away, and even more to clean it up and resell it.[8] Are your used goods actually worth that much?

Another favorite tactic is to warn families that no one will ever issue them another credit card after they file for bankruptcy. Many creditors hire agents to patrol the waiting rooms in the bankruptcy courts, typically friendly older ladies who make seemingly generous offers: "The company is willing to extend you a line of credit, *if* you'll agree to repay the balance on your credit card." But think again before you sign. These agents may seem like nice people, but they are peddling poison. Not only will you get stuck paying a bill you no longer owe, the effective interest rate on that new line of credit may be as high as 1,000 percent![9]

How will you get a new credit card if you forfeit your old one? By opening your mail. Within six months of filing for bankruptcy, *84 percent* of families had already received unsolicited offers for new credit.[10] Half of bankrupt families received more than thirty offers! You may find that after filing for bankruptcy you are *more* popular with credit card companies than ever before. Lenders know that you cannot declare bankruptcy again for six years, and they believe you may still be under enough financial strain that you will soon end up carrying a balance and making minimum monthly payments—rocketing you to number one on their list of favorite customers. So don't worry, there is life after bankruptcy. You will have a lot more credit at your disposal than you need (and probably a lot more than you should use). So just hang tough, and don't let yourself be bullied or threatened. The creditor is not your friend, and you should not sign away your future before the ink is dry on your bankruptcy petition.

We hear the chorus of self-blame and guilt tuning up. These companies lent you money, so aren't you obligated to pay them back? Yes, you are—up to a point. But you are also obligated to keep a roof over your children's head, to put food in their mouths, and to get them the medical care they need. Children take precedence over creditors.

Besides, most of those lenders *knew* you would have a tough time paying them back. They had your credit reports. They knew how much money you earned, and they knew how much you owed. *They took a calculated risk*. If everyone had stayed healthy and you hadn't lost your job, you would have paid your debts and your creditors would have made a handsome profit. But that didn't happen. Whenever a bank makes a loan, it hopes to make money, but lenders know that there is some chance that the money will never be repaid. The interest charges and penalty fees are designed to cover those risks, and the banks are doing just fine, even when they lose from time to time.

Think like a businessperson. Do you imagine the CEO of United Airlines and the president of K-Mart were wracked with guilt when their companies filed for bankruptcy? We doubt it. They did what they thought best for their shareholders and customers, and if that meant that some creditors ended up with the short end of the stick, then so be it. They saw it as simply a matter of business. When your family's welfare is at stake, so should you.

Stay Home?

Should you (or your spouse) quit your job and stay home so you won't be in any danger of falling into the Two-Income Trap? If you are like millions of parents, you are already up to your eyeballs in mortgage payments and tuition bills, and pulling out of the workforce will only make things worse. For you, the financial fire drill and some very angry calls to your senator are the best you can do.

For some families, keeping a parent at home is at least possible. But is it a good idea, financially speaking? It isn't a bad solution, if you can afford it. If you would prefer to have a parent at home full-time but were afraid that it would be too risky economically, then don't worry. The idea that it takes two incomes to be financially secure is dangerously wrongheaded. The data in this book show that a family with a stay-at-home parent has an important source of economic security, a backup earner and caregiver who can step in if anything goes wrong. So long as you can get by on a single income and the stay-at-home parent can enter the workforce if the need arises, then go right ahead and quit your job.

What if both parents prefer to work? By all means, do it. Two earners does not mean an inevitable dive into the Two-Income Trap; it just means there is more risk and the family must plan accordingly. The financial planning books typically treat one and two-income families the same, telling you to add up your family's income, divide by the expenses, and fill in the blanks. But they are not the same. Without a safety net, your two-income family must be careful not to budget as tightly as a one-income household. If at all possible, think of that second income as a safety net, a special reserve for bad times. When times are good, put something in savings, and spend the rest of the second paycheck on restaurants, nice clothes, and treats. If you can avoid committing it to the mortgage and the health insurance, you'll get to enjoy the benefits of having two incomes while staying secure.

The Other Solution: No Children?

Some women have found another way to avoid the Two-Income Trap. It doesn't involve loading up on insurance policies or conducting a financial fire drill; nor does it require you to keep a spouse at home full-time. And, unlike the other solutions we have presented, it is cost-free and highly effective. Their solution? Don't have children.

Childlessness may not be a calculated economic strategy, but it has powerful economic consequences. By forgoing childbearing, a woman decreases her chances of going bankrupt by 66 percent.[11] She reduces the likelihood that she will ever deal with a collection call or worry about a repo man, and she increases the chances that she will hold on to her home. And this improved financial security will last a lifetime: By remaining childless, a woman greatly improves her odds of having a comfortable retirement.[12]

A few generations ago, advising women not to have children would have seemed ridiculous. Not only would it have defied the social norms of the time (which assumed that everyone would become parents), but the advice would have been viewed as economically self-destructive. At one time, men and women viewed children as economic assets. Youngsters lent a hand on the farm or in the shop, they looked after their younger siblings, and, most important, they cared for their aging parents. Little wonder that parents were expected to shoulder the costs of bringing up those children. After all, parents reaped the rewards.

Children are still economic assets. Today's children will build the economy of tomorrow, defend the nation in future wars, care for the sick, construct new buildings, repair the roads, and support the next generation of elderly through Social Security. But there is a key difference: These benefits will go to society at large, not to specific parents. Moreover, most of the contributions from today's children will not occur until they have grown up and left home. In the modern economy, few children earn their keep by sweeping out the family store or gathering the next harvest; most will be a financial burden well into adulthood. In just a few generations, the calculus of raising children has changed dramatically. Middle-class parents are investing more and more in their own children; at the same time, society at large claims an ever-growing share of the rewards of those investments.

A column in *U.S. News & World Report* observed wryly: "At the individual family level, a child, financially speaking, looks more like a high-priced consumer item with no warranty. . . . For economic man in the late 20th century, child-rearing has become a crummy financial bargain."[13] The authors were fundamentally right. Bringing up children has indeed become a crummy financial bargain. But they were wrong in another regard. Signing on to have children is quite different from buying "a high-priced consumer item," with or without warranty. If having children were like buying, say, a Mercedes Benz, with a preset price tag that could be clearly accounted for, then prospective parents could make the usual set of financial choices posed by the typical economics textbook. They could choose among several options—the Mercedes, the BMW, or the pleasure of a tiny new person. Reasonable people could make informed choices, depending on their preferences, and they could abandon (or resell) their purchases if the costs got out of hand.

But the cost of a child is not so neatly packaged. It is not possible to calculate the eighteen-year (or twenty-two-year) price tag of an individual person, with her unique talents and needs, before she is even conceived. Nor does it matter that a prospective parent did not budget for the baby-with-asthma package or the costly diploma at a private college for the kid who was denied admission to State U. Parents make the commitment to meet their children's needs long before they know the full price. And that commitment will color the parents' financial prospects for the rest of their lives.

For a growing number of Americans, childlessness has become a serious option. Much has been made of the possibility of a looming shortfall in America's birth rate.[14] Over the past twenty years, the proportion of childless women has doubled, and demographers predict that as many as a quarter of today's young women will never have children.[15] If the word gets out that families with children are nearly three times more likely to collapse into bankruptcy, will even more women decide not to have children? And what about the children who grow up today watching mom and dad work hard all day, only to weep in frustration when bill collectors call them ugly names or repo men circle the family car? Will these children have any interest in becoming parents themselves?

Our crystal ball is cloudy, and it is quite possible that the biological drive to pass on our genes will continue to win out over seemingly more rational financial calculations. We certainly hope so. Not just for sentimental reasons, but also for economic ones. Many view parenthood as nothing more than another "lifestyle choice," not so different from joining a commune or developing a passion for windsurfing.[16] And that may be true from the perspective of an individual choosing whether or not to have a child, but it isn't true for society at large. What happens to a nation that rewards the childless and penalizes the parents? If middle-class men and women stop making that parental lifestyle choice, who will care for them in their old age? Who will pay taxes, build infrastructure, and keep the economy afloat? And most important, who will populate the great middle class of America's future?

We wish we could offer some clever advice that would tell everyone how to sidestep the financial land mines associated with parenthood, but we can't. The financial fire drill can help curb at least a few of the dangers of modern economic life, but it cannot negate the fundamental fact that having children has become an enormously risky undertaking. Nor can the financial fire drill protect an individual parent from the vagaries of the marketplace. So long as the only way parents can guarantee a decent education for their children is to buy an overpriced home in the suburbs, families will continue to take on ruinous mortgages. So long as the costs of preschool remain a family's responsibility rather than a public duty, parents will continue to struggle. So long as colleges can get away with doubling tuition every generation to pay for sports teams and armies of new administrators, families will be stretched even further. And so long as Congress refuses to impose some basic interest rate regulations, credit card companies and mortgage lenders will continue to drain tens of billions of dollars out of the pockets of middle-class American families each year.

Our advice here is born out of hope rather than sound financial reasoning. If you feel called to be a parent, we hope you will follow your heart. Yes, you may lose your home, and you may go bankrupt. We hope the joys will outweigh the financial pain. And besides, what other advice would you expect from two working mothers who believe in the great American middle class and who pray for its strong future?

But if you become a parent, we believe that you have an extra duty beyond providing for your child's needs; you also have a duty to speak up. The data in this book show that families cannot protect themselves alone. So write your representatives in Congress, petition your school board, and speak out. There are 63 million parents in America, and with them, you are strong enough to make a difference. If you are to survive financially, you and other parents must band together for change. The survival of your interest group—parents—depends on it.

Bankrupt Children

There is one more reason you should act. Not for yourself, or for other parents, or for future parents. You should take action on behalf of the children.

This book is certain to make some people angry. Those who are convinced that the problem with American families can be summed up by materialism and irresponsibility will denounce us as hopeless apologists. Spokespersons for the lending industry will puff about how much good all that debt has done for the American family. Politicians who have taken millions of dollars to protect the giant banks will pointedly ignore this book while they loudly reaffirm that they are "pro-family." And there will be no shortage of people who will continue to denounce the financially unlucky as moral failures.

But there is one fact that will be hard for even our most vocal critics to ignore. This year, an estimated 1.6 million children will go along for the ride when their parents declare bankruptcy. That means that more kids will be listed in their parents' bankruptcies than will sign up for Little League. Or adopt a dog from the humane society. Or get braces on their teeth.[17] If current trends continue, by the end of the decade *one of every seven children in the United States will have lived through their parents' bankruptcy*.[18]

Much like divorce, bankruptcy is about a destabilized family. A whole nation has focused on the difficulties that children face when their parents divorce, while the problem of financial distress among middle-class parents is widely ignored. And yet, in any given year *more children will live through their parents' bankruptcy than their parents' divorce*.[19] For these children, bankruptcy is not simply a matter of having less spending money or getting fewer new clothes. Like the children of divorce, the children of economic failure lose the life they once knew.

In some cases, the effects of deteriorating family finances are subtle, difficult for a child to comprehend. Mom cries a lot, Dad sits home all day, and the heat has been shut off. In other cases, the fallout is abrupt. A foreclosure notice stuck to the front door, a cramped apartment on the other side of town, a new school. And sometimes the spillover is totally unexpected. Sara Swerdling, a thirty-eight-year-old mother in California, tried to insulate her eleven-year-old son from the financial fallout of her husband's job loss. She carefully hid the past-due notices, told him the telephone was shut off due to a "mechanical difficulty," and said the car was towed away because the transmission was broken. But then came the phone call that forced her to admit that she and her husband could no longer shield him. "Our son has braces. When the dentist was informed of the bankruptcy, they called and said they wouldn't see him anymore." After a series of humiliating phone calls, she finally found an orthodontist who was willing to remove her son's braces—for cash in advance. Then she had to explain to her eleven-year-old what had gone wrong in their lives, why a stranger would take off his braces while his teeth were still crooked, and how his life was about to change.

When a radical change occurs in a child's life—divorce, a move to a new city, or even the birth of a new sibling—parents typically alert the other adults in the child's life, asking them to give additional support and to watch for signs of trouble. But middle-class parents don't tell the teachers, the pediatrician, the school counselor, or the babysitter that their youngster may be experiencing distress because Mom and Dad are on the brink of bankruptcy. This leaves children isolated, confused, and conscious that something shameful is going on.

The code of silence makes it difficult for these children to seek out friends who have lived through the same experience. Children become more isolated, cut off from their peers. Over time, this can evolve into keeping secrets and telling lies. Professor Katherine Newman, in her book *Falling from Grace*, quotes the advice an unemployed father gave to his son: "In his school, everybody's father is the head of this and that. So I said, 'You just tell them your Dad was VP of a company and he just refused to go on an overseas assignment. . . .' I told him if anybody asks, tell them I started my own firm."[20] When a parent advocates telling lies, what is a child to think? Politicians may contend that financial collapse has lost its stigma, but children living through it may not see it that way.

A handful of academic studies provides hints about the future these children face. The catalog of damages inflicted on children when their parents divorce—falling test scores, low self-esteem, discipline problems, depression—also applies for middle-class children whose parents are in financial trouble.[21] Financial collapse has an additional wrinkle less common among children of divorce: It often sends a child into adult roles long before his time. Newman observes: "For downwardly mobile families, it is the parents who need their kids' emotional support. . . . Their children want to be more independent, but a sense of responsibility and obligation pulls them back."[22]

Not all parents try to shield their children the way Sara Swerdling did. Sometimes the protection goes the other way. Many children, some as young as nine or ten, learn to screen the incoming phone calls to shield their parents from bill collectors. Charlene Dorset, a travel agent in a small town in Pennsylvania, describes a low point after her husband's business failed: "Two men came to our door [when I was at work]. They said that they read that we were going to be foreclosed on and that they would either buy the house [at auction] or give us loans to help us out. My son told them to get off the property and never come back. He must have looked so small and skinny next to those two men, but I don't think he even knew it, he was so mad."

If you care about children—about whether they succeed or fail academically, about whether they are self-confident or self-loathing, about whether they are thriving or under so much stress that they can't sleep at night—then you should care about family economics. If you care about children, then you should speak out.

Conservative columnist William F. Buckley Jr. describes the bankruptcy process as follows: "What has caused the acceleration of bankruptcies is the painlessness of the operation plus little avenues of abuse attractive to high-class bankrupts. . . . You come back one day from the corner lawyer and say, Whee! I don't owe anybody anything!"[23] We are not sure who was on Mr. Buckley's interview list as he developed his insights into how families respond to financial failure. We are pretty sure it was not one of the thousands of children who have just lost the home they grew up in. We also suspect it was not one of the millions of devastated parents who are watching the symbols and security associated with their children's place in the middle class crumble away. But we know that every person who read that column and who did not call Mr. Buckley to task for his cheap cynicism helped make life a little harder for a whole lot of children and their parents.

Playing by the Rules

The families we studied weren't so different from our own. There were people who made everyone laugh, people who dreamed big, and people who made some really stupid choices. More than anything else, the families whose lives animate this book worked hard, played by the rules—and failed. They made many of the same choices we made—they went to college, they bought homes, they sent both parents into the workforce—but they got caught in a trap of circumstances that would not let them go, and they ended up in a study of financial failure.

We believe in these families. But the rules they played by are no longer the rules that govern financial success for the middle class. In a single generation, the world has changed, and families are struggling to adapt. They committed themselves to thrift and hard work in exchange for a promise of economic security and a better future for their children. That promise has disappeared. There was a time when families sent mothers into the workplace only in times of distress. Today, women go to work every day just to maintain a tenuous grasp on a middle-class life. Plenty of families make it, but a growing number of those who worked just as hard and followed the rules just as carefully find themselves in a financial nightmare.

The collective pressures on the family—the rising costs of educating their children, the growing insurance payments and medical bills, the rising risks of layoffs and plant closures, and the unscrupulous tactics of an unrestrained credit industry—are pushing families to the breaking point. America's middle class is strong, but its strength is not unlimited.

The evidence we assemble is unrelenting, but we remain optimistic. The American middle class was forged by families who knew hardship and conflict and who dreamed of giving their children something better. It has survived wars, scandal, epidemics, the Great Depression, and massive transformations in the U.S. economy. It is under assault, but the families that make up the great middle are not quitters. They are ferocious fighters, for themselves and for their children. Their willingness to send 20 million mothers into the workplace had unintended fallout, but it was rooted in a powerful desire to create a better future for their children. Their failure to demand accountability from their politicians and the organizations that purport to speak for them has left them weakened. But we believe that collectively and individually these families have the tools to change the structure of their schools, to bring their politicians to heel, and to fight back against big businesses that would steal their economic vitality. They *can* release the trap.

APPENDIX
The Consumer Bankruptcy Project, 2001

In 1999 and 2000, a group of scholars began to assemble the pieces of what would become the Consumer Bankruptcy Project of 2001. A dozen professors from seven different research universities contributed to the design and implementation of the study. Dr. Teresa A. Sullivan, Executive Vice-Chancellor for Academic Affairs of the University of Texas System and Professor of Sociology; Professor Elizabeth Warren, Leo Gottlieb Professor of Law at Harvard University; and Professor Jay Lawrence Westbrook, Benno Schmidt Professor of Law at the University of Texas, took principal responsibility for designing the basic questionnaire and telephone survey questions for the 2001 study. In addition, Professor Michael Schill, Professor of Law at New York University and Director of the Furman Center for Real Estate and Urban Policy, and Dr. Susan Wachter, Professor of Real Estate and Finance at the Wharton School, University of Pennsylvania, were principal drafters of survey questions about housing and real estate. Dr. David Himmelstein and Dr. Steffie Woolhandler, both Associate Professors of Medicine at Harvard Medical School, designed the medical questions. Bruce Markell, Doris S. and Theodore B. Lee Professor of Law, and Robert Lawless, Professor of Law, both at the University of Nevada–Las Vegas, drafted the small business questions. Katherine Porter, Harvard Law School '01, John Pottow, Assistant Professor of Law at the University of Michigan, and Dr. Deborah Thorne, Assistant Professor of Sociology at Ohio University, served, in turn, as Project Director, each with a hand in both the design of portions of the project as well as direct oversight of the data collection. These dozen principal investigators brought expertise from a number of policy areas such as family economics, demographics, employment, health care finance, housing policy, small business, women's issues, law, sociology, business, and economics, as well as specific skills in data collection and analysis.

The 2001 Consumer Bankruptcy Project builds on three previous empirical studies of families that file for personal bankruptcy, conducted by Sullivan, Warren, and Westbrook. The earlier Consumer Bankruptcy Projects are detailed in the Appendices to *As We Forgive Our Debtors*[1] (1981 study) and *The Fragile Middle Class*[2] (1991 study). In addition, there was a supplementary study in 1999, the details of which are noted in Jacoby, Sullivan, and Warren's "Rethinking the Debates over Health Care Financing: Evidence from the Bankruptcy Courts."[3]

Development of the Sample

Debtors who file for Chapter 7 and Chapter 13 bankruptcies must attend a meeting with the bankruptcy trustee assigned to the case. The debtor's attorney nearly always attends the meeting with the debtor. The debtor's creditors receive formal notice of the meeting and are invited to attend as well. The 2001 core sample was constructed by distributing questionnaires to debtors who attended these meetings in the target cities on the target dates. The goal was to collect a quota of 250 questionnaires from each district, with the proportion of Chapter 7 and Chapter 13 questionnaires in the sample reflecting the proportion that occurred naturally in each district. For example, in the Central District of California, 80 percent of the petitions filed in 2000 were for Chapter 7 bankruptcies and 20 percent were for Chapter 13 bankruptcies. Thus, of the 250 questionnaires collected in this district in 2001, the researchers sought to match that same distribution: 200 Chapter 7 questionnaires and fifty Chapter 13 questionnaires. In order to achieve this distribution, questionnaires were distributed at Chapter 7 meetings until 200 debtors responded and at Chapter 13 meetings until fifty debtors responded. The same approach—quota sampling by district, by type of chapter—was followed in each of the other four districts until a full sample of 250 cases per district was collected. The total 1,250 cases (250 cases per district) constitute what is called the "core sample," which includes a split between Chapter 7 and Chapter 13 cases that is representative in each of the filing districts.

One questionnaire was completed per case. When couples filed jointly, they completed a *single* questionnaire. The questionnaire, however, collected separate demographic data for both husband and wife. The core sample consists of 1,250 cases, but because 320 of those cases were married couples filing jointly, there are 1,570 people in the core sample who filed for bankruptcy.

Core Sample

The 2001 core sample was drawn from California, Illinois, Pennsylvania, Tennessee, and Texas. This overlaps with the 1991 core sample, which was drawn from the same five states, and with the 1981 sample, which was drawn from three of the five states (Illinois, Pennsylvania, and Texas). Rather than drawing from multiple districts in each state, as in the earlier study, the 2001 Consumer Bankruptcy Project concentrated its resources by drawing a larger sample from one district per state:

the Central District of California, which includes Los Angeles; the Northern District of Illinois, which includes Chicago; the Eastern District of Pennsylvania, which includes Philadelphia; the Middle District of Tennessee, which includes Nashville; and the Northern District of Texas, which includes Dallas.[4] These five states represented 407,047 nonbusiness Chapter 7 and Chapter 13 filings in 2001, or about 26.4 percent of the 1,539,111 nonbusiness bankruptcy cases listed by the Administrative Office of the United States Courts nationwide.

Districts from five different states, each from a different region in the country, provided some geographic diversity. In addition, by drawing from some of the same districts as the 1981 and 1991 samples, the 2001 study maintains some continuity for researchers interested in longitudinal research. The choice of the specific districts within each state increased the size of the pools from which the sample was drawn, increasing the representativeness of the sample within the geographic location.

The five metropolitan areas captured in the core sample represent another form of diversity: the incidence of bankruptcy filings in the local population. To the extent that the decision to file for bankruptcy might be influenced by local legal cultures, variance in the filing rates per thousand may indicate differing bankruptcy practices as well.[5] According to data compiled by SMR Research Corporation, one area, Nashville, has higher rates of bankruptcy filings than most other U.S. cities, at 9.70 bankruptcy filings per 1,000 adults. Closer to the other end of the spectrum were Philadelphia (4.91) and Dallas (5.02), which have lower rates of bankruptcy filings than the U.S. population generally. In between were Chicago (5.83) and Los Angeles (8.02).[6]

This core sample varies from a representative national sample of bankrupt debtors in that it represents relatively few districts. The distribution and completion of the questionnaires also introduce an opportunity for nonresponse bias. This bias could be introduced if the people who complete the questionnaires differ systematically from the people who do not complete questionnaires in ways that might affect the variables of interest. It is possible, for example, that people who are very uncomfortable in the courthouse would reject the questionnaire. This discomfort (an unmeasured characteristic) might be linked to some other characteristic that was measured (such as size of total debt). By their very nature, such biases are difficult to detect.

Two events in 2001 might cause some speculation that our sample was prone to seasonality bias: the events of September 11, 2001, and their subsequent economic impact, and the publicity given the debates in Congress concerning revision of the bankruptcy laws. In fact, however, the sample was drawn earlier in 2001, before either of these events had occurred.

Supplemental Samples

To expand the analysis and to probe additional issues, two supplemental samples were developed. A central focus of the research is the relationships between hous-

TABLE A.1 Summary of core and supplemental samples

	Core sample	Supplemental sample		Totals
		Rural	*Homeowners*	
California	250		40	290
Illinois	250		231	481
Pennsylvania	250		250	500
Tennessee	250	168		418
Texas	250			250
Iowa		281		281
Total	1,250	449	521	2,220

ing, mortgages, and bankruptcy. To study these relationships with greater reliability, the research design included supplementary collections of homeowners in bankruptcy, drawn from Los Angeles, Chicago, and Philadelphia. In order to examine financial problems outside urban centers, an extended sample was drawn from rural areas in Tennessee and Iowa.

The quota sampling technique was also employed for both supplemental samples (homeowners and rural debtors), with the addition of more qualifying criteria. The supplemental rural sample consists only of those debtors living in certain predetermined rural zip codes; all respondents not in those zip codes were eliminated from the supplemental sample. The Los Angeles supplemental housing sample was developed by continuing to collect questionnaires beyond the original target of 250 until a total of 100 homeowners had been collected; nonhomeowner cases were discarded from this supplemental sample. The supplemental housing sample for Philadelphia and Chicago used two filters: The debtors were homeowners and they agreed to be interviewed by telephone; nonhomeowners and those who did not wish to be interviewed were omitted from those supplemental samples.

To recap: The core sample consists of 1,250 debtors, 250 from each of the first five states. This sample was supplemented by an extended sample of 970 debtors, which includes an extended selection of homeowners from the five core sample districts and an additional sample of rural debtors from Tennessee and Iowa. None of the supplemental data is part of the core sample.

Protection of Confidentiality

Before we entered the field, the study's procedures and instruments were reviewed by Harvard University and the University of Texas to guarantee protection of study participants. Consistent with those reviews, access to debtor identity has been limited to guarantee respondents' confidentiality. All researchers who had access to respondents' names and data were required to sign a statement promising to maintain confidentiality. Finally, responses are reported only in the aggregate. When individual quotations are used, the debtors' names and any other obvious identifiers have been changed.

Instruments

Data were collected using three types of instruments: debtor questionnaires, court records, and telephone interviews.

Questionnaires. The debtor questionnaires included the same demographic questions asked in the 1991 and 1999 research. In addition, many new questions were added in response to the data collected from the open-ended questions asked in 1991 and 1999, as well as developments in consumer law and practice. For example, the 2001 questionnaire asked debtors why they had filed for bankruptcy; the options provided on the questionnaire were based on the eight reasons most often given by debtors in 1991, plus an option to fill in a blank after "other." In addition, because so many debtors in 1991 and 1999 had indicated that an illness or injury was the catalyst for their bankruptcy, the 2001 questionnaire asked debtors if they had lost income as a result of their own or a family member's medical problems. The 2001 questionnaire also gathered information on health insurance, medical debt, child support, home ownership, mortgage debt, alternatives to bankruptcy, and number of dependents.

The majority of the questions were closed-ended and required the debtor only to check a box. One opened-ended question was for occupation: Debtors were asked for their occupations and, if married, the occupations of their spouses. Debtors' answers were entered verbatim into the database. Dr. Sullivan coded each entry using the 1970 U.S. Census codes and the corresponding prestige scores developed by the National Opinion Research Center.[7] Dr. Thorne recoded each entry to ensure accuracy and consistency.

In addition to the closed-ended questions, debtors were invited to use the back of the questionnaire to tell the story of their bankruptcies in their own words. The responses were included in the database as a text field.

At the bottom of the last page of the questionnaire, a form offered debtors $50 for participating in follow-up telephone interviews, with the possibility that they might eventually complete three such interviews over the next few years. Debtors who were willing to be interviewed signed the forms and provided their telephone numbers. Only those debtors who signed this form and provided a phone number were called. Debtors whose primary language was Spanish were given a Spanish version of the questionnaire. The questionnaire was translated into Spanish and back-translated into English to verify that the translation was accurate.

With the assistance of the Bankruptcy Court in Boston and the United States Trustee for Region One, the questionnaire was pretested in January 2001. Because this questionnaire was considerably more comprehensive than the one used in 1991, there was some concern about respondents' reactions to the amount of time it would take to complete it. The average time required to complete the questionnaire was six minutes, and no respondent expressed any concern about the length of the questionnaire. After testing, the questionnaires were refined and retested in the Boston courthouse. Once that was complete, the same questionnaire was used in all districts.

The questionnaires asked each debtor for more than thirty pieces of information, for a total of about 75,000 pieces of information gathered from the questionnaires. Copies of the questionnaire are available from the Consumer Bankruptcy Project, Harvard Law School.

Court Records. For every questionnaire that debtors returned, a copy of the corresponding court records was collected; thus the researchers coded court record data from all 2,220 cases in the core and supplemental samples. Court records for bankruptcy are a matter of public record. A photocopy of the court records or a printout from the online court records was added to each debtor's file.

Three people with legal training reviewed the court records, determined which information to code, and assisted in the development of a coding program for data entry. The information reported in the debtors' schedules, which are filed under penalty of perjury, includes income, assets, debts, household expenses, and several legal events. The research team entered approximately 160 pieces of information from each case into the database, for a total of more than 350,000 pieces of information gathered from the court records.

Telephone Surveys. The telephone survey comprised four specialized schedules: general questions presented to all respondents, a medical section presented to those who indicated that a medical problem had contributed to their bankruptcies, a small business section presented to current or former small business owners, and a homeowner section presented to those debtors who owned a home at the time of filing or who had owned a home within the previous five years but had lost it through foreclosure or other financial problems. Interviews took about twenty minutes for each section.

Telephone interviewers were all trained and supervised by Dr. Thorne. All initial interviewers were graduate students or postdoctoral students in sociology; later, other trained interviewers were added. All interview responses were entered directly into a Microsoft Access database designed specifically for this project. Approximately 226,000 pieces of data from the telephone survey were entered in the database.

Response Rates

In some districts, the Chapter 7 and Chapter 13 trustees distributed and collected the questionnaires; in other districts, we trained a local person to complete the distribution and collection, with the cooperation of the trustees. In almost all cases, the questionnaires were distributed and completed when the debtors attended a mandatory meeting at the courthouse, although a few people took their questionnaires home and returned them by mail a few days later.

Without the cooperation of the trustees, it would have been almost impossible to gather a useful sample from among the debtors attending these meetings. The need to rely on the trustees, however, meant that we lost some degree of control over the distribution of the questionnaires. Although we can be nearly certain that the questionnaires were distributed to every debtor who attended a meeting scheduled on a particular day, on some days the trustees did not distribute questionnaires, often because they had no help, because they felt especially pressed for time, or because they forgot. In one district, the Middle District of Tennessee, the trustees went far beyond our expectations and maintained especially careful records, and we could determine that the response rate was 99 percent. In the remaining four districts, however, we could not impose on the trustees to keep similar records, so it is not possible to identify the questionnaire response rates with precision. We estimate that in Texas and Illinois, response rates were approximately 90 percent on the days the trustees distributed the questionnaires. In Illinois, California, and Pennsylvania, when someone other than the trustee distributed the questionnaires, the response rates were lower, estimated at about 60 percent, 55 percent, and 45 percent, respectively.

Because court records are public data, we collected court records for each debtor in the sample, effectively a 100 percent response rate.

Debtors from the core sample and the supplemental homeowner samples were eligible to participate in the telephone survey. Participants in the Iowa supplemental rural sample were not part of the telephone interview portion of the study because those questionnaires were gathered later.

From the core sample of 1,250, 875 debtors (70 percent) agreed to a telephone interview. Of these, it was possible to contact and complete at least one schedule of the telephone survey with 609 debtors, for a response rate of 69.6 percent of those who agreed to be interviewed, or 48.7 percent of all debtors in the core sample. In the supplemental housing sample, 521 debtors were eligible to be interviewed; of these, 328 completed telephone surveys, for a response rate of 62.9 percent. In total, 930 telephone interviews were completed between the core and the supplemental samples.

Coding Accuracy

Data from both the questionnaires and court records were entered into a Microsoft Access database designed specifically for this instrument. Training was extensive, particularly for collecting data from court records. Ten percent of all questionnaire entries were rechecked for errors. The error rate was approximately 0.7 percent. Because the court record data coding was extremely complex, on completion of the data entry, the researchers arranged to recode 500 cases. All mistakes were corrected; therefore, the accuracy of these 500 cases approaches 100 percent. Of the remaining approximately 1,720 cases, 15 percent were randomly selected for quality control checks. On average, there was one error per 160 data points, which translates into accuracy exceeding 99 percent.

ACKNOWLEDGMENTS

In a book about debt, we now acknowledge our own debts, which are substantial. No work involving so much data, so many different areas of expertise, and so many ideas could emerge without the contributions of many different actors.

We begin our thanks with those who provided the support that made this book possible. The Ford Foundation (grant 1010-1838) and the Robert Wood Johnson Foundation (grant 042425) provided generous support for the collection of the bankruptcy data that are used in this book. The Fellowship Program at the Radcliffe Institute for Advanced Study was the first to invest in a project about middle-class mothers and children in financial trouble, generously supporting one of us (Elizabeth) for the year of research that laid the foundation for this book. The Harvard Law School and the New York University School of Law both made substantial contributions to the Consumer Bankruptcy Project as well; we are particularly grateful to the respective former deans, Robert Clark and John Sexton, for their ongoing support for empirical work so that the project could begin.

As we noted in the appendix, the 2001 Consumer Bankruptcy Project was built on the hard labor put into the 1981 and 1991 Consumer Bankruptcy Projects. Dr. Teresa Sullivan and Professor Jay Westbrook have been my (Elizabeth's) longtime coauthors, coinvestigators, and coconspirators. When it was time to put together the 2001 Project, they brought their considerable talents and energies to yet another empirical study. No one could ask for better fellow travelers—and friends.

The 2001 project opened up new lines of inquiry, requiring participation by people with expertise in diverse specialties. We are grateful to Dr. David Himmelstein and Dr. Steffie Woolhandler, both of the Harvard Medical School, for their contributions on health care finance issues. We wish to thank Dr. Susan Wachter, of the Wharton School, University of Pennsylvania, and Professor Michael Schill, of the New York University Law School, for structuring the research on housing policy issues. We thank Professors Bruce Markell and Robert Lawless, University of Nevada–Las Vegas, for developing the interview questions for the self-employed. Their substantial contributions transformed the Consumer Bankruptcy Project into a richly complex, multifaceted study.

In addition, three former students (now moving into academic positions in their own right) served at different times as project directors: Katherine Porter provided the energy and enthusiasm to help design and initiate the data collection and see the project take life. Professor John Pottow added expertise as we began the work on court records. Professor Deborah Thorne completed the data collection and painstakingly assured the accuracy of the data. Each enriched and strengthened the Consumer Bankruptcy Project, and we express our thanks for their hard work.

Everyone associated with the project benefited from the continuing support of Alex Warren, who designed and managed the database with great skill. He was always willing to do "just one more run" and always alert to new ways to test our hypotheses. We are grateful for his help.

The bankruptcy judges and trustees made data collection possible. We offer our lasting thanks to the Honorable Keith Lundin, of the United States Bankruptcy Court for the Middle District of Tennessee, who provided the kind of advice and encouragement that makes empirical work possible, and to his very able assistant Cindy Odle, who did much of the ground work in Tennessee. We are also grateful for the support and cooperation of the chief judges of the districts we studied: the Honorable Steven Felsenthal, the Honorable Bruce Fox, the Honorable Lee Jackwig, the Honorable Carol Kenner, the Honorable Geraldine Mund, and the Honorable Susan Sonderby. We also appreciate the ready cooperation of the Office of the United States Trustee and the Assistant United States Trustees, the individual bankruptcy trustees, and the bankruptcy clerks of Boston, Chicago, Dallas, Des Moines, Los Angeles, Nashville, and Philadelphia. We owe them an incalculable debt. Without their generous contributions of time and energy to this project, there would have been no 2001 Consumer Bankruptcy Project.

We owe other debts as well. Eric Keil, an economist at the Bureau of Labor Statistics, was a patient and resourceful guide through much of the government data, and we offer our thanks. We also thank Margaret Brinig, Brenda Cossman, David Himmelstein, Michael Schill, Teresa Sullivan, Susan Wachter, Brady Williamson, and Steffie Woolhandler for reading and commenting on chapter drafts and suggesting additional data sources. Jean Avnet Morse provided thoughtful advice across a range of topics, making literally hundreds of useful suggestions that have made this a better book. Bruce H. Mann read the entire draft and listened to endless interpretations of the data; he provided wise counsel, gentle advice, and unconditional support, for which we publicly acknowledge our gratitude.

This book reports on original data from the Consumer Bankruptcy Project, but it also incorporates data from more than three dozen other data sources, both public and private. We were blessed with superb research assistance from Harvard Law School students who added their energy to this project by helping us track down particularly elusive data and by fact checking our findings. Yolanda Rodriquez, Harvard Law '03, was a thoroughgoing professional, working through citations and locating financial data. James Hart, Harvard Law '04, also checked references, while he dug into various calculations and engaged in spirited conversations about how best to understand the federal data. Daniel Ebner, Harvard Law '04, rechecked all the Consumer Bankruptcy Project data runs, assuming the huge task of verifying their accuracy down to the second decimal point. Lea Krivinskas, Harvard Law '04, tirelessly verified hundreds of facts. Angie Littwin, Harvard Law '02; Susan Lee, Harvard Law '02; Amy McNutt, Harvard Law '04; Nathan Oman, Harvard Law '03; Michael Roh, Harvard Law '04; and Daniel Volchok, Harvard Law '03, also provided important assistance with the research work. Catherine Dick, Harvard Law '05, was the lifesaver at the end whose creativity, initiative, and old-fashioned spunk helped us locate the last statistics we needed. To Yolanda, James, Dan, Lea, Angie, Sue, Amy, Nate, Mike, Dan, and Cassie—we say thank you for your hard work, your good brains, and your cheerful approach to difficult research assignments.

Our agent, Susan Rabiner, and our editor, Jo Ann Miller, have provided sound guidance. Their enthusiasm for the project has kept us warm, and their experience has kept us on track. Ann Deville, Cathleen Ellis, Candace Taylor, and Randi Segatore have given first-rate technical support, an addition of great value. Frank Carrere was our talented project photographer.

NOTES

Chapter 1

1. Ruth Ann and James and the other families whose stories appear in this book were interviewed as part of the 2001 Consumer Bankruptcy Project. In order to protect their privacy, all names and identifying information have been altered. See the appendix for more information.

2. My two longtime coauthors are Teresa A. Sullivan, a sociologist and now executive vice chancellor of the University of Texas, and Jay Lawrence Westbrook, a legal scholar who holds the Benno C. Schmidt Chair in Law at the University of Texas School of Law. For more on our earlier work, see the appendix.

3. The 1981 data are based exclusively on court records, which do not list marital status. We have therefore treated women filing alone as unmarried; joint filers are married. In 2001, since marital status is listed, this simplification is not needed. See more detailed discussion in chapter 5.

4. In 2001, the bankruptcy filing rate for couples with children was 14.7 per 1,000, compared with 7.3 for couples without children. For unmarried women with children, the filing rate was 21.3 per 1,000, compared with 7.2 for childless women and 6.1 for childless men.

5. The bankruptcy rolls increased rapidly during the late 1980s and again in the late 1990s, both of which were expansionary periods. Bankruptcy data from Administrative Office of the United States Courts.

6. This projection is based on a linear regression of personal bankruptcies in the United States between 1980 and 2002. The R-squared value was 0.937. This calculation assumes that the proportion of bankrupt families with children remained constant throughout this period. Based on these assumptions, 5.1 million families with children, or 13.5 percent of all households with children, would file for bankruptcy between 2003 and 2010.

7. In 2002, 2 million people filed for bankruptcy (including both husbands and wives who filed jointly). By comparison, 1.1 million Americans had a first or a recurrent coronary attack. American Heart Association, "Targeting the Facts: Our

Quick Guide to Heart Disease, Stroke and Risks" (2002). Available at http://www.americanheart.org/downloadable/heart/1014993119046targetfact.pdf [2/14/2003]. Approximately 1,284,900 new cancer cases were diagnosed. American Cancer Society, "Cancer Facts and Figures 2002." Available at http://www.cancer.org/downloads/STT/CancerFacts&Figures2002TM.pdf [2/14/2003]. In 2001, American universities and colleges awarded 1.2 million bachelor's degrees. U.S. Department of Education, National Center for Education Statistics, Table 247, Earned Degrees Conferred by Degree-Granting Institutions, by Level of Degree and Sex of Student: 1869–70 to 2010–11 (August 2001). Available at http://nces.ed.gov/pubs2002/digest2001/tables/dt247.asp [2/14/2003]. In 2001, there were 1.1 million divorces in the United States, compared with 1.5 million bankruptcy filings. Calculated from Centers for Disease Control and Prevention, "Births, Marriages, Divorces, and Deaths: Provisional Data for 2001," National Vital Statistics Report, vol. 50, no. 14 (September 11, 2002). Bankruptcy data from Administrative Office of the United States Courts, including unpublished data on joint filings.

8. "Late Payers," Cardweb.com (October 22, 2002). Available at http://www.cardweb.com/cardtrak/news/2002/october/22a.html [2/14/03].

9. Harvey Altes, the CEO of Time Finance Adjusters Inc., a trade association of accredited repossessors, "estimated that between 1998 and 2002 the number of cars repossessed nationally doubled from 1.2 million to around 2.5 million." Adam Fifield, "For the Repo Man, These Are Good Times: The Sluggish Economy Makes for Busy Nights in a Ticklish Job," *Philadelphia Inquirer*, December 29, 2002.

10. The proportion of mortgages in foreclosure proceedings at the end of the quarter increased from 0.31 percent in 1979 to 1.1 percent in 2002, an increase of 255 percent. Unpublished data, Foreclosure at End of Quarter, Mortgage Bankers of America (2002). For homeowners who were initially backed by FHA single-family mortgage insurance between 1982 and 2000, married couples with children were, on average, 39 percent more likely to undergo foreclosure by 2002 than married couples without children. Single parents were 28 percent more likely than single individuals without children. U.S. Department of Housing and Urban Development (HUD), unpublished data, FHA Single-Family Mortgage Insurance Cumulative Number and Percent of Foreclosures, 1982–2002.

11. Michelle J. White, "Why It Pays to File for Bankruptcy: A Critical Look at the Incentives Under U.S. Personal Bankruptcy Law and a Proposal for Change," *University of Chicago Law Review* 65 (Summer 1998), 685–732.

12. Among families in bankruptcy, 92 percent include a filer who completed at least some college (57 percent), held a job in the upper 80 percentile of occupational prestige (70 percent), and/or owned a home (58 percent). Two-thirds of filers met two or more criteria, and 27 percent met all three. Elizabeth Warren, "Financial Collapse and Class Status: Who Goes Bankrupt?" *Osgood Hall Law Review* 41, no. 1 (2003).

13. Our projection of the number of bankruptcies by single mothers between 2003 and 2010 is based on a linear regression of the number of women filing alone for bankruptcy in 1981 and 1991 and the number of single mothers filing in 2001. Chapter 5 has a further discussion of single mothers who file for bankruptcy.

14. Lillian P. Rubin, *Worlds of Pain: Life in the Working-Class Family* (New York: Basic Books, 1976). "Men manage the money in three-quarters of the [middle-class] families" (p. 107). Quoted in Deborah K. Thorne, "Personal Bankruptcy Through the Eyes of the Stigmatized: Insight into Issues of Shame, Gender, and Marital Discord," Ph.D. dissertation, Department of Sociology, Washington State University, Pullman, WA, May 2001.

15. Three-quarters of wives were exclusively responsible for assembling the necessary paperwork for credit counseling. Thorne, "Personal Bankruptcy Through the Eyes of the Stigmatized," p. 190. Similarly, we found that among families in bankruptcy, wives were about twice as likely as husbands to be exclusively responsible for paying the bills and dealing with bill collectors. Thorne concludes that once families get into financial trouble, the burden of "debt management and bankruptcy is overwhelmingly shouldered by women; husbands sidestep and off-load the responsibilities" (p. 219).

16. W. Jean Yeung and Sandra L. Hofferth, "Family Adaptations to Income and Job Loss in the U.S." *Journal of Family and Economic Issues* 19, no. 3 (Fall 1998): 255–283.

17. Foreclosure data, see HUD, unpublished data, 1982–2002. Custody was awarded to the wife in 72 percent of cases, compared with just 10 percent of awards going to the husband. The remainder were joint awards or awards to someone other than one of the spouses. Advance Report of Final Divorce Statistics 1989–1990. Available at http://www.cdc.gov/nchs/products/pubs/pubd/mvsr/supp/44–43/44–43.htm#43_9s [5/2/2003].

Chapter 2

1. John de Graaf, David Waan, and Thomas H. Naylor, *Affluenza: The All-Consuming Epidemic* (San Francisco: Barrett-Koehler, 2001), p. 13.

2. Graaf, Waan, and Naylor, *Affluenza,* p. 13.

3. Juliet B. Schor, *The Overspent American: Upscaling, Downshifting, and the New Consumer* (New York: Basic Books, 1998), p. 20.

4. Robert H. Frank, *Luxury Fever: Why Money Fails to Satisfy in an Era of Excess* (New York: Free Press, 1999), p. 45.

5. Schor, *The Overspent American,* p. 21.

6. Graaf, Waan, and Naylor, *Affluenza,* back cover.

7. Schor, *The Overspent American,* p. 11.

8. The Bureau of Labor Statistics maintains the Consumer Expenditure Survey (CES), a periodic set of interviews and diary entries that analyze the spending behav-

ior of over 20,000 consumer units. For much of our analysis we compare the results of the 1972–1973 CES with those of the 2000 CES. In some instances, we use prepublished tables from the 1980 or the 2000 survey in order to use the most comparable data available. We gratefully acknowledge the valuable assistance of Eric Keil, an economist at the Bureau of Labor Statistics, in locating and interpreting these data.

9. All comparisons of expenditures and income are adjusted for inflation using the Inflation Calculator, U.S. Department of Labor, Bureau of Labor Statistics. Available at www.bls.gov/cpi/home.htm [1/22/2003].

10. Daniel McGinn, "Maxed Out," *Newsweek*, August 27, 2001, p. 37.

11. U.S. Department of Labor, Bureau of Labor Statistics (BLS), *Consumer Expenditure Survey: Interview Survey, 1972–1973* (1997), Table 5, Selected Family Characteristics, Annual Expenditures, and Sources of Income Classified by Family Income Before Taxes for Four Person Families; *Consumer Expenditures in 2000,* BLS Report 958 (April 2002), Table 4, Size of Consumer Unit: Average Annual Expenditures and Characteristics, Consumer Expenditure Survey 2000 (data are for four-person families). See also Mark Lino, "USDA's Expenditures on Children by Families Project: Uses and Changes Over Time," *Family Economics and Nutrition Review* 13, no. 1 (2001): 81–86. According to USDA estimates, the total amount of money an average family will spend on clothing for a child between birth and age eighteen decreased 38 percent between 1960 and 2000 (Lino, p. 84).

12. Graaf, Waan, and Naylor, *Affluenza,* p. 28.

13. BLS, *Consumer Expenditure Survey: Interview Survey, 1972–1973,* Table 5; *Consumer Expenditures in 2000,* Table 4. See also Eva Jacobs and Stephanie Shipps, "How Family Spending Has Changed in the U.S.," *Monthly Labor Review* 113 (March 1990): 20–27.

14. Graaf, Waan, and Naylor, *Affluenza,* p. 28.

15. BLS, *Consumer Expenditure Survey: Interview Survey, 1972–1973,* Table 5; *Consumer Expenditure Survey, 2000* (prepublished data), Table 1400, Size of Consumer Unit: Average Annual Expenditures and Characteristics (data are for four-person families).

16. Walter L. Updegrave, "How Are We Doing? So Far, So Good. But Prosperity in the '90s Means Meeting Seven Basic Goals," *Money,* Fall 1990, p. 20.

17. BLS, *Consumer Expenditure Survey: Interview Survey, 1972–1973,* Table 5; *Consumer Expenditure Survey, 2000,* Table 1400.

18. BLS, *Consumer Expenditure Survey: Interview Survey, 1972–1973,* Table 5; *Consumer Expenditure Survey, 2000,* Table 1400. Electronics comparison includes expenditures on televisions, radios, musical instruments, and sound equipment. Computer calculation includes computer hardware and software.

19. For example, in 2000 the average family of four spent an extra $290 on telephone services. On the other hand, the average family spent nearly $200 less on floor coverings, $210 less on dry cleaning and laundry supplies, and $240 less on to-

bacco products and smoking supplies. BLS, *Consumer Expenditure Survey: Interview Survey, 1972–1973,* Table 5; *Consumer Expenditure Survey, 2000,* Table 1400.

20. Total revolving debt (which is predominantly credit card debt) increased from $64,500,000 in 1981 to $692,800,000 in 2000. SMR Research Corporation, *The New Bankruptcy Epidemic: Forecasts, Causes, and Risk Control* (Hackettstown, NJ, 2001), p. 14. Bankruptcy data calculated from data reported by Administrative Office of the United States Courts, Table F2 (total nonbusiness filings), 1980–2002.

21. Carolyn Setlow, "Home: The 'New' Destination," *Point of Purchase,* July 1, 2002.

22. Today the median sale price for an existing home is more than $150,000—up 32 percent in inflation-adjusted dollars from 1975. Joint Center for Housing Studies, Harvard University, *The State of the Nation's Housing, 2002* (Cambridge, MA, 2002), Table A-1, Housing Market Indicators, 1975–2001.

23. In 2001, 78.8 percent of married couples with children were homeowners. U.S. Department of Housing and Urban Development, Office of Policy Development and Research. U.S. Housing Market Conditions (Fourth Quarter, 2002), Table 30, Homeownership Rates by Household Type, 1983–Present. Although the data are not reported for subgroups, presumably this rate was lower for low-income families, and even higher for middle- and upper-income families. In the general population, middle-income households are 34 percent more likely than low-income households to own a home. Calculated from Joint Center for Housing Studies, *State of the Nation's Housing,* Table A-9.

24. Patric H. Hendershott, "Are Real House Prices Likely to Decline by 47 Percent?" *Regional Science and Urban Economics* 21, no. 4 (1991): 553–563. See also N. Gregory Mankiw and David N. Weil, "The Baby Boom, the Baby Bust, and the Housing Market," *Regional Science and Urban Economics* 19, no. 2 (1989): 235–258. Jonathan R. Laing, "Crumbling Castles: The Recession in Real Estate Has Ominous Implications," *Barron's,* December 18, 1989.

25. Updegrave, "How Are We Doing?" p. 20.

26. Joint Center for Housing Studies, *State of the Nation's Housing,* Table A-1.

27. The proportion of owner-occupied houses twenty-five years or older grew from 40 percent in 1975 to 59 percent in 1999. U.S. Department of Commerce, Bureau of the Census, *American Housing Survey, 1999,* Current Housing Reports, H150/99 (October 2000), Table 3-1, Introductory Characteristics—Owner Occupied Units; *American Housing Survey: 1975, General Housing Characteristics,* Current Housing Reports, H-150-75A (April 1977), Table A1, Characteristics of the Housing Inventory, 1975 and 1970.

28. Bureau of the Census, *American Housing Survey: 1975, General Housing Characteristics,* Current Housing Reports, H-150-75A, Table A1; *American Housing Survey, 1997,* Current Housing Reports, H150/97 (October 2000), Table 3-3, Size of Unit and Lot—Owner Occupied Units.

29. Bureau of the Census, *American Housing Survey: 1975, General Housing Characteristics,* Current Housing Reports, H-150-75A, Table A1; *American Housing Survey, 1999,* Current Housing Reports, H150/99, Table 3-3.

30. BLS, *Consumer Expenditure Survey, 1984*, Table 5, Composition of Consumer Unit. BLS, *Consumer Expenditure Survey, 2001*, Table 5, Composition of Consumer Unit, Average annual expenditures and characteristics . Data are mean estimated market value of owned home for "husband and wife only" consumer units. Similarly, the American Housing Survey shows that homeowners with no unmarried children (including both single and married homeowners) experienced a 20 percent increase in median home value between 1985 and 2001. *American Housing Survey for the United States in 1985*, Current Housing Reports, H-150-85 (December 1988), Table 3-22, Value by Selected Characteristics—Owner Occupied Units. *American Housing Survey for the United States: 2001*, Annual Survey (2001), Table 3-22, Value by Selected Characteristics—Owner Occupied Units.

31. BLS, *Consumer Expenditure Survey, 1984*, Table 5. BLS, *Consumer Expenditure Survey, 2001*, Table 5. Data are mean estimated market value of owned home for married couples with oldest child under age 6. We have focused on couples with young children because they are typically new entrants into the housing market and therefore feel most acutely increases in housing prices. Couples with the oldest child between age 6 and 17 also experienced a significant (though somewhat smaller) increase in average home value during this period, of 58 percent. The American Housing Survey indicates a somewhat less dramatic rise in median home values, showing that the average homeowner with two young children saw a 37 percent real increase in median home value between 1985 and 2001, compared with a 20 percent increase for homeowners without children. *American Housing Survey for the United States in 1985*, Current Housing Reports, H-150-85 (December 1988), Table 3-22. *American Housing Survey for the United States: 2001*, Annual Survey (2001), Table 3-22. The difference between BLS and American Housing Survey data may in part be due to the fact that BLS data separates married couples, whereas American Housing Survey lumps together both married and single homeowners. AHS data may be skewed by the growing number of single mothers, who live in much smaller and less expensive homes than their married counterparts, thus reducing the average amount spent by households with children.

32. BLS, *Consumer Expenditure Survey, 1980*, prepublished Table 5, Selected Characteristics and Annual Expenditures of All Consumer Units Classified by Composition of Consumer Unit, Interview Survey, 1980; *Consumer Expenditure Survey, 1999* (prepublished data), Table 1500, Composition of Consumer Unit: Average Annual Expenditures and Characteristics (data are for husband and wife with children).

33. "Americans Put Education at Top of Federal Spending Priorities," *Public Agenda Online,* April 2001. Available at http://www.publicagenda.org/issues/majprop.cfm?issue_type=education [1/20/2003].

34. See, for example, Arthur Levine, "American Education: Still Separate, Still Unequal," *Los Angeles Times,* February 2, 2003, p. M1.

35. David E. Clark and William E. Herrin, "The Impact of Public School Attributes on Home Sale Prices in California," *Growth and Change* 31 (Summer 2000): 385–407. "The elasticity of teacher-student ratio is nearly 8 times that of murder rate and just over 10 times that of the largest environmental quality measure [proximity to interstate]."

36. Sandra E. Black, "Do Better Schools Matter? Parental Valuation of Elementary Education," *Quarterly Journal of Economics* 114 (May 1999): 577–599.

37. The University of Pennsylvania made other modest investments in the neighborhood, including hiring trash collectors to remove litter from the streets and employing neighborhood safety "ambassadors." Those initiatives, however, did not represent major changes, since the university had already been policing the area for several years; many locals agree that the new elementary school was by far the most important change. Caitlin Francke, "Penn Area Revival Lures Many, Pushes Others Out," *Philadelphia Inquirer,* February 24, 2003.

38. George H. Gallup, "The Eleventh Annual Gallup Poll of the Public's Attitudes Toward the Public Schools," *Phi Delta Kappan* (September 1979), p. 37. "More Than Half of Americans Say Public Education Is Worse Today Than When They Were Students," *Public Agenda Online* (April 2000), available at http://www.publicagenda.org/issues/pcc_detail.cfm?issue_type=education&list=16 [1/20/2003].

39. Black parents are almost three times more likely than other parents to report that they are "completely dissatisfied" with the quality of their children's schools. Lydia Saad, "Grade School Receives Best Parent Ratings, Education Nationally Gets Modest Ratings," *Gallup Poll Analyses,* September 4, 2002.

40. Juliet Schor, *Do Americans Shop Too Much?* (Boston: Beacon Press, 2000), p. 11.

41. Thomas D. Snyder and Charlene M. Hoffman, *Digest of Education Statistics, 2001,* NCES 2001-130 (U.S. Department of Education, National Center for Education Statistics, February 2002), Table 150, Percent of Public Schools Reporting Crime Incidents and the Seriousness of Crime Incidents Reported, by School Characteristics, 1996–1997.

42. U.S. Department of Justice, Bureau of Justice Statistics, *Sourcebook of Criminal Justice, 2000,* NCJ 190251 (December 2001), Table 2.0001, Students Age 12 to 18 Reporting Fear of School-Related Victimization.

43. For a discussion of the financial effects of restrictive zoning, see Michael Schill, "Regulatory Barriers to Housing Development in the United States," in *Land Law in Comparative Perspective,* edited by Maria Elena Sanchez Jordan and Antonio Gambara (The Hague: Kluwer Law International, 2002), pp. 101–120.

44. "Violent Crime Fell 9% in '01, Victim Survey Shows," *New York Times,* September 9, 2002; the article cites a 50 percent decline in violent crime since 1993.

45. U.S. Department of Justice, *1995 Uniform Crime Reports* (1996), cited in Setha M. Low, "The Edge and the Center: Gated Communities and the Discourse of Urban Fear," *American Anthropologist* 103 (March 2001): 45–58. In a 1975 survey of homeowners, the U.S. Census Bureau found that people living in city centers were 38 percent more likely to complain of crime in their neighborhoods than their suburban counterparts. Today urban dwellers are 125 percent more likely than suburbanites to cite crime in their neighborhoods. Bureau of the Census, *American Housing Survey: 1975, Indicators of Housing and Neighborhood Quality*, Current Housing Reports, H-150-75B (February 1977), Table A-4, Selected Neighborhood Characteristics, 1975; *American Housing Survey, 1999*, Current Housing Reports, H150/99 (October 2000), Table 3-8, Neighborhood—Owner Occupied Units.

46. Danilo Yanich, "Location, Location, Location: Urban and Suburban Crime on Local TV News," *Journal of Urban Affairs* 23, no. 3-4 (2001): 221–241, Table 2, Rates of Selected Crimes in Baltimore and Philadelphia, 1977 and 1996.

47. Yanich, "Location, Location, Location," p. 222.

48. While this is not exclusively an urban-suburban dichotomy, urban dwellers are more than twice as likely as suburbanites to say that the public elementary schools are so bad that they would like to move. Similarly, parents who have young children and own homes in urban areas are almost 70 percent more likely to be unsatisfied with the public elementary schools in their neighborhoods than those living in the suburbs. Bureau of the Census, *American Housing Survey, 1999*, Current Housing Reports, H150/99, Table 3-8.

49. Lawrence Mishel, Jared Bernstein, and Heather Boushey, *The State of Working America, 2002–03* (Ithaca, NY: Cornell University Press, 2003) p. 103.

50. See, for example, Congressional Research Service, *Women and Credit: Synopsis of Prospective Findings of Study on Available Legal Remedies Against Sex Discrimination in the Granting of Credit and Possible State Statutory Origins of Unequal Treatment Based Primarily on the Credit Applicant's Sex or Marital Status.* Prepared for the Subcommittee on Consumer Affairs, House Committee on Banking and Currency; *Hearings on Credit Discrimination*, by Sylvia L. Beckey, U.S. House of Representatives, 93rd Congress, 2nd sess., May 2, 1974; and Margaret J. Gates, "Credit Discrimination Against Women: Causes and Solutions," *Vanderbilt Law Review* 27 (1974): 409–441.

51. Federal Trade Commission, *Equal Credit Opportunity*. Information sheet for consumers, available at http://www.ftc.gov/bcp/conline/pubs/credit/ecoa.htm [1/20/03].

52. Mark Evan Edwards, "Home Ownership, Affordability, and Mothers' Changing Work and Family Roles," *Social Science Quarterly* 82 (June 2001): 369–383; Sharon Danes and Mary Winter, "The Impact of the Employment of the Wife on the Achievement of Home Ownership," *Journal of Consumer Affairs* 24, no. 1 (1990): 148–169.

53. In a survey of 1,000 working mothers, 80 percent reported that their main reason for working was to support their families. Carin Rubenstein, "The Confident Generation: Working Moms Have a Brand New Attitude," *Working Mother,* May 1994, p. 42.

54. Calculated from Bureau of the Census, *Historical Income Tables—Families,* Current Population Survey, various Annual Demographic Supplements, Table F-14, Work Experience of Husband and Wife—All Married-Couple Families, by Presence of Children Under 18 Years Old and Median and Mean Income: 1976 to 2000.

55. Kristin Smith, Barbara Downs, and Martin O'Connell, "Maternity Leave and Patterns: 1961–1995," *Household Economic Studies,* U.S. Census Bureau, November 2001, Table I, Women Working at a Job, by Monthly Interval After First Birth, 1961–65 to 1991–94.

56. Stephanie Coontz, *The Way We Never Were: American Families and the Nostalgia Trap* (New York: Basic Books, 1992), p. 162.

57. Between 1979 and 2000, married mothers at all income levels increased their hours in the workforce. However, women whose husbands were in the bottom quintile added 334 hours per year, and those in the top quintile added just 315 hours per year, compared with an average increase of 428 hours per year for women in the middle three quintiles. Calculated from *The State of Working America 2002–2003,* Table 1.32, Annual Hours, Wives in Prime-Age, Married-Couple Families with Children, and Contributions to Change, 1979–2000, Sorted by Husband's Income.

58. Coontz, *The Way We Never Were,* p. 168.

59. Chris McComb, "Few Say It's Ideal for Both Parents to Work Full Time Outside of Home," Gallup News Service, April 20–22, 2001.

60. Both women and men who did not finish high school saw declines in real wages over the past twenty years. By contrast, among college graduates, women's earnings have increased 30 percent since 1979, while men's earnings have increased by 17 percent. U.S. Department of Labor, "Highlights of Women's Earnings in 2000," Report 952, August 2001, Table 15, Median Usual Weekly Earnings of Full-Time Wage and Salary Workers 25 and Over in Constant (2000) Dollars, by Sex and Educational Attainment, 1979–2000 Annual Averages.

61. Median earnings, which are the best measure of middle-class wages, have risen less than 1 percent for men since the early 1970s, while women's earnings have increased by more than one-third. Bureau of the Census, *Historical Income Tables—People,* Current Population Survey, various Annual Demographic Supplements. Available at http://www.census.gov/hhes/income/histinc/incperdet.html [1/5/2003], Table P-36, Full-Time, Year-Round Workers (All Races) by Median Income and Sex, 1955 to 2000.

62. Barbara J. Lipman, Center for Housing Policy, "Paycheck to Paycheck: Working Families and the Cost of Housing in America," *New Century Housing* 2 (June 2001): 24–26.

63. As we discuss in chapter 6, the proportion of middle-income families who would be considered "house poor" has quadrupled since 1975. Bureau of the Census, *Annual Housing Survey for the United States and Regions, 1975, Part C, Financial Characteristics of the Housing Inventory,* Annual Survey (1977), Table A-1, Income of Families and Primary Individuals in Owner and Renter Occupied Housing Units, 1975. Available at http://www.census.gov/prod/www/abs/h150.html [3/10/2003]; *American Housing Survey for the United States: 2001,* Annual Survey (2001), Table 2-20, Income of Families and Primary Individuals by Selected Characteristics—Occupied Units. Available at http://www.census.gov/hhes/www/housing/ahs/ahs01/tab313.html [3/4/2003]. In addition, the Consumer Expenditure Survey indicates that mortgage payments as a proportion of income has increased considerably since the early 1970s. Many indexes that measure housing affordability have shown no clear trend. These indices, however, typically calculate a *theoretical* housing cost, based on such factors as current mortgage rates and an imputed down payment amount. As a result, the indices are extremely sensitive to fluctuations in interest rates, ignoring the fact that many families have fixed-rate mortgages and do not refinance during periods of high interest. Similarly, these indexes typically assume that all buyers get a conventional mortgage, which ignores the extraordinary rise in high-cost subprime mortgages in recent years. Furthermore, they assume that the typical down payment has held constant over the past generation, when in fact first-time home buyers are putting down far smaller down payments today than twenty years ago. See, for example, Bureau of the Census, "Who Could Afford to Buy a House in 1995?" Table 4-2, Affordability Status of Families and Unrelated Individuals for a Modestly Priced Home, by Current Tenure and Type of Financing, United States, 1984, 1988, 1991, 1993, and 1995. See also Joint Center for Housing Studies, *State of the Nation's Housing,* Table A-3. We continue to believe that the best evidence of real housing costs is the direct data on what families report they are actually paying.

64. BLS, *Consumer Expenditure Survey: Interview Survey, 1972–1973,* Table 5; *Consumer Expenditure Survey, 2000,* Table 1400. Note that in 2000, 74 percent of married couples with children owned their own homes; in 1972/73 this figure was 71 percent. In order to isolate the effects of changing supply and demand for owner-occupied housing, this calculation only accounts for changes in mortgage expenditures (including both interest and principal) by families who owned their own homes. Federal Reserve data produce similar results (see above).

65. Martha Minow argues that "daring changes" are needed to increase parental involvement and promote accountability in the schools. *Partners, Not Rivals: Privatization and the Public Good* (Boston: Beacon Press, 2003).

66. Laurent Belsie, "Preschools Are Popping at the Seams," *Christian Science Monitor,* July 9, 2002, p. 13.

67. Belsie, "Preschools Are Popping at the Seams," p. 13.

68. Children's Defense Fund, *Key Facts: Essential Information About Child Care, Early Education, and School-Age Care* (Washington, DC: CDF, 2000).

69. Anna Quindlen, "Building Blocks for Every Kid," *Newsweek*, February 12, 2001.

70. Vicki Iovine, *The Girlfriends' Guide to Toddlers: A Survival Manual to the "Terrible Twos" (and Ones and Threes) from the First Step, the First Potty, and the First Word ("No") to the Last Blankie* (New York: Berkley Publishing Group, 1999): 240.

71. Suzanne Helburn et al., *Cost, Quality, and Child Care Outcomes in Child Care Centers* (Denver: Center for Research in Economic and Social Policy, University of Colorado at Denver, 1995).

72. National Council of Jewish Women, *Opening a New Window on Child Care: A Report on the Status of Child Care in the Nation Today* (New York: NCJW, 1999), p. 6.

73. Kate N. Grossman, "Pre-kindergarten Lures Middle Class to Public School," *Chicago Sun-Times*, June 10, 2002; in-state tuition and fees at the University of Illinois are $5,748. University of Illinois Web site, at http://www.oar.uiuc.edu/current/tuit.html [12/19/2002].

74. Karen Schulman, *The High Cost of Child Care Puts Quality Care Out of Reach for Many Families* (Washington, DC: Children's Defense Fund, 2000), Table A-1, Comparison of Average Annual Child Care Costs in Urban Area Centers to Average Annual Public College Tuition Costs.

75. See, for example, Center on Education Policy, "Gore's Preschool and Child Care Proposals," Policy Paper (Washington, DC: CEP, June 2000).

76. "Landing a Man on the Moon: The Public's View," *Gallup Poll Analyses*, July 20, 1999.

77. John Immerwahr and Tony Foleno, Center for Public Policy and Higher Education, *Great Expectations: How the Public and Parents—White, African American, and Hispanic—View Higher Education* (Washington, DC: Public Agenda, May 2000), Table 1.

78. Immerwahr and Foleno, *Great Expectations*, Table 3.

79. Immerwahr and Foleno, *Great Expectations*, p. 1.

80. "57 Percent of UW Freshmen in Top 10 Percent of Class," *Wisconsin State Journal*, August 5, 2002.

81. A private college education costs $25,300 a year, about half the entire annual income for an average, middle-class family. Thomas D. Snyder and Charlene M. Hoffman, *Digest of Education Statistics, 1999*. NCES 2000-031 (Washington, DC: U.S. Department of Education, National Center for Education Statistics, March 2000), Table 317, Average Undergraduate Tuition and Fees and Room and Board Rates Paid by Full-Time Equivalent Students in Institutions of Higher Education, by Type and Control of Institution, 1964–65 to 1998–99.

82. Immerwahr and Foleno, *Great Expectations*, Table 1.

83. U.S. Department of Education, National Center for Education Statistics, *Digest of Education Statistics, 1999*, Table 317.

84. BLS, *Consumer Price Index Detailed Tables, Annual Averages, 2001*. Available at http://www.bls.gov/cpi/cpid01av.pdf [12/19/2002]. Table 1A, Consumer Price

Index for All Urban Consumers: City Average, by Expenditure Category and Commodity and Service Group. Thomas D. Snyder and Charlene M. Hoffman, *Digest of Education Statistics, 1999*. NCES 2000-031 (Washington, DC: U.S. Department of Education, National Center for Education Statistics, March 2000), Table 240, Average Salary of Full-Time Instructional Faculty on 9-month Contracts in Institutions of Higher Education, by Academic Rank, Sex, and Control and Type of Institution, 1970–71 to 1997–98.

85. Snyder and Hoffman, *Digest of Education Statistics, 1999*, Table 317; Bureau of the Census, *Historical Income Tables—Families*, Current Population Survey, various Annual Demographic Supplements. Table F-10, Presence of Children Under 18 Years Old by Type of Family—Families by Median and Mean Income. Available at http://www.census.gov/hhes/income/histinc/incfamdet.html [1/22/2003].

86. Immerwahr and Foleno, *Great Expectations*, Table 8.

87. American Council on Education, *The Cost of College: Perceptions, Reality, and Value*. ACE Issue Brief (Washington, DC: ACE, January 1997): 3–4. The Report cites a number of causes for rising costs, including economic market conditions, state budget cuts, financial aid, student expectations, scientific needs, regulatory compliance, and an increase in the federal minimum wage.

88. American Council on Education and National Affairs, "Hearing Focuses on Rising College Tuition," *Higher Education and National Affairs*, July 29, 1996, p. 2.

89. *Statement of the American Association of University Professors to the National Commission on the Cost of Higher Education*, October 1997, p. 3.

90. American Council on Education, *The Cost of College*, p. 3.

91. Charles T. Clotfelter, *Buying the Best: Cost Escalation in Elite Higher Education* (Princeton, NJ: Princeton University Press, 1996), pp. 188–198.

92. James L. Schulman and William G. Bowen, *The Game of Life: College Sports and Educational Values* (Princeton, NJ: Princeton University Press, 2001), pp. 244–245.

93. Daniel L. Fulks, *Revenues and Expenses of Division I and II Intercollegiate Athletics Programs: Financial Trends and Relationships—1999* (Indianapolis: National Collegiate Athletic Association, 2000). Between 1993 and 1999, the average deficit, excluding subsidies from the university's general funds, increased by 57 percent for Division I-AA colleges, by 127 percent for I-AAA colleges, and by 50 percent for Division II colleges.

94. Michael Arnone, "The Wannabes," *Chronicle of Higher Education*, January 3, 2003.

95. American Council on Education, "Senate Hearing Focuses on College Costs," *Higher Education and National Affairs*, February 14, 2000.

96. Immerwahr and Foleno, *Great Expectations*, p. 1.

97. U.S. Department of Education, "Accountability for Results Works: College Loan Default Rates Continue to Decline," press release, September 19, 2001.

Available at http://www.ed.gov/PressReleases/09-2001/09192001a.html [1/5/2003]. The Department of Education heralded the success of its programs to reduce the default rate on student loans, but the reduction does not mean that families can afford the loans. Student loans are almost never dischargeable in bankruptcy, so many have learned that they must pay their student loans even if it means losing the house, the car, and the furniture.

98. Stephen Burd, "How Much Is Too Much?" *Chronicle of Higher Education*, January 24, 2003.

99. Calculated from Glenn B. Canner, Thomas A. Durking, and Charles A. Lucket, "Recent Developments in Home Equity Lending," *Federal Reserve Bulletin*, April 1998.

100. Center for Public Policy and Higher Education, *Losing Ground: A National Status Report on the Affordability of American Higher Education* (San Jose, CA: National Center for Public Policy and Higher Education, 2002), p. 13; see also Snyder and Hoffman, *Digest of Education Statistics, 2001*, Table 331, Current Fund Revenue of Degree-Granting Institutions, by Source of Funds, 1919–20 to 1995–96. Current fund revenue at public universities from state, local, and federal tax appropriations increased 34 percent between 1980 and 1997, inflation adjusted.

101. BLS, *Consumer Expenditure Survey: Interview Survey, 1972–1973*, Table 5; *Consumer Expenditures in 2000*, Table 4.

102. Graaf, Waan, and Naylor, *Affluenza*, pp. 25–26.

103. According to the Bureau of Labor Statistics, the average four-person family had 1.7 vehicles a generation ago; today they have 2.5, an increase of nearly one (0.8) car per family. This is a big jump, but it isn't clear that over-consumption is to blame. The trick is in the averages. Many four-person families have more than two adults at home, such as a son in college, an elderly grandparent, or even a brother-in-law who doesn't have his own place. The number of adults in the average family of four is 2.4 today (up just slightly from 2.3 a generation ago). This means that the average family has shifted from owning 0.7 vehicles per adult to 1.0 vehicles per adult. In other words, as Mom headed to the office and families moved deeper into the suburbs, they did indeed splurge, seeing to it that each adult had his or her own vehicle so they could get to work, school, and market. BLS, *Consumer Expenditure Survey: Interview Survey, 1972–1973*, Table 5; *Consumer Expenditures in 2000*, Table 4.

104. Homeowners' median distance to work increased from 7.9 miles in 1975 to 10 miles in 1999. Bureau of the Census, American Housing Survey, 1975, General Housing Characteristics, Current Housing Reports H-150-75A, Table A1, Bureau of the Census, *American Housing Survey, 1999*, Current Housing Reports H150/99 (October 2000), Table 2-24, Journey to Work—Occupied Units.

105. U.S. Department of Energy, Office of Transportation, "Automobile Affordability, 1979–1999," *OTT Fact of the Week* 121, March 20, 2000. Available at www.ott.doe.gov/facts/archives/fotw121.shtml [12/19/2002].

106. Patricia S. Hu and Jennifer R. Young, *Summary of Travel Trends: 1995 Nationwide Personal Transportation Survey* (Washington, DC: U.S. Department of Transportation, Federal Highway Administration, December 1999), Table 20, Distribution of Vehicles by Vehicle Age and Vehicle Type, 1969, 1977, 1983, 1990, and 1995 NPTS (percentage of total vehicles).

107. BLS, *Consumer Expenditure Survey: Interview Survey, 1972–1973,* Table 5; *Consumer Expenditures in 2000,* Table 4.

108. "Volvo Saved My Life," *Volvo.com*. Available at http://new.volvocars.com/whyvolvo/why_save_my_life.asp [12/19/2002].

109. Melanie Haiken, "Car Seat Safety: How to Choose and Use a Car Seat: Why Does my Child Need a Booster Seat?" Parentcenter.com, http://www.parentcenter.com/refcap/39413.html [12/19/2002].

110. Insurance Institute for Highway Safety, *Fatality Facts—Children, 2001* (Arlington, VA: IIHS, October 2001).

111. Bureau of the Census, *Historical Income Tables—People,* Table P-36.

112. BLS, *Consumer Expenditure Survey: Interview Survey, 1972–1973,* Table 5. In 1972/73, the average family of four spent $160 (inflation adjusted to $640) on private health insurance (not including expenditures on Medicare). However, 38 percent of these families spent nothing whatsoever on health insurance, typically because they were uninsured, although in some cases because they were covered by a government program such as Medicaid or because they had a particularly generous employer who paid the entire bill. In order to get a more accurate picture of the average health insurance burden on a middle-income, insured family (who would not typically qualify for Medicaid), we have included in our calculation only those families who spent at least $1 on health insurance. For our estimate for a middle-class family's typical expenditures on health insurance, the calculation is as follows: $640 (average expenditures on health insurance) divided by 62 percent (the portion of families who reported expenditures on private health insurance) = $1,027.

113. Average mortgage principal and interest paid by a home-owning, four-person family; for methodology, see note 64 above. BLS, *Consumer Expenditure Survey: Interview Survey, 1972–1973,* Table 5.

114. BLS, *Consumer Expenditure Survey: Interview Survey, 1972–1973,* Table 5. As we noted earlier, the average family of four actually owned 1.7 vehicles in 1972/73 and 2.5 vehicles in 2000. We also noted, however, that the average family of four has 2.5 adults. A family with more than two adults is presumably more likely to have more vehicles, while a family with two or fewer adults would have fewer vehicles. Since our focus here is on the nuclear family with two adults and two young children, we assume, for simplicity's sake, that the family owns just one car in 1972/73 and just two cars in 2000. We will use this calculation again in chapter 5 when we calculate the postdivorce budget.

115. Claire M. Hintz, *The Tax Burden of the Median American Family,* Tax Foundation Special Report 96 (Washington, DC: Tax Foundation, March 2000),

Table 1, Taxes and the Median One-Income American Family. For our 1973 calculation, we apply the Tax Foundation's estimate of the tax rate for a single-income family in 1975. This report has the only data we can locate that attempts to estimate the entire state, local, and federal tax burden on middle-income families, using a consistent methodology over the past forty years. Most other estimates only account for federal income taxes, which underrepresents the true tax burden on families, and most offer only current estimates, without historical context. In addition, this report differentiates between the tax burdens on two-income and one-income families, which is critical for this analysis. We have made a few minor adjustments to the Tax Foundation's basic methodology. First, we have omitted employer-paid payroll taxes from both the income and the tax burden calculations. This does not change the comparison between 1973 and 2000 in any substantial way, but it prevents us from the need to gross up income by including the employer's contribution to payroll taxes, only to have that income deducted on the tax side. Second, we use median wages for a fully employed male, rather than median income for a single-income family, as the basis for applying the taxes, in order to be consistent with our model—a married couple in which the male was employed. The results should be quite similar either way: In 1975, the Tax Foundation reported that the median income for a single-income family was $12,560; according to the U.S. Census Bureau, median earnings for full-time, year-round male workers was $12,934 that year—a difference of less than 3 percent—which would indicate that a family living on median earnings for a fully employed male would be in roughly the same tax bracket as the family living on the median income for all one-income families. Third, we have adjusted the Tax Foundation calculations by omitting imputed corporate taxes, again avoiding the problem of overstating income by including an imputed distribution from corporate profits only to have that amount then deducted in taxes. Imputed corporate income taxes are from Ed Harris, David Weiner, and Roberton Williams, "Effective Federal Tax Rates, 1979–1997" (Washington, DC: Congressional Budget Office, Tax Analysis Division, October 2001). We have not included any itemized deductions, since average tax burdens already account for average deduction levels, and there would be a considerable risk of double-counting a family's deductions.

116. Bureau of the Census, *Historical Income Tables—People,* Table P-36.

117. BLS, *Consumer Expenditure Survey, 2000,* Table 1400. For methodology, see note 64 above.

118. Kristin Smith, *Who's Minding the Kids? Child Care Arrangements: Spring 1997*, Bureau of the Census, Current Population Reports P70-86 (July 2002), Table 6, Average Weekly Child Care Expenditures by Employed Mothers of Children 5 to 14, Spring 1999. Day-care costs are calculated from average child-care costs for mothers employed full-time with a child aged five to fourteen, and preschool costs are calculated from average child-care costs for mothers employed full-time with a child under five.

119. BLS, *Consumer Expenditure Survey, 2000,* Table 1400. The calculation of health insurance and car costs was made in the same manner as the calculation for 1972/73; see notes 112 and 114 above.

120. Hintz, *The Tax Burden of the Median American Family*. For our 2000 calculation, we apply the Tax Foundation's estimate of the tax rate for a two-income family in 1998, the most recent year for which this calculation was available. Because they own a more expensive home than their one-income counterparts in the early 1970s, the two-income family pays more property taxes in 2000, in addition to higher income taxes. See note 115 for an explanation of methodology.

121.

TABLE Typical budget, four-person family

	Tom and Susan *Single-income family, early 1970s* (Inflation adjusted)	**Justin and Kimberly** *Dual-income family, early 2000s*	*Percentage change*
Husband's income	$38,700	$39,000	1%
Wife's income	0	$28,800	1000%++
Total Family Income	**$38,700**	**$67,800**	**75%**
Tax rate (% of income: local, state, and federal)	24%	33%	35%
Taxes	$9,386	$22,256	137%
After-tax income	**$29,314**	**$45,544**	**55%**
Major fixed expenses			
Home mortgage	$5,309	$8,978	69%
Day care (7-year-old)	$0	$4,354	1000%++
Preschool (3-year-old)	$0	$5,321	1000%++
Health insurance	$1,027	$1,653	61%
Automobile: Car 1 (Purchase, upkeep, insurance)	$5,144	$4,097	-20.4%
Automobile: Car 2	$0	$4,097	1000%++
Total fixed expenses	**$11,480**	**$28,499**	**148%**
Discretionary income (food, clothes, utilities, extras, etc.)	**$17,834**	**$17,045**	**-4%**

(Note that all figures were rounded off to the nearest $10 in the text.)

122. Only 52 percent of all families have a retirement account. Ana Aizcorbe, Arthur Kennickell, and Kevin Moore, "Recent Changes in U.S. Family Finances: Evidence from the 1998 and 2001 Survey of Consumer Finances," *Federal Reserve Bulletin,* January 2003, Table 5B, Family Holdings of Financial Assets, by Selected Characteristics of Families and Type of Assets, 2001 Survey of Consumer Finances.

Chapter 3

1. Rosalind C. Barnett and Caryl Rivers, *She Works/He Works: How Two-Income Families Are Happier, Healthier, and Better-Off* (San Francisco: HarperSanFrancisco, 1996), pp. 2, 5.

2. In 1973, the median income for a woman who worked full-time, year-round was $6,488, or $21,913 adjusted for inflation to 2000 dollars. U.S. Census Bureau, Table P-36, Full-Time, Year-Round Workers (All Races) by Median Income and Sex: 1955 to 2000. Available at http://landview.census.gov/hhes/income/histinc/p36.html [1/10/2003]. A longtime stay-at-home wife with fewer skills might have earned somewhat less than the median income on entering the workforce. Such differences, however, should be relatively modest. In the late 1970s, for example, women in their early twenties (who were presumably less experienced than average) earned only 12 percent less than the median income for all working women. In addition, middle-class women generally had higher levels of education than many lower-income working mothers. U.S. Department of Labor, "Highlights of Women's Earnings in 2000," August 2001, Table 13.

3. Unemployment Insurance Fact Sheet, Department of Labor. Available at http://workforcesecurity.doleta.gov/unemploy/uifactsheet.asp.

4. There have been conflicting studies of what sociologists call "the added worker effect," that is, the magnitude and direction of changes in workforce participation of wives of unemployed men. For example, some researchers have examined whether a wife's labor force participation increases in the same year of or in the year immediately following the husband's unemployment, and found no significant effect. See, for example, Tim Maloney, "Unobserved Variables and the Elusive Added Worker Effect," *Economica* 58 (May 1991): 173–187; see also W. Jean Yeung and Sandra L. Hofferth, "Family Adaptations to Income and Job Loss in the U.S.," *Journal of Family and Economic Issues* 19 (Fall 1998): 255–283. However, more recent research has shown that wives' entrance into the workforce is gradual, beginning one or more years before a husband's job loss and continuing for multiple years after the job loss. When this is taken into account, a significant "added worker effect" has been documented. See Melvin Stephens Jr., "Worker Displacement and the Added Worker Effect," National Bureau of Economic Research, Working Paper 8260 (April 2001).

5. See Stephens, "Worker Displacement and the Added Worker Effect." Stephens found that the greater the number of children under age six, the less likely the wife was to increase her participation in the workforce. See also Jonathan Gruber and Julie Berry Cullen, "Spousal Labor Supply as Insurance: Does Unemployment Insurance Crowd Out the Added Worker Effect?" National Bureau of Economic Research, Working Paper 5608 (June 1996).

6. Black women living in areas of high unemployment are less likely to increase their participation in the workforce, presumably because of the difficulty in finding a job. See Yeung and Hofferth, "Family Adaptations to Income and Job Loss."

7. A wife is significantly more likely to increase her hours in the workforce if her husband suffers a large wage loss than if he finds a new job with similar or higher wages. See Stephens, "Worker Displacement and the Added Worker Effect." As the duration of a husband's unemployment increased, the probability that his wife would enter the workforce nearly doubled. Craig B. Little, "Technical-Professional Unemployment: Middle-Class Adaptability to Personal Crisis," *Sociological Quarterly* 17 (Spring 1976): 262–274; interviews were conducted with 100 unemployed male technical-professional workers during the aerospace-defense-electronics recession of early 1972. See also Gruber and Cullen, "Spousal Labor Supply as Insurance," in which the authors argue that unemployment insurance tends to crowd out spousal labor supply: "Our estimates imply that in the absence of [unemployment insurance], wives' total hours of work would rise by 30% during their husbands' spells of unemployment."

8. See Stephens, "Worker Displacement and the Added Worker Effect."

9. Shannon Brownlee, Matthew Miller, Susannah Fox, Amy Saltzman, Brendan I. Koerner, and Jason Vest, "Lies Parents Tell Themselves About Why They Work," *U.S. News & World Report*, May 12, 1997.

10. William R. Johnson and Jonathan Skinner, "Accounting for Changes in the Labor Supply of Recently Divorced Women," *Journal of Human Resources* 23 (Fall 1988): 417–436; U.S. Census Bureau, Table F-7, Type of Family (All Races) by Median and Mean Income, 1947 to 2001. Available at http://landview.census.gov/hhes/income/histinc/f07.html [1/10/2003].

11. Robyn Stone, Gail Lee Cafferata, and Judith Sangl, "Caregivers of the Frail Elderly: A National Profile," *Gerontologist* 27 (October 1987): 616–626.

12. Sociologists have documented immediate adjustments families make during a period of unemployment, noting that families often reduce their food expenses or postpone major household purchases. See Rand D. Conger and Glen H. Elder Jr., *Families in Troubled Times: Adapting to Change in Rural America* (New York: Aldine De Gruyter, 1994). See also Yeung and Hofferth, "Family Adaptations to Income and Job Loss," pp. 269–276.

13. Betty Friedan, *The Feminine Mystique* (New York: W. W. Norton, 1984), pp. 206–207 (emphasis omitted).

14. This is the title of a book edited by renowned conservative Phyllis Schlafly: *Who Will Rock the Cradle? The Battle for Control of Child Care in America* (Nashville, TN: W Publishing Group, 1990).

15. IRAs and 401(k) plans, which allow workers to set aside pretax earnings for retirement, are the best-known examples. In addition, employer-sponsored Flexible Spending Accounts enable workers to put pretax dollars aside for qualified medical expenses. The Economic Growth and Tax Relief Reconciliation Act of 2001 grants federal tax exemption on earnings from state education saving plans when the money is used to pay for qualified higher education expenses.

16. "Saving the Wealthy," *Baltimore Sun,* February 7, 2003.

17. SMR Research Corporation, *The New Bankruptcy Epidemic: Forecasts, Causes, and Risk Control* (Hackettstown, NJ, 2001), 94.

Chapter 4

1. 147 Cong. Rec. S1934 (2001) (statement of Sen. Hatch). Available at www.senate.gov/~hatch, "Statements," April 15, 1999.

2. 147 Cong. Rec. S1934 (2001) (statement of Sen. Hatch).

3. Henry J. Hyde, News Advisory, U.S. House of Representatives, Committee on the Judiciary (March 10, 1999). Available at http://www.house.gov/judiciary/031099a.htm [3/14/2003].

4. "Administration of the Bankruptcy Act," *Report of the Fifty-third Annual Meeting of the American Bar Association Held at Chicago, Illinois, August 20, 21, and 22, 1930* (statement of Hon. Thomas D. Thacher, Solicitor General of the United States), p. 255. In the 1930s, Yale University researchers teamed up with the Department of Commerce to study the rise in personal bankruptcies. Their conclusion? The stigma associated with bankruptcy "has been gradually diminishing." Victor Sadd and Robert T. Williams, *Causes of Bankruptcies Among Consumers* (Washington, DC: Government Printing Office, 1933), p. 5.

5. Cotton Mather, *Fair Dealing Between Debtor and Creditor* (Boston: 1716): "People there are, too many, who do bring Debts upon themselves, in such a manner, and in such a measure, that a Folly nothing short of Criminal, is to be charged upon them. And when they have brought such Debts upon themselves, their Delay to get from under them, is what also amounts unto a Crime, for which they are to be Indicted, as not having the Fear of God before their Eyes."

6. Thorough histories of the early republic, such as Bruce Mann's *A Republic of Debtors: Bankruptcy in the Age of American Independence* (Cambridge, MA: Harvard University Press, 2002), are replete with stories of the battles between debtors and creditors, and the canny ways in which each side tried to outmaneuver the other.

7. In one paper, the authors claim that stigma could be measured on a state-by-state basis. The authors identify several measurable economic factors, then claim that any rise in bankruptcy filings that is not explained by those economic factors must be caused by a decline in stigma. For example, they suggest that the people of Tennessee (who have relatively higher bankruptcy filing rates) must feel less shame than the people of Hawaii (who have relatively lower bankruptcy filing rates). See Scott Fay, Erik Hurst, and Michelle J. White, "The Bankruptcy Decision: Does Stigma Matter?" Working Paper 98-01, Department of Economics, University of Michigan (January 1998). In a later paper, the same authors use similar data to show that families who could benefit the most from bankruptcy (that is, the families whose debts are highest relative to their assets and state law exemptions) are most

likely to file for bankruptcy, thus proving—at least to these authors—that these families are somehow "strategic" in their use of bankruptcy, which supposedly means they feel no stigma. Scott Fay, Erik Hurst, and Michelle J. White, "The Household Bankruptcy Decision," *American Economic Review* 92 (June 2002): 706–718. Another study takes a similar approach, explaining as much of the variation in the use of credit cards as possible on the basis of economic factors, then declaring that families were more likely to file for bankruptcy in 1997 than they had been in 1995 because of a decline in stigma during that two-year period. David B. Gross and Nicholas S. Souleles, "An Empirical Analysis of Personal Bankruptcy and Delinquency," 98-28-B, Financial Institutions Center, the Wharton School, University of Pennsylvania (November 1999). Other researchers look at social factors as well as economic factors. For example, one study focuses on the role of religion. The study assumes that Catholics have more moral qualms about filing for bankruptcy than, say, Methodists, Jews, or agnostics. F. H. Buckley and Margaret F. Brinig, "The Bankruptcy Puzzle," *Journal of Legal Studies* 27 (January 1998): 187–207.

8. Fay, Hurst, and White, "The Household Bankruptcy Decision." The Panel Study of Income Data, a long-term study of family finances conducted by the University of Michigan, is held up as about as perfect a cross-section of American households as researchers can construct. Only aggregate data are reported, and individual responses are held in the strictest confidence. The families in the study willingly share information about their incomes, their purchases, their debts, their investments, and scores of other financial data with the researchers. And yet, when these families were asked about whether they had filed for bankruptcy, only about half of the predicted number confessed to a bankruptcy filing. Either the sample is badly skewed, which no researcher has claimed, or the families concealed their bankruptcy filings. The authors report these facts, although they do not draw the inference that the study subjects were reluctant to report their bankruptcy filings.

9. Michelle J. White, "Why It Pays to File for Bankruptcy: A Critical Look at the Incentives Under U.S. Personal Bankruptcy Law and a Proposal for Change," *University of Chicago Law Review* 65 (Summer 1998): 685–732. White shows that about 17 percent of U.S. households would profit from filing for bankruptcy—and yet, for some reason (presumably at least somewhat influenced by a sense of shame or stigma), they don't file. Despite this finding, White is one of the coauthors of another paper (cited above) claiming that stigma has declined.

10. Congressman Rick Boucher is one of many who have used this term: "Bankruptcies of convenience are driving this increase [in bankruptcy filings]. Bankruptcy was never meant to be used as a financial planning tool, but it is becoming a first stop rather than a last resort. . . ." Congressman Rick Boucher, Hearing on Bankruptcy Reform and Financial Services Issues, Senate Banking Committee (March 25, 1999). Available at http://banking.senate.gov/99_03hrg/032599/boucher.htm [3/14/2003].

11. 147 Cong. Rec. S2374 (2001) (statement of Sen. Murray).

12. Constance M. Kilmark, "Inside the World of the Troubled Debtor," *Journal of Bankruptcy Law and Practice* 10 (March-April 2001): 257–278.

13. The exact figure is 84.3 percent of the families interviewed.

14. Judge Edith H. Jones and Todd J. Zywicki, "It's Time for Means-Testing," *Brigham Young University Law Review* (February 1999): 177–249.

15. The bankruptcy laws have their own section of the United States Code, 11 U.S.C. sections 101 et seq. Within that section are the various "chapters." The first chapters in the code lay out rules applicable to all bankruptcies. Chapter 7 governs the liquidation bankruptcies of both individuals and businesses, Chapter 11 deals primarily with business reorganizations, Chapter 12 governs the restructuring of family farms, and Chapter 13 is for families trying to repay debts over time.

16. Businesses may file for Chapter 11 if they want to try to reorganize, or Chapter 7 if they are to be liquidated immediately.

17. 11 U.S.C. section 541.

18. The variation is extreme. Half of all the states have exemptions of $20,000 or less, and six states permit multimillion-dollar exemptions. The National Bankruptcy Review Commission recommended that Congress put a floor and a ceiling on homestead exemptions. At various times, the Senate proposed to cap homestead exemptions pegged variously at $125,000 to $250,000, although the House rejected such caps. But neither the House nor the Senate ever moved to create any floor for homestead exemptions. For many families with high mortgages relative to value, the exemption debate is a distant abstraction: They have no home equity to protect.

19. 11 U.S.C. section 523.

20. 11 U.S.C. sections 727(a)(8) and (a)(9). The law is more specific: A debtor is eligible for a discharge only after six years have passed. In fact, many families file for Chapter 13, try to make payments, and then drop out of the system when they cannot pay. They received no discharge, so they are eligible to file again. In our study, 5 percent of the Chapter 7 filers had filed for bankruptcy at least once before, and 31 percent of the Chapter 13 filers had been in bankruptcy previously, presumably filing, refiling once, and even refiling a second time, trying to get their financial lives straightened out.

21. 11 U.S.C. section 1325(b).

22. 11 U.S.C. section 1328(a).

23. In 1981, the median nonmortgage debt-to-income ratio for families in bankruptcy was 0.79. In 1991, the ratio had climbed to 1.06. In 2001, the ratio was 1.5.

24. *Personal Bankruptcy: A Literature Review*, CBO Papers (September 2000). Available at http://www.cbo.gov/showdoc.cfrm?index=2421&sequence=0 [3/3/2003], See Marianne Culhane and Michaela White, "Taking the New Consumer Bankruptcy Model for a Test Drive: Means Testing Real Chapter 7 Debtors," *American Bankruptcy Institute Review* (Spring 1999): 28–75. In a sam-

ple of 1,041 Chapter 7 cases, the authors found only six debtors who could repay their debt. See discussion in chapter 6.

25. Adam Fifield, "For the Repo Man, These Are Good Times: The Sluggish Economy Makes for Busy Nights in a Ticklish Job," *Philadelphia Inquirer,* December 29, 2002. The rate of mortgage foreclosure increased from 0.31 percent in 1979 to 1.1 percent in 2002. Unpublished data, "Foreclosure at End of Quarter, U.S. (Unadjusted %)," Mortgage Bankers Association of America (2002).

26. Statement of Senator Orrin Hatch Before the United States Senate Committee on the Judiciary (May 21, 1998). Available at http://judiciary.senate.gov/oldsite/ogh52198.htm [3/14/2003]: "[The proposed bankruptcy bill] has new safeguards against the fraud and abuse that costs hardworking Americans." The American Bankers Association estimates that 10 percent of all bankruptcy filings (approximately 150,000 filings in 2001) are fraudulent. Eric Gillin, "Events Conspire Against Bankruptcy Reform," *The Street.com,* posted January 10, 2002. Available at http://www.thestreet.com/markets/ericgillin/10006456.html [3/14/2003]. "What we have a problem with are the individuals who understand how the system works but choose to abuse it, and we estimate that's about 10 percent of all bankruptcy filers," said Catherine Pulley, spokeswoman for the American Bankers Association. *All Things Considered,* National Public Radio, July 26, 2002. The industry meaning of "fraud and abuse" is fairly aggressive: The industry also claims that about 10 percent of all families currently in Chapter 7 (or 7 percent of bankrupt families overall) could pay *something* to their creditors if they went on a stringent, court-imposed budget for five years. Evidently failure to pay that "something" by giving up every dollar of disposable income to creditors is, according to this group, "fraudulent." It is important to note that the credit industry does not accuse these families of any acts that would be considered fraudulent in a legal sense, such as providing false information on a credit application, violating the bankruptcy laws, or lying under oath. Indeed, there is no accusation that these families have deceived anyone (which is usually the meaning of "fraud"), either the courts or their creditors. The industry claims of how many families could repay has never been corroborated by any independent source. See discussion in chapter 6.

27. 18 U.S.C. sections 152, 157.

28. For a more detailed discussion of how a bankruptcy case is initiated, see Teresa A. Sullivan, Elizabeth Warren, and Jay Lawrence Westbrook, *As We Forgive Our Debtors: Bankruptcy and Consumer Credit in America* (New York: Oxford University Press, 1989), pp. 20–45.

29. Many of the families in the bankruptcy system go to high-volume attorneys who advertise widely and who make their money by standardizing procedures and minimizing the time the attorney spends with the client. Often called "bankruptcy mills," these law offices may or may not give good legal advice, but it is clear that what they tell their clients is fairly routinized. See, e.g., Teresa A. Sullivan, Eliza-

beth Warren, and Jay Westbrook, "The Persistence of Local Legal Culture: Twenty Years of Evidence from the Bankruptcy Courts," *Harvard Journal of Law and Public Policy* 17 (1994): 846–850; reprinted in Charles J. Tabb, *Bankruptcy Anthology* (Westbury, NY: Foundation Press, 2002).

30. In 1980 there were 291,000 personal bankruptcies, just 19 percent of the 1.5 million personal bankruptcies that were filed in 2002. If fraud alone accounted for the entire increase in bankruptcy filings, then there would have been more than 1.2 million (1.5 million minus 291,000) fraudulent filings in 2002—or 80 percent of the total filings.

31. Among bankrupt families with children, 71.5 percent report a job loss, a reduction of income, or other job-related problem as a reason for filing. Fifty-three percent report a medical problem, which includes all filers who reported $1,000 or more in unpaid medical bills, who had at least two weeks of unpaid leave from work because of an illness or disability, or who explained that they filed for bankruptcy because of a medical problem. Family breakup, cited by 19 percent of families with children, includes those who reported "divorce or family breakup" as a cause of bankruptcy. Families with children cite at least one of these problems in 86.9 percent of all cases. The remaining 13.1 percent give either a different reason or no reason at all.

32. Johanne Boisjoly, Greg J. Duncan, and Timothy Smeeding, "The Shifting Incidence of Involuntary Job Losses from 1968 to 1992," *Industrial Relations* 37 (April 1998): 207–231, Figure 4. From 1968 to 1979, the average annual rate of job loss because of layoffs or company closing among men aged twenty-five to fifty-nine was 2.5 percent.

33. This calculation assumes that husbands and wives face roughly the same risk of getting laid off in a single year. See, e.g., Peter Gottschalk and Robert Moffitt, "Job Instability and Insecurity for Males and Females in the 1980s and 1990s," Working Paper 408, Department of Economics, Boston College (January 1999), p. 9. The authors found that men and women had similar rates of job exits during the period 1981–1991.

34. For simplicity's sake, this calculation assumes no correlation in the risk of job loss between husbands and wives. In fact, there is some evidence that the likelihood that a husband and a wife will both lose their jobs is weakly correlated. Husbands and wives tend to work in the same geographical area, for example, so both may face increased chances of layoff at the same time; also, they sometimes work for the same employer, who may cut back many jobs at once. As a result, the estimate in the text may slightly overstate the portion of couples in which one spouse loses a job. At the same time, however, it necessarily underestimates the proportion of couples experiencing a job loss for both spouses in a single year.

35. See Boisjoly, Duncan, and Smeeding, "The Shifting Incidence of Involuntary Job Losses." The authors found a 28 percent increase in the incidence of involuntary

job loss between the 1968–1979 period and the 1980–1992 period. See also Daniel Polsky, "Changing Consequences of Job Separation in the United States," *Industrial and Labor Relations Review* 52 (July 1999): 565–580. Both studies found evidence that workers were more likely to lose their jobs in the 1980s and 1990s than they were in the 1970s. There is some evidence that the job loss rate improved during the expansion of the late 1990s. See Henry S. Farber, "Job Loss in the United States, 1981–1999," Working Paper 453, Industrial Relations Section, Princeton University (June 2001). That trend, however, may have reversed during the 2001–2002 recession, when mass layoffs were 40–50 percent higher than in the 1996–1999 period. Statistics from the U.S. Department of Labor, Bureau of Labor Statistics, Archived News Releases for Extended Mass Layoffs. Available at http://0-www.bls.gov.library.csuhayward.edu/schedule/archives/mslo_nr.htm [3/14/2003]. There are no published studies that compare involuntary terminations during the 1970s with the early 2000s, so we have chosen, for simplicity's sake, to document the increase between the 1970s and the early 1990s, and then to assume that the 2000s rate is comparable to that of the 1980s and early 1990s. We note, however, that sociologists and labor economists have not come to a consensus about the incidence of job loss over the past generation. Their empirical findings differ, depending on the data sets they use, the specific variables on which they focus, and the populations they examine. Several studies using the Panel Study of Income Dynamics (PSID) data detected a rise in involuntary job losses in the 1980s and 1990s compared with the 1970s. Researchers relying on Current Population Survey (CPS) data have found little increase in job instability overall, although they have noted rising instability for certain subgroups. For a review of the literature, see, e.g., John Fitzgerald, "Job Instability and Earnings and Income Consequences: Evidence from SIPP 1983–1995," Economics Department, Bowdoin College (July 26, 1999), paper prepared for the Joint Center for Poverty Research. We also note that we have not accounted for differences in age or skill among workers. Younger parents may actually be more likely to suffer a job loss, because of a relative lack of work experience. See Boisjoly, Duncan, and Smeeding, "The Shifting Incidence of Involuntary Job Losses."

36. Although most studies focus exclusively on men, we assume that husbands and wives, both working full-time, face an equal chance of job loss. This places the odds that one spouse would lose a job at 3.2 percent from 1980 to 1992. See Boisjoly, Duncan, and Smeeding, "The Shifting Incidence of Involuntary Job Losses." We assume once again that there is no correlation between the chances of job loss between husbands and wives. We have not accounted for possible changes in the odds of job loss after 1992; see previous note.

37. Fully 79 percent of married women who file for bankruptcy are in the labor force, compared with 62 percent of married women in the general population. Bureau of the Census, Table F-7, Type of Family (All Races) by Median and Mean Income, 1947 to 2000, February 8, 2002.

38. Among two-income families filing for bankruptcy, about 83.3 percent identified a job problem as leading to their bankruptcy. Among married couples with only one income, the percentage identifying a job problem was 74.6 percent. Among single filers, that is, men and women who filed for bankruptcy without a spouse, the proportion identifying a job problem is even lower: 63.6 percent.

39. Among all respondents, 68.0 percent identify a job problem in the two-year period before they filed for bankruptcy. In 2001, this amounted to an estimated 1,047,000 households in bankruptcy in the aftermath of a job problem.

40. Rosalind C. Barnett and Caryl Rivers, *She Works/He Works: How Two-Income Families Are Happier, Healthier, and Better-Off* (San Francisco: HarperSanFrancisco, 1996), pp. 2, 5. See discussion in chapter 3.

41. John M. Broder, "Problem of Lost Health Benefits Is Reaching into the Middle Class," *New York Times*, November 25, 2002.

42. D. U. Himmelstein, S. Woolhandler, and O. Carrasquillo, unpublished analysis of data from the Current Population Survey and the National Health Interview Survey.

43. Comparisons between bankruptcy filers in the early 1980s and today are difficult, because no one collected precisely the same data then as now. The best comparative estimate can be made from a 1981 survey that the San Antonio courts required of all families who filed for bankruptcy, which shows that about 8 percent of the filers cited a medical reason for filing. Sullivan, Warren, and Westbrook, *As We Forgive Our Debtors*, p. 175, n. 1. Extrapolating that sample to all filers in 1980 would suggest that about 23,000 families filed for bankruptcy in the wake of a medical problem. Other reports from about the same time estimate a lower number of medical-related bankruptcies, but they rely exclusively on court records to identify medical debt still outstanding at the time of filing and do not ask the debtors directly what happened. For example, a 1978 study in Albany, New York, found that medical bills constituted less than 2 percent of scheduled debts, but the study was based entirely on identifying medical bills in court records. B. A. Gold and E. A. Donahue, "Health Care and Personal Bankruptcy," *Journal of Health Politics and Law* 7 (1982): 734–739. For comparability to the 1981 data, the 2001 calculation includes only families who specifically identified a medical reason, thus excluding those who identified lost time at work because of medical problems. That subset would suggest that about 424,500 families in 2002 filed because of an identified medical reason—more than a twentyfold increase. For more information on current filings for medical reasons, see David Himmelstein, Deborah Thorne, Elizabeth Warren, and Steffie Woolhandler, "Illness and Injury as a Cause of Bankruptcy in the United States" (forthcoming, 2003).

44. Bureau of the Census, Current Population Reports, Special Studies, P23-190, *65+ in the United States*, 1996, Table 2-1, Elderly Population by Age: 1900–2050.

45. Twenty-two percent of working parents report receiving at least one hour of unpaid assistance from their own parents each month, compared with 38 percent of

working parents who report providing at least one hour of unpaid assistance to their own parents each month. Jody Heymann, *The Widening Gap: Why America's Working Families Are in Jeopardy and What Can Be Done About It* (New York: Basic Books, 2000), pp. 103–104.

46. In 2000, there were 36 million hospital discharges in the United States. Centers for Medicare and Medicaid Services, Health Care Indicators, Table 1, Selected Community Hospital Statistics, 1998–2002.

47. In 2001, approximately 27,500 single-income couples, or 0.13 percent of all single-income couples in the United States, filed for bankruptcy after missing two or more weeks of work without pay because of the illness of the worker or of another family member. By comparison, 82,800 two-income couples, or 0.25 percent of the total, filed for bankruptcy after missing work because of illness.

48. Approximately 43 percent of marriages end in divorce. Data from the National Center for Health Statistics, cited in Margaret F. Brinig and Steven L. Nock, "Marry Me, Bill: Should Cohabitation Be the Default Option?" paper prepared for the Emory Series on Marriage and Religion, March 2003.

49. Barnett and Rivers, *She Works/He Works,* p. 22.

50. Scott J. South, "Time-Dependent Effects of Wives' Employment on Marital Dissolution," *American Sociological Review* 66 (April 2001): 226–245. See also Steven L. Nock, "When Married Spouses Are Equal," *Virginia Journal of Social Policy and the Law* 9 (Fall 2001): 48–70. Nock found that marriages between equally dependent spouses (defined as marriages in which each spouse earns at least 40 percent of the total family income) are 57 percent more likely than other marriages to end in divorce.

51. For a discussion of contributors to changing divorce rates among working and nonworking women, see South, "Time-Dependent Effects."

52. Bureau of the Census, Table CH-5, Children Under 18 Years Living With Mother Only, by Marital Status of Mother: 1960 to Present (June 29, 2001).

53. The number of unmarried, opposite-sex-couple households with children under age fifteen increased from 204,000 in 1977 to 1.7 million in 2000. Bureau of the Census, Table UC-1, Unmarried-Couple Households, by Presence of Children: 1960 to Present (2001). In 2000 there were 27.1 million married couples with children under eighteen. Bureau of the Census, Table F-10, Presence of Children Under 18 Years Old by Type of Family and Median and Mean Income, 1974–2001.

54. Larry Bumpass and Hsien-Hen Lu, "Trends in Cohabitation and Implications for Children's Family Contexts in the United States," *Population Studies* 54 (2000): 29–41.

55. Wendy D. Manning and Pamela J. Smock, "The Relative Stability of Cohabiting and Marital Unions for Children," unpublished paper (2002). See also Larry L. Bumpass and James A. Sweet, "National Estimates of Cohabitation," *Demography* 26 (November 1989): 615–625. Cited in Renata Forste, "Prelude to Marriage or Al-

ternative to Marriage? A Social Demographic Look at Cohabitation in the U.S.," Symposium on the ALI's Family Dissolution Principles: Blueprint to Strengthen or to Deconstruct Families? Brigham Young University, February 3, 2001. The authors found that 29 percent of cohabiting unions end within the first two years, compared with only 9 percent of marriages.

56. See, for example, W. Jean Yeung and Sandra L. Hofferth, "Family Adaptations to Income and Job Loss in the U.S.," *Journal of Family and Economic Issues* 19 (Fall 1998): 255–283.

57. Among families with children, 38.7 percent gave only one of these three reasons (job loss, medical problems, or a family breakup), 40.4 percent gave two reasons, and 7.8 percent identified all three reasons.

58. Among those in bankruptcy with out-of-pocket medical expenses of more than $1,000, 62.0 percent, or about 243,000 families, had continuous medical insurance coverage. Calculated from Himmelstein et al., "Illness and Injury as a Cause of Bankruptcy."

59. Calculated from Himmelstein et al., "Illness and Injury as a Cause of Bankruptcy."

60. Only 43 percent of workers have long-term disability coverage, and only 19 percent have at least six months of short-term coverage. Helen Levy, "Disability Insurance: Where Are the Gaps in Coverage?" unpublished paper (July 2002).

61. In Texas, for example, an individual "must be physically and mentally able to perform full time work" in order to qualify for unemployment benefits. Texas Workforce Commission, "Unemployment Insurance Benefits, Frequently Asked Questions." Available at http://m06hostp.twc.state.tx.us/CLAIMS/common/help.html#faqs [3/23/03].

62. The proportion of families reporting that the debtor or spouse lost two or more weeks without pay because of illness or injury was 21.3 percent.

63. U.S. Office of Personnel Management, "Long Term Care Insurance Background." Available at http://www.opm.gov/insure/ltc/ltcbackground.pdf [3/22/03].

64. Statement of Senator Orrin Hatch Before the United States Senate Committee on the Judiciary, S.1301—The Consumer Bankruptcy Reform Act of 1998 (May 21, 1998). Available at http://judiciary.senate.gov/oldsite/ogh52198.htm [3/22/03].

Chapter 5

1. Lenore J. Weitzman, *The Divorce Revolution: The Unexpected Social and Economic Consequences for Women and Children in America* (New York: Free Press, 1985): 323.

2. A subsequent analysis of Weitzman's data showed the decline for women to be 27 percent and an increase for men of 10 percent. Richard R. Peterson, "A Re-evaluation of the Economic Consequences of Divorce," *American Sociological Review* 61

(June 1996): 528, 532; see also Lenore J. Weitzman, "The Economic Consequences of Divorce Are Still Unequal: Comment on Peterson," *American Sociological Review* 61 (June 1996): 537; Richard R. Peterson, "Statistical Errors, Faulty Conclusions, Misguided Policy: Reply to Weitzman," *American Sociological Review* 61 (June 1996): 539. While Weitzman's study is controversial and her reported numbers are disputed, the overall effect of divorce on women and the greater economic suffering that divorce inflicts on women are generally well established in the scholarly literature.

3. Suzanne M. Bianchi, Lekha Subaiya, and Joan R. Kahn, "The Gender Gap in the Economic Well-Being of Nonresident Fathers and Custodial Mothers," *Demography* 36 (May 1999): 195–203.

4. Danielle Crittenden, *What Our Mothers Didn't Tell Us: Why Happiness Eludes the Modern Woman* (New York: Simon and Schuster, 1999): 133–134.

5. U.S. Department of Education, National Center for Education Statistics, Table 177, "Total Fall Enrollment in Degree-Granting Institutions, by Level of Enrollment, Sex, Attendance, Status, and Type and Control of Institution, 1999." Available at http://nces.ed.gov/pubs2002/digest2001/tables/dt177.asp [11/21/02].

6. Women now constitute 45 percent of managers, compared with just 18 percent in 1970. James Heintz, Nancy Folbre, and the Center for Popular Economics, *The Ultimate Field Guide to the U.S. Economy* (New York: New Press, 2000), p. 54; Diana Furchtgott-Roth and Christine Stolba, *Women's Figures: An Illustrated Guide to the Economic Progress of Women in America* (Washington, DC: AEI Press, 1999) p. 19; U.S. Department of Education, National Center for Education Statistics, Table 226.

7. Furchtgott-Roth and Stolba, *Women's Figures,* p. xvii.

8. In 2000, fully employed women with children under eighteen had median weekly earnings of $479, compared with $499 for women with no children. U.S. Department of Labor, Bureau of Labor Statistics, *Highlights of Women's Earnings in 2000,* BLS Report 952 (August 2001), Table 9.

9. Even though 2001 was a recession year, the unemployment rate among women, at less than 5 percent, was still lower than it was at any point during the 1970s. The number of women-owned businesses has grown from fewer than 1 million in 1972 to more than 8 million in 1997. Furchtgott-Roth and Stolba, *Women's Figures,* p. 37. The proportion of wives with higher annual earnings than their husbands nearly doubled in just sixteen years, from 11 percent in 1980 to 21 percent in 1996. Richard B. Freeman, "The Feminization of Work in the U.S.: A New Era for (Man)kind?" in *Gender and the Labor Market: Econometric Evidence on Obstacles in Achieving Gender Equality,* edited by Siv S. Gustaffson and Daniele E. Meulders (New York: Palgrave Macmillan, 2000), Table 1.4, Percentage of Women with Higher Earnings Than Their Husband, 1970–96.

10. In 1975, Congress passed Title IV-D of the Social Security Act, which expanded child support enforcement by states. The 1984 Child Support Enforcement

Amendments required states to withhold wages from noncustodial parents who fell behind in their child support payments. In 1988, Congress enacted immediate wage withholding, which went into effect in January 1994 for all new child support orders. For a discussion of child support enforcement reforms, see Elaine Sorensen and Ariel Halpern, "Child Support Enforcement: How Well Is It Doing?" Urban Institute, Assessing the New Federalism, Discussion Paper 99-11 (Washington, DC: Urban Institute, December 1999), pp. 11–16.

11. For example, a California assemblyman, James Hayes, was involved in a brutal alimony battle with his wife of twenty-five years at the same time he played a leadership role in the adoption of the California no-fault statute in the 1970s. At one point, he was able to cut his wife's alimony to $200 a month, with the trial judge telling her "to get a job," despite her having spent a quarter-century as a homemaker and having completed only one year of college. The decision was overturned on appeal. Allen M. Parkman, *No-Fault Divorce, What Went Wrong?* (Boulder: Westview Press, 1992), pp. 56–63; see also Weitzman, *The Divorce Revolution,* p. 211. A number of similar horror stories under Maryland's 1980 statute are told in a report of a 1986 study in Montgomery County, Maryland. Rosalyn B. Bell, "Alimony and the Financially Dependent Spouse in Montgomery County, Maryland," *Family Law Quarterly* 22 (Fall 1988): 225. In 1984, the federal government required states to adopt support guidelines, although judges were not required to follow them. In 1988, under the Family Support Act, Congress required states to make support guidelines binding on judges unless a written finding was issued.

12. Elaine Sorensen and Ariel Halpern, "Child Support Enforcement Is Working Better Than We Think," Urban Institute: New Federalism, Issues and Options for States, Series A, No. A-31 (March 1999), p. 4.

13. Elaine Sorensen and Ariel Halpern, "Child Support Enforcement."

14. The bankruptcy filing rate for single mothers is 21.3 per 1,000 compared with 14.7 for married parents, 7.2 for unmarried childless women, and 6.1 for unmarried childless men.

15. Federal Reserve Board, Survey of Consumer Finances, 1998 Full Public Dataset. Available at http://www.federalreserve.gov/pubs/oss/oss2/98/scf98home.html [1/5/2003].

16. U.S. Department of Housing and Urban Development, Federal Housing Authority Single Family Mortgage Insurance Foreclosures, Cumulative by Number and Percent, 1982–2002. Unpublished Data. More than 10 percent of FHA-insured mortgages issued to single parents and originated between 1982 and 1990 have since resulted in foreclosure. The foreclosure rate for mortgages issued in the early 1980s is more than one in four.

17. Teresa A. Sullivan, Elizabeth Warren, and Jay Lawrence Westbrook, *As We Forgive Our Debtors: Bankruptcy and Consumer Credit in America* (New York: Ox-

ford University Press, 1989). The 1981 data are based exclusively on court records, which listed only the type of case filed (joint petition or single petition), not the marital status of the person filing. We assumed that those filing jointly were married, as stipulated by the bankruptcy laws. Because there are significant legal advantages for a married couple to file on joint petition rather than two separate petitions, it is not unreasonable to assume that the single filers are not married or are separated. Data from 2001 suggest that a small number of the women who file for bankruptcy alone are in fact married, but this is offset by a small number who file jointly even though they are separated or divorced.

18. In 2000, 19.3 percent of not-married women were raising children on their own, compared with 16.9 percent in 1980. Calculated from data from U.S. Census Bureau, Table MS-1, Marital Status of the Population 15 Years Old and Over, by Sex and Race, 1950 to Present (June 29, 2001); Table FM-2, All Parent/Child Situations, by Type, Race, and Hispanic Origin of Householder or Reference Person, 1970 to Present (June 29, 2001). Available at http://landview.census.gov/population/socdemo/hh-fam/tabFM-2.txt [11/3/02].

19. In 1981, the filing rate per 1,000 was only 2.1 for women filing alone, compared with 4.3 for men filing alone and 2.7 for couples filing jointly, providing another indication that we are likely overstating the filing rates for unmarried mothers in bankruptcy in 1981 and therefore understating the magnitude of the increase over the past two decades. Calculated from data from Warren, Westbrook, and Sullivan, *As We Forgive Our Debtors*; Statistical Abstract of the United States 1984, Table 50, Marital Status of the Population, by Sex, 1940 to 1982, and Table 51, Marital Status of the Population, by Sex and Age, 1982.

20. Calculated from data available on number of bankruptcy filings in 2002 from the Administrative Office of the United States Courts; U.S. Census Bureau, Table F-10, Presence of Children Under 18 Years Old by Type of Family and Median and Mean Income, 1974 to 2000. Available at http://www.census.gov/hhes/income/histinc/f10.html [3/27/03].

21. Our projection is based on a linear regression of women filing for personal bankruptcy alone in the United States in 1981, 1991, and 2001. The R-squared value was 0.988. The calculation assumes that single mothers as a proportion of all single women filing for bankruptcy remained constant throughout this period. As we noted in the text, this assumption likely overstates the number of single women with children in the early 1980s and thus understates the growth in filings among this group from 1981 through 2001. The calculation also assumes that in 1981 and 1991 all single-filing women were not married and all joint-filing women were married. For 2001, actual marital status is used. Data for 1981 are from Warren, Westbrook, and Sullivan, *As We Forgive Our Debtors*. Data for 1991 are from Teresa A. Sullivan, Elizabeth Warren, and Jay Lawrence Westbrook, *The Fragile Middle Class: Americans in Debt* (New York: Oxford University Press, 2000).

22. Calculated from U.S. Census Bureau, Table F2, Family Households, by Type, Age of Own Children, Educational Attainment, and Race and Hispanic Origin of Householder, March 2000 (June 21, 2001). Available at http://landview.census.gov/population/socdemo/hh-fam/p20-537/2000/tabF2.pdf [12/3/02].

23. Fifty-six percent of single mothers in bankruptcy had occupational prestige scores in the middle 40 percent for women in the general population.

24. Bankruptcy data include current homeowners and women who lost their home in the past five years because of financial reasons. The home ownership rate among all single parents is from U.S. Department of Labor, Bureau of Labor Statistics, Consumer Expenditure Survey, 1999 (prepublished data), Table 1500, Composition of Consumer Unit: Average Annual Expenditures and Characteristics (data are for single person with children).

25. According to the papers she filed with the court, her workout with her mortgage lender required her to pay monthly mortgage costs (including back payments) of $1,435. In addition, she paid utility costs of $600 and property taxes of $2,700, for a total of $2,260 a month. Her take-home pay before her most recent raise was about $3,000 per month. Gayle later got a substantial raise, so the proportion of her paycheck dedicated to housing dropped to two-thirds of her total take-home pay.

26. "Full-time employment within marriage does not necessarily protect women from a declining standard of living after marital disruption. Full-time working women who contributed a relatively small amount to family income (either because of their own low wages or their husband's high wages) experienced much larger declines in living standards than other women. Whereas women who did not work or worked only part-time before separation could enter the workforce or increase the number of hours they worked, full-time working women would have a harder time increasing their incomes without further training." Bianchi, Subaiya, and Kahn, "The Gender Gap in the Economic Well-Being of Nonresident Fathers and Custodial Mothers," pp. 192–200.

27. During the 1980s and 1990s, child support payment levels among men who paid in full averaged 18 percent of their income. Patricia A. McManus and Thomas A. Diprete, "Losers and Winners: The Financial Consequences of Separation and Divorce for Men," *American Sociological Review* 66 (April 2001), footnote on p. 260. Other studies have shown that real average child support payments changed only modestly between the 1970s and the mid-1990s, so, for simplicity's sake, the same 18 percent estimate was used for the 1970s and the 2000 calculations. Anne Case, I-Fen Lin, and Sara McLanahan, "Understanding Child Support Trends: Economic, Demographic, and Political Contributions," National Bureau of Economic Research, Working Paper 8056, Figure 1b. For a tabulation of Tom and Susan's predivorce expenditures, see "Typical budget, four-person family" for "Tom and Susan" in note 121, chapter 2. The calculation of Susan's postdivorce discretionary income adds full-time child-care costs for a preschooler and a grade-schooler. Child-care

costs based on the average expenditures for nonfamily care outside a child's home for a mother working full-time (2,000 hours per year). Calculated from Richard L. Shortlidge and Patricia Brito, "How Women Arrange for the Care of Their Children While They Work: A Study of Child Care Arrangements, Costs, and Preferences in 1971," Center for Human Resource Research, College of Administrative Science, Ohio State University, Table 15, Unadjusted and Adjusted Expenditures for Child Care, by Socioeconomic and Demographic Characteristics, 1971 (White Women with Youngest Child 3 to 5 Years of Age), and Table 17, Unadjusted and Adjusted Expenditures for Child Care, by Socioeconomic and Demographic Characteristics, 1971 (White Women with Youngest Child 6 to 13 Years of Age). The calculation assumes that Susan will keep the car or purchase another one of similar value. It also assumes that she keeps the same, predivorce expenses for the mortgage and health insurance.

28. For a tabulation of Justin and Kimberly's predivorce expenditures, see "Typical budget, four-person family" for "Justin and Kimberly" in note 121, chapter 2. As in the 1970s example, child support is calculated at 18 percent of the ex-husband's income. The calculation assumes that Kimberly keeps one car and Justin takes the other. It also assumes that Kimberly keeps the same, predivorce expenses for the mortgage, health insurance, and child care. We note that one-quarter of noncustodial parents provide health insurance for their children. Timothy Grall, U.S. Department of Commerce, U.S. Census Bureau, "Child Support for Custodial Mothers and Fathers" (October 2000), p. 5. If we assumed instead that the father provides health insurance for his ex-wife and his children, the family's discretionary income would decline slightly less precipitously after divorce. Under this scenario, postdivorce discretionary income as a proportion of predivorce income would be 21 percent in 1973 and 6 percent in 2000—an improvement of 2 percentage points in both years.

29. In 1977 only 38 percent of families had a bank-type credit card, compared with 68 percent in 1998. Thomas A. Durkin, "Credit Cards: Use and Consumer Attitudes, 1970–2000," Federal Reserve Bulletin (September 2000), Table 1. Available at http://www.federalreserve.gov/pubs/bulletin/2000/0900lead.pdf [12/3/02].

30. SMR Research Corporation, *The New Bankruptcy Epidemic: Forecasts, Causes, and Risk Control* (Hackettstown, NJ, 2001), pp. 14, 94. Credit card debt calculated as revolving credit per adult divided by income per adult. The earliest year in which consistent data on both credit card debt and savings rates are available is 1981. We note, however, that by beginning in 1981, we understate the magnitude of the change over the past generation. In the early 1970s, credit card debt for the average family was even lower. In 1968, for example, total revolving credit outstanding was just $2 billion, compared with $626 billion in 2000. Durkin, "Credit Cards," p. 623.

31. The difference between median income of single mothers and married couples with children calculated from U.S. Census Bureau, Table F-10, Presence of Children Under 18 Years Old by Type of Family and Median and Mean Income,

1974 to 2000. Available at http://www.census.gov/hhes/income/histinc/f10.html [3/27/03].

32. Pamela J. Smock, "The Economic Costs of Marital Disruption for Young Women over the Past Two Decades," *Demography* 30 (August 1993): 359.

33. Never-married women constitute 37 percent of all divorced, never married, separated, and widowed mothers in bankruptcy, compared with 43.2 percent in the general population. Jason Fields and Lynne M. Casper, *America's Families and Living Arrangements, 2000.* Bureau of the Census, Current Population Reports P20-537 (June 2001), Detailed Table F61.

34. About one in seven never-married mothers specifically identify the reason for their bankruptcy as "divorce/family breakup."

35. Federal law restricts wage garnishment for child support at 50 percent of disposable income when the payer is supporting another spouse or dependent child, and 60 percent of disposable income when, as in the case of Brad, the payer is unattached. *Consumer Credit Protection Act* (CCPA), 15 U.S.C. 1673(b)(2) (2003).

36. Calculated from data in Daniel R. Meyer, "The Effect of Child Support on the Economic Status of Nonresident Fathers," in *Fathers Under Fire,* edited by Irwin Garfinkel et al. (New York: Russell Sage Foundation, 1998), p. 87; see also Cynthia Miller, Irwin Garfinkel, and Sara McLanahan, "Child Support in the U.S.: Can Fathers Afford to Pay More?" *Review of Income and Wealth* 43 (September 1997): 274.

37. Sanford L. Braver, *Divorced Dads* (New York: Jeremy P. Tarcher/Putnam, 1998), p. 33.

38. Irwin Garfinkel, Sara S. McLanahan, and Thomas L. Hanson, "A Patchwork Portrait of Nonresident Fathers," in *Fathers Under Fire,* p. 52.

39. Miller, Garfinkel, and McLanahan, "Child Support in the U.S.," p. 274.

40. Garfinkel, McLanahan, and Hanson, "A Patchwork Portrait," p. 54.

41. Braver, *Divorced Dads,* p. 33.

42. Weitzman, *The Divorce Revolution,* p. 391.

43. See, for example, Miller, Garfinkel, and McLanahan, "Child Support in the U.S.," pp. 261, 274, and 276.

44. Elaine Sorensen, "A Little Help for 'Deadbeat' Dads," *Washington Post,* November 15, 1995.

45. Ann Crittenden, *The Price of Motherhood* (New York: Metropolitan Books, 2001), p. 153.

46. Under a typical support arrangement, Justin would pay roughly 18 percent of his income, or $7,020, bringing his income to $32,000 while Kimberly's rises to nearly $36,000. This would put Justin at 3.6 times the poverty level, while Kimberly and her two children would live at 2.6 times the poverty level. Under the Share-the-Pain approach, in order for Justin, Kimberly, and the children to all live at the same level (roughly three times the poverty level), Justin would need to pay $12,400 in child sup-

port, so that Kimberly's income (including child support) would rise to $41,200 while Justin's would drop to $26,600. See note 29 above for additional information about these calculations. The poverty level is calculated from Bureau of the Census, Table 21, Poverty Thresholds by Size of Family and Number of Related Children, 2000. Available at http://ferret.bls.census.gov/macro/032001/pov/new21_000.htm [3/22/03].

47. Under the Share-the-Pain approach, Kimberly's postdivorce discretionary income would be $7,770. See notes 29 and 47 above and "Typical budget, four-person family" for "Justin and Kimberly" in note 121, chapter 2 for additional information about these calculations.

48. Sally C. Clarke, *Advance Report of Final Divorce Statistics 1989 and 1990,* Centers from Disease Control and Prevention, National Center for Health Statistics, Monthly Vital Statistics Report 43, no. 9 (Hyattsville, MD: NCHS, March 1995), Table 19.

49. Lisa Kocian, "Father Continues His Quest to Reform State Custody Law," *Boston Globe,* March 17, 2002.

50. In one-third of joint custody cases, no child support is ordered, compared with only 11 percent of cases where the mother is awarded legal and physical custody. Eleanor E. Maccoby and Robert H. Mnookin, *Dividing the Child: Social and Legal Dilemmas of Custody* (Cambridge, MA: Harvard University Press, 1992), Figure 6.11, Child Support Orders by Custody Arrangement.

51. Garfinkel, McLanahan, and Hanson, "A Patchwork Portrait," p. 49.

52. Elaine Sorensen, "A National Profile of Nonresident Fathers and Their Ability to Pay Child Support," *Journal of Marriage and the Family* 59 (November 1997): 785–797, Table 1.

53. The limitations of the data make it impossible to calculate a precise filing rate for nonresident fathers. The Consumer Bankruptcy Project asked petitioners to identify whether they owe "child support or alimony." Unfortunately, accurate data on the number of people obliged to pay alimony in the general population are not available. In addition, some men with informal support arrangements might have answered yes in the bankruptcy questionnaire, although they would not appear in other reports on the number of men in the general population who are legally obligated to pay support. If the number of men who say that they owe support (including alimony and informal arrangements) is compared with the approximate number of men in the population whose ex-wives and ex-girlfriends report that they are owed child support (usually through a formal arrangement and excluding alimony), the filing rate for men paying child support would be 22.5 per 1,000. The number of men in the general population who owe child support is estimated at 7.1 million, which is the number of custodial mothers who were owed child support in 2000. Timothy Grall, "Custodial Mothers and Fathers and Their Child Support, 1999."

54. Henry Hyde, news release, March 10, 1999. Available at http://www.house.gov/judiciary/031099a.htm [3/22/03].

Chapter 6

1. Elizabeth Warren, "Bankrupt? Pay Your Child Support First," *New York Times*, April 27, 1998. See also Elizabeth Warren, "In Serious Jeopardy; Lies vs. Unadulterated Statistics Muddle Bankruptcy Reform," *Chicago Tribune*, March 19, 1998.

2. Katharine Q. Seelye, "First Lady in a Messy Fight on the Eve of Her Campaign," *New York Times*, June 27, 1999. In her book, Mrs. Clinton writes: "Proposed bankruptcy reform moving through Congress threatened to undermine the spousal and child support many women depend on." Hillary Rodham Clinton, *Living History* (New York: Simon&Schuster, 2003), p. 384.

3. According to Seelye, "[Mrs. Clinton] wrote dozens of personal notes to lawmakers last year as the [bankruptcy] bills made their tortuous way through the Congressional process. And she, along with Senator Edward M. Kennedy, Democrat of Massachusetts, played what the bill's opponents say was a decisive role in helping to kill the legislation last year." Seelye, "First Lady in a Messy Fight."

4. Corporations do not contribute directly, but their employees make coordinated contributions. The *Philadelphia Inquirer* reported: "By orchestrating mass contributions from its employees, the Wilmington-based company has become Bush's single largest source of campaign money. MBNA employees have given more than $250,000 to the Republican's presidential bid, an Inquirer analysis found." Robert Zausner and Josh Goldstein, "Bush's Largest Funding Source: Employees of Credit Card Firm," *Philadelphia Inquirer*, July 28, 2000, p. A1.

5. Senator Clinton claimed in her press release that she supported passage of the bankruptcy bill because "I have worked with a number of people over the past three years to make improvements." She then cited a provision that moved child support claims higher in the distributional pecking order in bankruptcy, by permitting single mothers to stand first in line for distributions from the liquidation of an ex-husband's assets. Office of Senator Hillary Rodham Clinton, "Senator Hillary Rodham Clinton Statement for the Record," news release, March 15, 2001. While this amendment may have provided some political cover, it offers virtually no financial help to single mothers, since the overwhelming majority of ex-husbands don't pay anything in distributions during bankruptcy. Of far more importance was the fact that the bill would permit credit card companies to compete with women *after* bankruptcy for their ex-husbands' limited income, and this provision remained unchanged in the 1998 and 2001 versions of the bill. Senator Clinton claimed that the bill improved circumstances for single mothers, but her view was not shared by any women's groups or consumer groups.

6. Alexander Bolton, "Bankruptcy Bill Is Conflict for Daschle," *The Hill*, March 14, 2001.

7. Consumer nonrevolving debt grew from $500 billion in 1993 to $1 trillion in 2002 (not adjusted for inflation). Federal Reserve, *Consumer Credit Historical*

Data, Federal Reserve Statistical Release G.19 (January 8, 2003), Table, Consumer Credit Outstanding, Nonrevolving. Available at http://www.federalreserve.gov/releases/g19/hist/ [1/28/2003]. Mortgage debt as a share of disposable personal income grew from 39.6 percent in 1973 to 73.2 percent in 2001. Lawrence Mishel, Jared Bernstein, and Heather Boushey (Economic Policy Institute), *The State of Working America: 2002–2003* (Ithaca, New York: Cornell University Press, ILR Press, 2002), p. 296, Table 4.14, Household Debt, by Type, 1949–2001.

8. By 1997, the outstanding home equity debt of American homeowners had reached one-third the size of total nonmortgage consumer debt. Glenn B. Canner, Thomas A. Durkin, and Charles A. Luckett, "Recent Developments in Home Equity Lending," *Federal Reserve Bulletin* 74 (April 1998), pp. 242, 248.

9. Eric Gillin, "Events Conspire Against Bankruptcy Reform," in *The Street.com,* January 10, 2002. Available at http://www.thestreet.com/markets/ericgillin/10006456.html [3/2/2003].

10. Among first-time home buyers a generation ago, 70.9 percent reported that their down payments came entirely from savings, and 20.4 percent said they also had help from relatives. U.S. Bureau of the Census, Data User Services Division, *Statistical Abstract of the United States 1982–83,* 103rd ed. National Data Book and Guide to Sources, compiled by Glenn W. King under the direction of Paul T. Zeisset (Washington, DC, 1982), p. 762, Table 1367, Recent Home Buyers—General Characteristics and Downpayments, 1976 to 1981.

11. Chris Pummer, "GOP in Danger of Misreading Election 'Mandate'," in *CBS-Marketwatch.com,* November 6, 2002.

12. See, e.g., Kathleen C. Engel and Patricia A. McCoy, "A Tale of Three Markets: The Law and Economics of Predatory Lending," *Texas Law Review* 80 (May 2002): 1255, 1271–1279, in which the authors describe the mortgage market of the 1970s as a limited steady business, not aimed toward attracting high-risk borrowers.

13. Diane Ellis, "The Effect of Consumer Interest Rate Deregulation on Credit Card Volumes, Charge-Offs, and the Personal Bankruptcy Rate," *Bank Trends,* no. 98-05 (March 1998). Available at http://www.fdic.gov/bank/analytical/bank/bt_9805.html [3/3/2003]. See also Christopher C. DeMuth, "The Case Against Credit Card Interest Rate Regulation," *Yale Journal on Regulation* (Spring 1986): 200–244.

14. The Supreme Court ruling in *Marquette National Bank of Minneapolis v. First of Omaha Service Corporation* in 1978 allowed a Nebraska bank to export credit card rates to Minnesota. 439 U.S. 299 (1978). The federal government approved this reinterpretation of the McFadden Act in 1983. Financial Institutions Reform, Recovery, and Enforcement Act (FIRREA), U.S. Code, vol. 12, sec. 1831d (1994).

15. In the late 1970s, the usury cap in New York was 18 percent on the first $500 and 12 percent for loans above that amount. Robert D. Manning, *Credit Card Nation: The Consequences of America's Addiction to Credit* (New York: Basic Books,

2000), p. 88. For a review of the calculations behind and evolution of New York's usury statute, see New York, *General Obligations Law, Compiled* (Bender 2002), sec. 5-501.

16. Manning, *Credit Card Nation,* p. 94.

17. For example, Citibank moved its credit card headquarters from New York to South Dakota in 1981. Manning, *Credit Card Nation,* p. 89.

18. Credit card delinquencies were at or below 3 percent for most of the early 1980s, compared with more than 4 percent in 2001 and 2002. "Delinquency Tumbles," in *Cardweb.com,* September 30, 2002. Available at http://www.cardweb.com/cardtrak/2002/september.html [2/12/2003]. Even as delinquencies climbed, credit card lending has remained about twice as profitable as other forms of lending. *The Profitability of Credit Card Operations of Depository Institutions,* Annual Report submitted to Congress (2002). For longer-term profitability trends, see Lawrence M. Ausubel, "Credit Card Defaults, Credit Card Profits, and Bankruptcy," *American Bankruptcy Law Journal* 71 (Spring 1997): 258–260.

19. Calculation based on the following data: Five billion direct-mail card offers were sent out in 2001. "In Brief: 5 Billion Direct-Mail Card Offers Last Year," *American Banker,* April 19, 2002, p. 10. In 2002, direct-mail card offers grew by 300 million mailings over 2001. "Foggy 2003," in *Cardweb.com,* January 3, 2003. Available at http://www.cardweb.com/cardtrak/2003/january.html [2/12/2003]. The average credit line per credit card was $7,160 in 1999; for the purposes of this calculation, we have assumed that this figure remained unchanged in 2002. Leslie Beyer, "The Outer Limits," *Credit Card Management,* November 1999, p. 28. There are 105 million households in the United States. U.S. Bureau of the Census, 2000 Summary File, Table DP-1, Profile of General Demographic Characteristics, 2000.

20. Calculated from Thomas A. Durkin, "Credit Cards: Use and Consumer Attitudes, 1970–2000," *Federal Reserve Bulletin* 76 (September 2000): 623.

21. See Gillin, "Events Conspire Against Bankruptcy Reform."

22. Todd Mason, "Jobless Relying on Credit Cards, Home Equity," *Philadelphia Inquirer,* April 17, 2003; Manning, *Credit Card Nation,* pp. 4, 131.

23. Matt Olson, "Medical Debtors to the Poorhouse: Credit Card Companies Singing All the Way to the Bank," *The Progressive* 5, no. 7 (July 1, 2001): 30.

24. In 1997, 61 percent of homeowners who had taken a traditional home equity loan reported that they took the loan to repay other debts, compared with just 1 percent who took the loan to pay for a vacation. Among homeowners with a line of credit (a somewhat more affluent group than those with traditional home equity loans), 49 percent took a loan to repay debts, and 13 percent did so to take a vacation. Canner, Durkin, and Luckett, "Recent Developments in Home Equity Lending," p. 248.

25. "Lobbyists Battle Over Bankruptcy Bill," in *MSNBC.com,* August 5, 2002. Available at http://www.msnbc.com/news/790231.asp#BODY [3/6/2003].

26. Among all homeowners in bankruptcy, 34 percent had either taken out a second or third mortgage or refinanced to obtain cash. Among homeowners with minor children, the figure is essentially the same, 32.4 percent.

27. Among families filing for bankruptcy, 49.7 percent reported credit card debts exceeding six months' income. For this calculation, we excluded all families reporting no income, even though many of them were carrying large balances on their credit cards. As a result, we probably understate the magnitude of the problem facing these families.

28. "Credit card debt" or "trouble managing money" was listed by 55 percent of all the households filing for bankruptcy, but only 5.7 percent of all families, and only 3.7 percent of families with children, listed either of those reasons without also listing a job loss, a medical problem, or a family breakup as a reason for filing.

29. Judge Edith H. Jones and Todd J. Zywicki, "It's Time for Means-Testing," *Brigham Young University Law Review* (1999): 177–249.

30. In 1980, Congress passed the Depository Institutions and Monetary Control Act (DIDMCA), which phased out Regulation Q, thus allowing banks to pay higher interest to depositors. It also preempted state usury laws as they applied to depositTyr institutions making loans secured by a first-lien home mortgage. After passage of the DIDMCA, the courts extended the usury law preemption to apply to non-purchase price first-lien home mortgages. Cathy Lesser Mansfield, "The Road to Subprime 'HEL' Was Paved with Good Congressional Intentions: Usuary Deregulation and the Subprime Home Equity Market, *South Carolina Law Review* 51 (Spring 2000): 473, 492-495, and 511-521

31. Fannie Mae, *Becoming A Homeowner: How Much House Can You Afford?* In the "Homepath" section of FannieMae.com. Available at http://www.fanniemae.com/homebuyers/findamortgage/becoming/started/houseafford.jhtml?p=Find+a+Mortgage&s=Becoming+a+Homeowner&t=Getting+Started&q=How+Much+House+Can+You+Afford? [3/2/2003].

32. U.S. Bureau of the Census, *House-Poor/House-Rich*, Statistical Brief (August 1991).

33. Calculated from U.S. Bureau of the Census, *Annual Housing Survey for the United States and Regions: 1975, Part C, Financial Characteristics of the Housing Inventory,* Annual Survey (1977). Available at http://www.census.gov/prod/www/abs/h150.html [3/10/2003]. Table A-1, Income of Families and Primary Individuals in Owner and Renter Occupied Housing Units, 1975. U.S. Bureau of the Census, *American Housing Survey for the United States: 2001,* Annual Survey (2001). Available at http://www.census.gov/hhes/www/housing/ahs/ahs01/tab313/html [3/4/2003]. Table 2-20, Income of Families and Primary Individuals by Selected Characteristics—Occupied Units. Note that because of the limitations of the standard survey reporting tables, for the 2001 survey we have defined middle class as earning between $20,000 and $100,000 a year. For the 1975 survey we have defined

middle class as earning between $7,000 and $35,000 a year, or $21,000 and $108,000 in inflation-adjusted dollars. "House poor" includes all families spending more than 35 percent of their income on housing, which was the highest level the government even bothered to report in the 1970s. The proportion of these middle-class homeowners spending more than 35 percent of their income increased from 2.8 percent in 1975 to 13.5 percent in 2001.

34. U.S. Bureau of the Census, Data User Services Division, *Statistical Abstract of the United States 1993,* 113th ed. *The National Data Book,* compiled by Glenn W. King under the direction of Marie Argana (1993), p. 734, Table 1247, Recent Home Buyers—General Characteristics, 1976 to 1992.

35. Ruth Simon and Michelle Higgins, "Stretched Buyers Push Mortgage Levels to a New High," *Wall Street Journal,* June 12, 2002.

36. Calculated from Yongheng Deng, John M. Quigley, Robert Van Order, "Mortgage Default and Low Downpayment Loans: The Costs of Public Subsidy," National Bureau of Economic Research, Working Paper No. 5184 (July 1995), p. 12.

37. White House, Office of the Press Secretary, "President Hosts Conference on Minority Homeownership," press release, October 15, 2002.

38. There are several companies affiliated under the "Citigroup" logo. For ease of identification throughout the chapter, we refer to all of these companies under this organization's best-known moniker—Citibank. Likewise, we use "Chase" as the moniker for J.P. Morgan Chase & Co. For a list of the largest subprime lenders active in the United States, see U.S. Department of Housing and Urban Development (HUD), *HUD Subprime and Manufactured Home Lender List,* data set (2001). Available at http://www.huduser.org/datasets/manu.html [2/1/2003].

39. Lew Sichelman, "Community Group Claims CitiFinancial Still Predatory," *Origination News,* January 2002 (reporting on new claims of CitiFinancial's predatory practices after settlements with state and federal regulators).

40. Senate Banking, Housing, and Urban Affairs Committee, "Predatory Mortgage Lending," statement made by Jeffrey Zeltzer on behalf of the National Home Equity Mortgage Association (NHEMA), 107th Cong., 1st sess., July 26, 2001. See also National Home Equity Mortgage Association, "Join NHEMA," in NHEMA.org. Available at http://www.nhema.org/Join/ [3/4/2003].

41. HUD, *Unequal Burden: Income and Racial Disparities in Subprime Lending in America.* Subprime Lending Report (April 2000). Available at http://www.hud.gov/library/bookshelf18/pressrel/subprime.html [2/1/2003].

42. See Sichelman, "Community Group Claims CitiFinancial Still Predatory."

43. HUD, *Unequal Burden.* To be sure, subprime lenders have focused more of their efforts among poorer homeowners; 26 percent of low-income homeowners end up with subprime refinancing, more than twice the rate of moderate-income families.

44. See, e.g., Howell E. Jackson and Jeremy Berry, "Kickback or Compensation: The Case of Yield Spread Premiums," Working Paper, Harvard Law School (January 2002).

45. Dennis Hevesi, "A Wider Loan Pool Draws More Sharks," *New York Times*, August 31, 2001.

46. The charges alleged that Citibank's consumer finance unit employed deceptive practices to sell home loan insurance. To settle the case, Citibank agreed to pay $240 million, the largest settlement to date of a Federal Trade Commission consumer protection case. "Citigroup $240 Mln Lending Unit Settlement Approved," *Bloomberg News*, November 15, 2002.

47. Paul Beckett, "Citigroup's 'Subprime' Reforms Questioned," *Wall Street Journal*, July 18, 2002.

48. For a thorough discussion of discrimination in mortgage lending, see Stephen Ross and John Yinger, *The Color of Credit: Mortgage Discrimination, Research Methodology, and Fair-Lending Enforcement* (Cambridge, MA: MIT Press, 2002).

49. Association of Community Organizations for Reform Now, *Separate and Unequal: Predatory Lending in America* (Washington, DC: ACORN, November 2002). Available at http://www.acorn.org/acorn10/predatorylending/plreports/SU2002/index.php [2/01/03]. See also Randall M. Scheessele, "1998 HMDA Highlights," Working Paper HF-009, HUD, Office of Policy and Research (September 1999). Available at http://www.huduser.org/publications/hsgfin/workpapr9.html [2/18/2003].

50. HUD, *Unequal Burden*.

51. Congress recently considered legislation specifically targeting "loan to own" practices as an amendment to the current Truth in Lending laws. See "Illinois Association of Mortgage Brokers Backs Important Consumer Protection Legislation," *PR Newswire*, April 17, 2000; Consumer Mortgage Protection Act of 2000, 106th Cong., 2nd sess., H.R. 4213.

52. Margot Saunders, director of the National Consumer Law Center, explained in testimony before Congress: "Based on equity, a lender is in an advantageous situation: either the borrower pays the loan back with high interest or foreclosure on the home permits a recovery from the property directly. In fact, when foreclosure occurs and the borrower's property is sold to the lender for less than fair market value (as it generally is), the lender can resell the property after foreclosure and realize the homeowner's equity. These anticipated windfalls encourage some lenders to make loans designed to result in foreclosure." National Consumer Law Center, "Testimony Regarding the Rewrite of Truth in Lending Act and Real Estate Settlement Procedures Act," Before the Subcommitees on Housing and Community Opportunity and Financial Institutions and Consumer Credit, House Committee on Banking, Financial Institutions and Consumer Credit, U.S. House of Representatives, 105th Cong., 2nd sess., September 16, 1998.

53. Mortgage Bankers Association of America, Foreclosure at End of Quarter, U.S. (Unadjusted %), unpublished data, December 2002. By comparison, foreclosures grew from 0.15 percent of all mortgages in the first quarter of 1979 to 0.37 percent in the first quarter of 2002, an increase of nearly 150 percent. We note that the number of homes in foreclosure grew faster than the number of foreclosures started. Little has changed in the legal procedures of foreclosure, so the difference in the proportion of homes in foreclosure is primarily attributed to the fact that today, once foreclosure proceedings have been started, a home is more likely to proceed through the foreclosure process than it was a generation ago. This suggests that families today are less likely than families were twenty-five years ago to come up with the money to pay the mortgage company or to sell the house rather than lose it in foreclosure.

54. Mary Kane, "Creditors Happy to Lend to Bankrupt Consumers, New Credit Lines Are Often Higher," *New Orleans Times-Picayune,* July 20, 1997.

55. In the past few years, business consulting firms have given lenders essentially the same advice. For example, in 1997 Fair, Isaac & Co. released a bankruptcy predictor program that it claimed could eliminate 54 percent of bankruptcy losses by screening potential nonpayers from the bottom 10 percent of credit card holders. Available at www.fairisaac.com. "Credit Cards: Fight for Bankruptcy Law Reform Masks Truth," *American Banker* 162 (September 8, 1997): 30.

56. A dozen years later, his view had clearly become part of the conventional wisdom among credit card insiders. Industry analysts routinely explain how hard it is "to differentiate between customers who are the most profitable from those most likely to file for bankruptcy. . . . These customers' accounts often look exactly the same." "Bankruptcy Losses on Cards," *Nilson Report* 779 (January 2003): 6.

57. David S. Evans and Richard L. Schmalensee, *The Economics of the Payment Card Industry* (Cambridge, MA: National Economic Research Associates, 1993). Banks are "fighting back" against borrowers who pay off their loans early by charging these customers more money. Teresa Dixon Murray, "Being Good Can Be Bad in Borrowing: Banks Hit Early Payers," *Plain Dealer,* May 6, 2001. Beneficial National Bank of Delaware canceled the MasterCards of 12,000 customers who paid their bills in full; they are expected to cancel another 30,000 customers soon. Other lenders, such as NationsBank and GE Rewards MasterCard, have imposed fees or canceled cards for customers who pay their bills in full. Bruce Mohl, "The Careful Debtor Loses Credit at BJ's," *Boston Globe,* September 25, 1997. A Federal Judge recently struck down a California law that required card issuers to warn cardholders how long it would take for them to pay off their debt if they only made their minimum payments. "Federal Judge Strikes Down California Card Law," *CardLine,* December 27, 2002.

58. For a discussion of consumer credit during the 1920s and 1930s, see Lendol Calder, *Financing the American Dream* (Princeton, NJ: Princeton University Press,

1999): 156–208, 262–290. Calder reports, "The 1930s were prosperous years for consumer credit agencies. They prospered not by lending to the unemployed and destitute, but by expanding services to people who were fortunate enough to hold on to their jobs" (p. 292).

59. Between 1996 and 2001, total late fee revenues generated to bank credit card issuers increased from $1.7 billion to $7.3 billion. "Late Fee Bug," in *Cardweb.com,* May 17, 2002. Available at http://www.cardweb.com/cardtrak/news/2002/may/17a.html [1/28/2003]. The average credit card late fee increased from $11.60 in February 1994 to $30.04 in November 2002. "Late Fees Slow," in *Cardweb.com,* December 11, 2002. Available at http://www.cardweb.com/cardtrak/news/2002/december/11a.html [1/28/2003].

60. Revenues of the top 100 contingent collections agencies grew from $1.7 billion in 1995 to $4.2 billion in 2000. Mike Ginsberg, "State of the Collection Industry," Powerpoint presentation of the Kaulkin Ginsberg Company, March 19, 2001. Available at http://www.kaulkin.com/pptfiles/l-the_state_of_the_collection_industry.ppt [1/28/2003]. For additional industry statistics, see Association of Credit and Collection Professionals, "Collection Facts," in AcaInternational.org, November 15, 2002. Available at http://www.acainternational.org/intcontent.aspx?via=pn&cid=1362&sid=1 [1/28/2003].

61. *In re Francis Michael Latanowich*, 207 B.R. 326 (Bankr. D. Mass. 1997).

62. Professor Jay Westbrook remarked, "Sears looked the bankruptcy laws straight in the eye and defied them"—to the tune of $160 million. Barnaby J. Feder, "Bankrupt See Sears' Strong-Arm Side: Heavy-Handed Debt Collection," *Austin American-Statesman,* July 22, 1997. Sears conceded as much, agreeing to pay a $60 million criminal fine and additional restitution pegged at $600 million.

63. United States Trustee's Response Regarding Reaffirmation Agreements Between Debtors and Sears, Roebuck & Company, *In re Francis Michael Latanowich*, 207 B.R. 326 (Bankr. D. Mass. 1997) (No. 95-18280-CJK).

64. We spoke with Millard Land, president and CEO of Adjuster's Inc., a Texas-based repossession, collateral collection, and investigations agency, and a member of the Board of Directors and Grievance Chairman for Time Finance Adjusters. He told us that his firm typically charges $350–$400 to repossess a small item such as a television set, and $400–$500 to repossess something larger, such as furniture. He also said that in his experience, it is virtually unheard of to repossess personal goods, such as clothing and car batteries. These costs would far exceed the amount Sears could recoup in selling many of these goods. For example, Sears sells brand-new Walkmans for $29.99–$49.99 and new car batteries for $39.99–$99.99. Sears, "Automotive: Batteries" and "Electronics: Personal Radios and Cassettes" at Sears.com (2003).

65. Quoted by Susan Chandler, "Stuck in the Middle," *Chicago Tribune,* August 20, 2000, C1.

66. Kate Griffin, "How Hard Is Too Hard?" *Credit Card Management* (December 1997), pp. 26–30 (discussing AT&T practices); "GE to Pay $100 Million Settlement," *AP Online,* January 22, 1999; "Stores Chain Settles Cases on Bankruptcy Violations," *Fulton County Daily Report,* February 25, 1998 (reporting Federated Department Stores' $11.3 million settlement covering twenty states); "May Stores Settles Suit over Collection Tactics, Will Pay $22 Million," *Wall Street Journal,* November 3, 1998; "Card Notes: Another Retailer Settles Reaffirmation Suit," *Credit Card News,* December 1, 1998 (detailing a Circuit City subsidiary's agreement to pay $6 million to an estimated 11,000 customers); Lynn Arditi, "Bankrupt Credit-Card Holders to Be Reimbursed by JCPenney," *Providence Journal-Bulletin,* December 10, 1998 (discussing the company's $11.7 million settlement spanning forty-two states and covering 11,000 consumers). After this rapid-fire round of settlements, a few court opinions put an end to the reaffirmation suit frenzy, declaring that there was no private right of action available to debtors in these situations. See William L. Stern, "The End of 'Re-Aff' Class Actions," *Consumer Bankruptcy News,* March 6, 2001. Not all of these companies threatened to seize families' goods. Some sent bills, made collection calls, or threatened to take people to court—all in violation of federal law. See, e.g., Bruce Mohl, "Federated, 20 States in $10m Settlement," *Boston Globe,* February 18, 1998.

67. According to the Federal Trade Commission, in most states, used mattresses can be resold as long as they meet certain labeling and processing requirements. U.S. Federal Trade Commission, "Consumers Can 'Rest Easy' Following FTC Settlements with Two Used Mattress Resellers," news release, June 14, 2000. Available at http://www.ftc.gov/opa/2000/06/mattress2.htm [3/6/2003]. However, we have no evidence that Sears is in the used mattress processing business. So, even though the woman was incorrect about the law of mattress sales, it was certainly reasonable to be skeptical of Sears's intent to repossess.

68. United States Trustee's Response Regarding Reaffirmation Agreements Between Debtors and Sears, Roebuck & Company, *In re Francis Michael Latanowich,* 207 B.R. 326 (Bankr. D. Mass. 1997) (No. 95-18280-CJK).

69. Barnaby J. Feder, "Spending It: The Harder Side of Sears," *New York Times,* July 20, 1997.

70. David Snyder, "Is Sears a Bank Or a Retailer? It Must Come Clean on Credit," *Crain's Chicago Business,* November 3, 1997. Since that time, Sears has substantially expanded its credit card operations, launching a MasterCard that can be used outside the store. Today it is the third largest MasterCard issuer in the world. Joe Hallinan and Amy Merrick, "Credit Cards Swipe Sears Profits," *Wall Street Journal,* February 11, 2003.

71. Today many states have technical usury laws on the books, but in many cases the caps are so high that they provide little protection. Because out-of-state lenders can evade those laws, local lenders have pressed state legislatures to raise usury caps

so that they are not put at a competitive disadvantage. Moreover, even if a state keeps its rates low, that provides little protection for its residents, since out-of-state lenders simply override local laws by incorporating in other states and marketing higher-rate loans across state borders.

72. Jerry W. Markham, *A Financial History of the United States,* volume 3, *From the Age of Derivatives into the New Millennium (1970–2001)* (Armonk, NY: M. E. Sharpe, 2002), pp. 73–74.

73. Jones and Zywicki, "It's Time for Means-Testing."

74. Federal Deposit Insurance Corporation (FDIC), Historical Statistics on Banking, Commercial Bank Reports, Table CB04, Net Income, FDIC-Insured Commercial Banks (Washington, DC: 2002). Available at http://www2.fdic.gov/hsob/ [3/20/2003].

75. The nine interest rate cuts by the Federal Reserve in 2001 did not affect most fixed-rate cards and had only modest effects on variable-rate cards. Cecily Fraser, "A $10 Billion Windfall: Credit Card Lenders Don't Pass on Full Interest-Rate Cuts," *CBS MarketWatch.com,* October 3, 2001. Available at http://www.cbs.marketwatch.com [2/2/2003].

76. Interest on so-called payday loans can be in the 300–1,000 percent range. FDIC, *Payday Lending FYI: An Update on Emerging Issues in Bankruptcy* (January 29, 2003).

77. Mansfield, "The Road to Subprime 'HEL'," pp. 492–495. The initial Depository Institutions and Monetary Control Act (DIDMCA), which allowed banks to pay higher interest to depositors and preempted state usury laws, passed the House on September 11, 1979, by a vote of 367 to 39, and passed the Senate on November 1, 1979, by a vote of 76 to 9. U.S. Library of Congress, *Bill Summary and Status for the 96th Congress: H.R. 4986,* Thomas Legislative Information on the Internet (1995). Available at http://thomas.loc.gov [3/3/2003].

78. Progressive reformers actually made the first major campaign to "democratize credit" in the early twentieth century. Calder, *Financing the American Dream,* pp. 124–155.

79. Even the most aggressive advocates of expanding home-ownership rates in America are beginning to call for reregulation of the mortgage market, recognizing that the impact on the number of families buying homes is likely to be small. National Training and Information Center, *The Devil's in the Details: An Analysis of Federal Housing Administration Default Concentration and Lender Performance in 20 U.S. Cities* (Chicago: NTIC, October 1997). See also National Training and Information Center, *Preying on Neighborhoods: Subprime Mortgage Lending and Chicagoland Foreclosures* (Chicago: NTIC, September 21, 1999).

80. HUD, Office of Policy Development and Research, *U.S. Housing Market Conditions,* Historical Data, 3rd Quarter, 2002 (November 2002), Table 27, Homeownership Rates by Age of Householder, 1982–Present. Available at http://www.huduser.org/periodicals/ushmc/fall02/histdat27.htm [2/18/2003].

81. National Community Reinvestment Corporation, "About Us," in NCRC.org (2002). Available at http://www.ncrc.org/about/aboutindex.html [2/2/2003]. (The organization's primary mission is "to increase the flow of private capital into traditionally underserved communities.")

82. "Federal Regulators Drop Subprime Proposal," *CardLine* 3, no. 2 (January 10, 2003): 1.

83. *Economist*, "Hunting the Loan Sharks," August 31, 2002.

84. Jeanette Bradley and Peter Skillern, "Predatory Lending: Subprime Lenders Trick Homeowners into Expensive Loans," in the National Housing Institute's *Shelter Force Online,* no. 109, January/February 2000.

85. To be fair, efforts to regulate predation are better than nothing. After North Carolina enacted some limits on predatory lending, at least one subprime lender left the state's markets entirely and headed for easier pickings in other states. See Noel C. Paul, "Homeownership Can Be Short-lived in Inner Cities," *Christian Science Monitor,* May 1, 2001.

86. Hevesi, "A Wider Loan Pool."

87. There have been numerous private efforts to bring lower-cost capital to underserved communities. See, for example, Woodstock Institute, *Doing Well While Doing Good,* Reinvestment Alert Number 18 (Chicago: Woodstock Institute, September 2002). Available at http://www.woodstockinst.org/alert18.pdf [3/22/03].

88. Democratic National Committee, *The 2000 Democratic Party Platform: Prosperity, Progress, and Peace* (Washington, DC: DNC, 2000). Available at http://www.democrats.org/about/2000platform.html [2/2/2003]. Republican National Committee, *Republican Platform 2000: Renewing America's Purpose, Together* (Washington, DC: RNC, 2000). Available at http://www.rnc.org/gopinfo.platform [2/2/2003].

89. Ellis, "The Effect of Consumer Interest Rate Deregulation."

90. National Bankruptcy Review Commission, *Bankruptcy: The Next Twenty Years. Final Report* (Washington, DC, 1997): 77–95 (NBRC Report). For the reasons families file for bankruptcy, see p. ii. The Commission recommended, for example, that the practice of permitting credit card companies to pressure families to agree to repay debts discharged in bankruptcy should be outlawed. Recommendation 1.2.1. It also recommended that unlimited homestead exemptions should be capped at $100,000, which would prevent wealthier families from shielding their assets in an expensive home. Recommendation 1.2.2.

91. For additional background on this organization, see, e.g., Steve Cocheo, "In Debt and Loving It," *ABA Banking Journal* 89, no. 8 (August 1, 1997); "The Curtain Rises on the Latest Bankruptcy Drama," *Credit Card News* (December 15, 1996).

92. Industry analysts estimate that about 31 percent of credit card chargeoffs are listed in bankruptcy, while the remaining 69 percent are simply written off as uncollectable even if the family never files for bankruptcy. "Bankruptcy Losses on Cards," *Nilson Report* 779 (January 2003): 6.

93. The bankruptcy lobby group and the supporters of the current bankruptcy bill readily acknowledge that their goal is to reduce the number of families eligible to file for bankruptcy. See, for example, testimony of longtime credit industry lobbyist George J. Wallace, Subcommittee on Administrative and Commercial Law of the Committee on the Judiciary, House of Representatives (March 4, 2003). They do not, however, point out that this means that more families would end up mired in debt for the rest of their lives.

94. "Bankruptcy Efforts 'Worsen' Chargeoffs," *Card News* 12, no. 21 (October 27, 1997).

95. The bill morphed through multiple versions. To read it, it was necessary to hold a copy of the already lengthy bankruptcy code beside it and try to parse through the proposed changes. The final Engrossed Senate Amendment version was 222 pages long. *Bankruptcy Reform Act of 2001*, 107th Cong., 1st session, H.R. 333 (Engrossed Senate Amendment version, last updated on 7/18/2001).

96. Common Cause, "Controversial Bankruptcy Bill Moves Forward: Creditor Interests Gave $63 Million," in CommonCause.org (September 19, 2002). Available at http://www.commoncause.org/moneyinpolitics/img/091902bankruptcy_study.pdf [2/12/2003].

97. American Bankruptcy Institute, *Statements Made Upon the Introduction of the "Bankruptcy Reform Act of 1999"* (February 24, 1999). Available at http://www.abiworld.org/legis/bills/statements2-24-99.html [3/3/2003].

98. For a detailed discussion of this aspect of the credit industry's campaign to justify a change in the bankruptcy laws, including dissemination of the claim that bankruptcy costs average families, see Elizabeth Warren, "The Market for Data: The Changing Role of the Social Sciences in Changing the Law" (Fairchild Lecture), *Wisconsin Law Review* 2002 (2002): 1–43. Note that the figure was originally quoted as $400 per family, but that later commentators inflated the figure, so that $550 is now the figure most commonly cited. The new number has no more factual basis than the original.

99. The creditor coalition hired Ernst & Young (E&Y) to produce some numbers for their public relations campaign. E&Y initially estimated that 15 percent of the families in Chapter 7 might have the ability to pay something under the proposed legislation. Because the debtors in Chapter 13 were already paying, they were left out of the calculation. Nonetheless, the proposed bankruptcy bill would impose several new burdens on Chapter 13 filers as well. Under current legislation, for example, families are permitted to focus their available income on making up home mortgage arrearages; the proposed legislation would require that credit card issuers and car lenders receive more repayments or the family would be denied access to Chapter 13 protection. A year later, E&Y lowered their estimate of potential payers to 10 percent of Chapter 7 filers. (For a review of these two studies, see U.S. Congressional Budget Office, *Personal Bankruptcy: A Literature Review*, CBO Papers

[September 2000]. Available at http://www.cbo.gov/showdoc.cfrm?index=2421& sequence=0 [3/3/2003].) In 2002, 1,036,410 families filed for Chapter 7 bankruptcy. Multiplying that figure by the E&Y claim that 10 percent of them could pay something yields a total of about 103,600 families. Independent academics estimate that only 3.6 percent of those in Chapter 7 might be able to repay more under the new legislation. The lower estimate, of course, just makes the $550 per family estimate more absurd, requiring those Chapter 7 filers to come up with over $1.5 million apiece. Marianne B. Culhane and Michaela M. White, "Taking the New Consumer Bankruptcy Model for a Test Drive: Means Testing Real Chapter 7 Debtors," *American Bankruptcy Institute Law Review* 7 (Spring 1999): 27, 59.

100. Senator Hillary Rodham Clinton, Bankruptcy Floor Statement, July 12, 2001.

101. Phil Shenon, "Abortion Issue Holds up Bill on Bankruptcy," *New York Times,* April 30, 2002. Shenon writes: "The provision would bar abortion opponents from declaring bankruptcy to avoid paying court-imposed fines or damages that result from violent protests at abortion clinics. In recent years, a number of prominent abortion foes have used the bankruptcy laws for that purpose, among them Randall Terry, the founder of Operation Rescue. In declaring bankruptcy in 1998, Mr. Terry said he wanted to avoid paying debts, which then totaled more than $1 million, 'to those who would use my money to promote the killing of the unborn.'"

102. Philip Shenon, "Lenders' Ads Urge Senator to Drop Item from Debt Bill," *New York Times,* May 21, 2002.

103. Bolton, "Bankruptcy Bill Is Conflict for Daschle."

104. The bankruptcy filing rates in 2001 were 39.9 per 1,000 for black homeowners, 14.4 for Hispanic homeowners, and 5.8 for white homeowners. National data on the number of homeowners by racial group from U.S. Bureau of the Census, American Housing Survey for the United States: 2001, Annual Survey (2001). Available at http://www.census.gov/hhes/www/housing/ahs/01adtchrt/tab3-1.html [3/22/03].

105. HUD, Federal Housing Authority Single Family Mortgage Insurance Foreclosures, Cumulative by Number and Percent, 1982–2002, unpublished data.

106. In Chicago, 41 percent of the city's subprime refinancing occurs in black neighborhoods, although only 10 percent of the overall refinancing takes place in these same neighborhoods. HUD, *Unequal Burden.* An Illinois study found that there are 37 percent more payday loans issued in minority neighborhoods than in white neighborhoods. Woodstock Institute, *Unregulated Payday Lending Pulls Vulnerable Consumers into Spiraling Debt*, Reinvestment Alert Number 14 (Chicago: Woodstock Institute, March 2000). Available at www.woodstockinst.org/alert.pdf [2/2/2003].

107. In 1996, a Texaco employee revealed secret tape recordings he had made of Texaco executives disparaging African-American employees and discussing the shredding of documents pertaining to a discrimination case. After this release, civil

rights leaders called for a boycott against the company, a number of customers cut up their Texaco credit cards, and some investors sold their Texaco stock. Within two weeks of the disclosure, Texaco agreed to pay $140 million to settle the case. The outrage over these tapes prompted the company to adopt new policies to promote equality and erase discrimination within its organization. See, e.g., Adam Bryant, "How Much Has Texaco Changed?" *New York Times,* November 2, 1997; Tim Whitmire, "Tapes Don't Stick in Court: Ex-Texaco Executives Walk," *Chicago Sun-Times,* May 13, 1998.

108. See chapter 1, note 10, and chapter 5, notes 17 and 21, for more information on these calculations.

109. Letter from American Association of University Women, Children NOW, Children's Defense Fund, Center for Law and Social Policy (CLASP), Feminist Majority Foundation, National Association of Commissions for Women (NACW), National Center for Youth Law, National Organization for Women, National Partnership for Women and Families, National Women's Conference, National Women's Law Center, National Youth Law Center, NOW Legal Defense and Education Fund, OWL, The Women Activist Fund, Inc., Wider Opportunities for Women, Women Employed, Women Work!, Women's Law Center of Maryland, Inc., YWCA of the USA, March 2, 2000 (on file with the authors). The leading organizations are the National Women's Law Center, the NOW Legal Defense and Education Fund, and the National Partnership for Women and Families.

110. There was a glossy photograph of Senator Biden in the NOW Legal Defense annual report, which is sent to thousands of politically active women. No other politician rated a mention.

111. Pamela Barnett, "Sources Say Addition of Biden Increased Its Size," *Congressional Daily,* June 23, 2001; Pamela Barnett, "Large Bankruptcy Conference Dismays Bill Supporters," *Congressional Daily,* July 23, 2001.

112. During the 2002–2003 academic year, 714,000 women were awarded bachelor's degrees. National Center for Education Statistics, *Digest of Education Statistics*, 2001, 37th ed. Compilation of Statistical Information, by Valerie White Plisko (Washington, DC, 2001), Table 247, Earned Degrees Conferred by Degree-Granting Institutions, by Level of Degree and Sex of Student, 1869–70 to 2010–11. Available at http://nces.ed.gov/pubs2002/digest2001/tables/dt247.asp [2/6/2003]. In an average month in 1999, 1.8 million children received day care subsidized by the federal Child Care and Development Block Grant/Child Care and Development Fund, the primary federal program for subsidized day care. U.S. Department of Health and Human Services, Administration for Children and Families, *Child Care and Development Block Grant/Child Care and Development Fund,* news release December 6, 2000. Table, Children Served in Fiscal Year 1999 (average monthly). Many of these children will be in the same program for several years. By comparison, in a two-year period, approximately 3.1 million children will go through their

parents' bankruptcies. Each year, approximately 1.5 million women in the United States are raped and/or physically assaulted by an intimate partner; about 375,000 of these women seek police protection. Patricia Tjaden and Nancy Thoennes, *Extent, Nature, and Consequences of Intimate Partner Violence: Findings from the National Violence Against Women Survey* (Washington, DC: U.S. Department of Justice, National Institute of Justice, July 2000). Available at http://ncjrs.org/txtfiles1/nij/181867.txt [2/19/2003]. Callie Marie Rennison, *Rape and Sexual Assault: Reporting to Police and Medical Attention, 1992–2000, Selected Findings* (Washington, DC: U.S. Department of Justice, Bureau of Justice Statistics, August 2002). Available at http://www.ojp.usdoj.gov/bjs/abstract/rsarp00.htm [2/19/2003].

113. Open letter to Congress (February 28, 2001). Signers include American Friends Service Committee, McAuley Institute, MidAmerica Leadership Foundation, Unitarian Universalist Association of Congregations, Unitarian Universalist Service Committee, Washington Ethical Action Office/American Ethical Union, Religious Action Center of Reform Judaism, and NETWORK, A National Catholic Social Justice Lobby.

Chapter 7

1. See calculation in chapter 4, notes 33–36.

2. Ernst & Young LLP, et al. *Ernst & Young's Financial Planning for Women: A Woman's Guide to Money for All of Life's Major Events* (New York: John Wiley & Sons, 1999), p. 15.

3. *Consumer Reports*, "What Price Insurance?" July 1999. Available at http://www.consumerreports.org [3/22/03]. As we noted in chapter 6, a creditor has a right to collect against the estate, but surviving family members have no obligation to pay.

4. "Credit Protection," *CardTrakOnline*, September 20, 2002. Available at http://www.cardweb.com/cardtrak/news/2002/september/30a.html [3/22/03].

5. A thoughtful overview with a lot of practical advice is James P. Caher and John M. Caher, *Personal Bankruptcy for Dummies* (New York: Wiley, 2003).

6. See discussion in chapter 4.

7. Court records showed reaffirmation for 24.5 percent of the families in Chapter 7. Families who have filed for Chapter 13, which account for 30 percent of all bankruptcy filings, have already committed their entire disposable incomes to debt repayment, making reaffirmation irrelevant for them.

8. See discussion of the economics of repossession in chapter 6.

9. For example, a California debtor was offered $251 in new credit if she would reaffirm a debt for $250.93. If she used that new $251 credit in full, the court notes that she would be paying more than 100 percent interest for the new credit. If she used less, say $25 of the credit, she would be paying an effective interest rate in excess of 1,000 percent. Nonetheless, the debtor agreed to the deal. In re Kamps, 217

B.R. 836, 851 (Bankr. C.D. C.A. 1998). Similar examples of debtors signing such one-sided deals abound throughout the bankruptcy system.

10. Among respondents, 84.3 percent said they had received preapproved credit cards and other debt solicitations within six months of their bankruptcy filings. The median number of solicitations was thirty.

11. The filing rate for not-married women with minor children was 21.3 per 1,000; the filing rate for single women without children was 7.2 per 1,000, or 66 percent lower.

12. E. R. Kingson and R. O'Grady-LeShane, "The Effects of Caregiving on Women's Social Security Benefits," *Gerontologist* 33 (1993): 230–239.

13. Phillip J. Longman and Amy Graham, "The Cost of Children," *U.S. News & World Report,* March 30, 1998, p. 58.

14. See, for example, Ben Wattenberg, *The Birth Dearth: What Happens When People in Free Countries Don't Have Enough Babies?* (New York: Pharos Books, 1988).

15. Stephanie Mencimer, "The Baby Boycott," *Washington Monthly,* June 2001, p. 14.

16. Elinor Burkett, *The Baby Boon: How Family-Friendly America Cheats the Childless* (New York: Free Press, 2000), p. 197.

17. In 2001, Little League had an estimated 1.1 million new members. Private correspondence, Director of Media Relations and Communications, March 5, 2003. Approximately 34 million households own dogs. Of those, 20 percent, or 6.8 million, adopted the dog(s) from the humane society. The average family's dog is five to six years old, with a life expectancy of more than ten years, suggesting that approximately 680,000 families adopt a dog from the humane society every year, including both families with and without children. According to the American Association of Orthodontics, approximately 1.6 million children and teenagers begin orthodontic treatment each year. Communication with American Association of Orthodontics, March 4, 2003.

18. Based on a linear regression of personal bankruptcies in America, 1980–2002, with an R-squared value of 0.937. The calculation assumes that the average number of children listed on their parents' bankruptcy filing as dependent stays constant throughout this period.

19. Approximately 1 million children go through their parents' divorce each year. "U.S. Divorce Statistics," *Divorce Magazine.com* (2000). Available at http://www.divorcemag.com/statistics/statsUS.shtml [4/1/03].

20. Katherine S. Newman, *Falling from Grace: The Experience of Downward Mobility in the American Middle Class* (New York: Free Press, 1988), p. 97.

21. Susan E. Mayer, *What Money Can't Buy: Family Income and Children's Life Chances* (Cambridge, MA: Harvard University Press, 1997), pp. 76–77. Five- to seven-year-olds whose parents experienced a drop in income of 35 percent or more

between two adjacent years were more likely to experience lower test scores and behavior problems in the classroom. Mayer controlled for other factors, such as parents' marital status, race, and parents' age at the birth of the child. Les B. Whitbeck, Ronald L. Simons, Rand D. Conger, Frederick O. Lorenz, Shirley Huck, and Glenn H. Elder Jr., "Family Economic Hardship, Parental Support, and Adolescent Self-Esteem," *Social Psychology Quarterly* 54 (December 1991): 353–363. The authors found that adolescents from families in financial distress are more likely to experience low self-esteem. Diana S. Clark-Lempers, Jacques D. Lempers, and Anton J. Netusil, "Family Financial Stress, Parental Support, and Young Adolescents' Academic Achievement and Depressive Symptoms," *Journal of Early Adolescence* 10 (February 1990): 21–36. The study reported that adolescents from families in financial distress are more likely to experience greater strain in their relationships with their parents.

22. Newman, *Falling from Grace,* p. 105.

23. William Buckley Jr., "On Going Broke," *The Washington Times* (July 2, 1999), p. A14.

Appendix

1. Teresa Sullivan, Elizabeth Warren, and Jay Lawrence Westbrook, *As We Forgive Our Debtors: Bankruptcy and Consumer Credit in America* (New York: Oxford University Press, 1989). The study examined court records for 1,529 randomly chosen debtors filing in all the judicial districts of three states—Illinois, Pennsylvania, and Texas—in 1981.

2. Teresa Sullivan, Elizabeth Warren, and Jay Lawrence Westbrook, *The Fragile Middle Class: Americans in Debt* (New Haven, CT: Yale University Press, 2000). The study examined both court records and a one-page questionnaire for 2,400 randomly chosen families filing for bankruptcy in all the judicial districts of five states—California, Illinois, Pennsylvania, Tennessee, and Texas—in 1991.

3. Melissa Jacoby, Teresa Sullivan, and Elizabeth Warren, "Rethinking the Debates over Health Care Financing: Evidence from the Bankruptcy Courts," *New York University Law Review* 76 (2001): 375. The study collected questionnaire data from a random sample of 1,455 families who filed for bankruptcy in eight federal judicial districts: the Northern District of California, the Northern District of Illinois, the Eastern District of Kentucky, the Southern District of Ohio, the Eastern District of Pennsylvania, the Middle District of Tennessee, the Northern District of Texas, and the Eastern District of Wisconsin in 1999.

4. Because one focus of the 2001 study was the relationship between home ownership and bankruptcy, the Northern District of Texas (Dallas) was chosen over the Western District, which included San Antonio. It was the belief of the researchers that the housing market of Dallas was more typical and provided a more accurate representation of an urban center. San Antonio's housing market was considered

atypical for two reasons: proximity to the Mexico border and the fact that San Antonio is home to three major military installations. Each debtor must file in the district where he or she is a resident (legally defined), but some districts have more than one office to accept filings. So, for example, if the debtor resides in the Northern District of Illinois, he or she can file in Chicago or Rockford, a suburb, although very few are filed in Rockford. The researchers sampled only in the big cities, which is where the overwhelming majority of bankruptcies are filed in four of the five districts. In the Central District of California, the researchers sampled only Los Angeles, but in that district a larger proportion of cases are also filed in outlying areas. As we note in the text, this may result in a bias toward larger cities and an underrepresentation of rural and small-town areas.

5. For a discussion of this phenomenon, see Teresa A. Sullivan, Elizabeth Warren, and Jay Lawrence Westbrook, "The Persistence of Local Legal Culture: Twenty Years of Evidence from the Bankruptcy Courts," *Harvard Journal of Law and Public Policy* 17 (1994), reprinted in Charles J. Tabb, *Bankruptcy Anthology* (Westbury, NY: Foundation Press, 2002).

6. Mean bankruptcy filing rate per 1,000 adults, 1990–2000. SMR Research Corporation, *The New Bankruptcy Epidemic: Forecasts, Causes, and Risk Control* (Hackettstown, NJ, June 2001), pp. 181–187.

7. The 1970 occupational codes have been used in all of the preceding Consumer Bankruptcy Projects. They are also still widely in use as the last "pure" occupational codes used by the Census Bureau. They have been used in major studies such as the General Social Survey. Since the 1970 census, the Bureau has adopted sets of codes that incorporate industry as well as occupation, but several "walkovers" are available that permit correspondence from one set of codes to another.

INDEX

ABOUT THE AUTHORS

Elizabeth Warren is the Leo Gottlieb Professor of Law at Harvard Law School. She has coauthored six books on bankruptcy and commercial law, including the prizewinning *As We Forgive Our Debtors* and *The Fragile Middle Class.* She was senior adviser to the 1997 Congressional Bankruptcy Review Commission on Bankruptcy. In 1998, the *National Law Journal* named her one of the Fifty Most Influential Women Lawyers in America. She is the mother of two grown children, and she lives in Cambridge, Massachusetts, with her husband.

Amelia Warren Tyagi holds degrees from Brown University and the Wharton School at the University of Pennsylvania. She worked as a consultant for McKinsey & Company, where she specialized in health care and public education. In 1999, she cofounded a health benefits firm, HealthAllies. She lives in Los Angeles with her husband and their two-year-old daughter.

Warren and Tyagi are mother and daughter. This is their first book together.